# A Handbook of English Grammar

A Handbook of

# ENGLISH GRAMMAR

on Functional Principles

Second Edition

*By Bent Preisler*

AARHUS UNIVERSITY PRESS

Copyright: Aarhus University Press, 1992, 1997
Printed on acid-free paper by Bogtrykkeriet, Skive
ISBN 87 7288 655 2

AARHUS UNIVERSITY PRESS
Building 170, University of Aarhus
DK-8000 Aarhus C, Denmark

73 Lime Walk
Headington, Oxford OX3 7AD
Fax (+ 44) 1865 750 079

Box 511
Oakville, Conn. 06779
Fax (+ 1) 860 945 9468

# PREFACE

The conceptual framework of this book (*HEG*) is, to a large extent, based on the work of M.A.K. Halliday, whose influence is also to be seen (directly or indirectly) in various particulars of the description. Hence the word *functional* in the title. Halliday (1985: xiii-xiv) defines the word in terms of several related aspects of his theory: (1) a functional grammar "is designed to account for how the language is **used**"; (2) "following from this, the fundamental components of **meaning** in language are [seen to be] functional components"; (3) "each **element** in a language is explained by reference to its function in the total linguistic system" (p. xiii). It must be pointed out, however, that the conceptual framework of *HEG* is not *identical* to that of Halliday's work, and that, for instance, the "fundamental components of meaning" referred to as communicative functions in *HEG* (§ 9.15) are based on a model by Arndt and Ryan (1986), not Halliday's model of metafunctions, despite some natural points of affinity between the two.

The basic structure of this book derives from a larger one, *Kompendium i Engelsk Grammatik*, which I co-authored with Hans Arndt and Frede Østergaard (1977), and which is now out of print. Many of the examples and a few tabulations, too, reflect this heritage. However, *HEG* is not just a short, English version of the *Kompendium*. It represents a thorough revision of the description in terms of what I think should be required of a structure-function handbook of English grammar for use in the otherwise "communicatively" oriented university language course of the 1990's. It is intended for advanced students of English, whether native speakers or foreign learners. It was written because, at this department, we have for a long time felt the need for a descriptive English grammar of this type and size, to fill the gap between shorter grammars like Crystal's *Rediscover Grammar* (Longman), on the one hand, and bulkier ones like Quirk & Greenbaum's *A University Grammar of English* (Longman), on the other.

Although *HEG* is not a "communicative" grammar, it has come about within the framework of communicative language teaching. It introduces a number of concepts which are important in this respect, and several sections have been organized on semantic/pragmatic principles. Communicative skills presuppose linguistic creativity — the ability to come up with a variety of different ways in which the same basic message could be phrased depending on the specific context, audience etc. Grammar should stimulate the student's linguistic imagination by presenting language as a system of options, with a view to the construction of texts. Reference grammars do not meet this requirement; grammar course books sometimes do, but their organization is based solely on pedagogical considerations, which makes them difficult to use for reference. *HEG* is based on my experience that, at an advanced level, it is the linguistic structure itself (involving syntactic as well as semantic structure) which provides the most efficient organizing principle of a handbook of English Grammar.

However, *HEG* does contain all the detailed information of a reference book, each detail being presented as an integrated manifestation of the linguistic system. From the point of view of English proficiency, the book aims at imparting the grammatical "facts" as well as an awareness of linguistic structure. Explicit clause and phrase analyses are employed throughout, enabling the reader to understand how every element of the description relates to the underlying system. I have thought it best not to discuss competing analyses, which I think could make the material difficult to digest. At continental universities, after all, it is normal for students to be required to study the grammatical system of English at undergraduate level. On the other hand, the strict adherence to a theoretical framework, and the emphasis on explanation and analysis, would also make the book suitable for postgraduate students. Postgraduate students would be able to go on to consider other models and possible analyses under the guidance of their teachers, but in my experience the success of comparative studies depends on the extent to which the students are first given a firm grasp of the essentials of linguistic description, through the systematic application of a particular approach.

It is a special feature of this grammar that it can be used equally well by students of British and American English. The description and examples aim at being generally neutral in this respect, but characteristic differences between the two varieties are pointed out systematically and explicitly. This should accommodate the increasing number of students who, after spending a year or more in the U.S. as exchange students, return to their European university with a wish to develop their newly acquired American English proficiency.

Two general comments on the exemplification need to be made:

"Common-core" examples have been chosen so as not to contain *any* variety-specific features in terms of American/British English, which also means that they do not contain words that are spelled differently in the two varieties (in the running text, in the rare instances where there *are* any differences, the spelling is American English).

I have deliberately chosen not to base this grammar purely on unamended data from a particular corpus, despite the current tendency to use corpus data for the purpose of livening up reference grammars. There are good reasons for this: (1) the unedited, authentic example usually contains at least two or three more grammatical problems than the one which the student is trying to focus on; (2) unedited, authentic examples are often incomprehensible when occurring out of context, or they contain too much irrelevant material. However, many of the examples of *HEG* are in fact either authentic or based on slightly amended corpus data.

My indebtedness to Hans Arndt and Frede Østergaard is obvious. If I should have failed here and there to do justice to our former joint achievement, I hope they will forgive me. Special thanks are due to Hans Arndt and Althea Ryan for allowing me to base my outline of communicative functions directly on their work (op.cit.). I owe a tremendous debt of gratitude to Shirley Larsen and Tim Caudery for taking on the thankless task of testing the book chapter by chapter in their teaching, and for the many hours they spent providing me with invaluable feedback and suggestions. I am also grateful to Knud Sørensen, Gerda Poulsen, Jody Pennington, Peter Harder and Anders Iversen for their willingness to read through and comment on the MS. My discussions with these colleagues have resulted in a much better book than the first version, and I may yet be sorry that I did not follow their advice more often. Finally, I would like to thank the students for putting up with the inconvenience of using a book in the making.

*July, 1992*                                                                                    *Bent Preisler*

The second edition contains minor changes and corrections (particularly in §§ 2.7.11, 8.3.2., 10.8.7, 15.2, 19.4.4).

*March, 1997/BP*

# CONTENTS

# ABBREVIATIONS AND SYMBOLS

| | |
|---|---|
| A | *adverbial* |
| AE | *American English* |
| AP | *adjective/adverb phrase* |
| BE | *British English* |
| C | *complement* |
| D | *determiner* |
| DO | *direct object* |
| E | *event point* (point on the time line), or *epithet* (premodifier in NP) |
| F-pos | *final position* |
| H | *head* |
| IO | *indirect object* |
| I-pos | *initial position* |
| J | *junctive* |
| N | *nominator* |
| NP | *noun phrase* |
| O | *ordinator* |
| OC | *object complement* |
| Pf | *prefix* |
| POM | *postmodifier* |
| PrD | *predeterminer* |
| PRM | *premodifier* |
| R | *root* (word constituent), or *reference point* (point on the time line) |
| S | *subject* |
| SC | *subject complement* |
| Sf | *suffix* |
| U | *utterance point* (point on the time line) |
| V | *verbal*, or *main verb* |
| v | *verb-phrase premodifier, auxiliary verb* |
| Voc | *vocative* |
| VP | *verb phrase* |
| V-pos | *verb-neighbor position* |
| - | (as in V- S -V) *structurally divided constituent* |
| → | (as in: V→ |
| ← | ←V)  *orthographically divided constituent* |
| S= | *preliminary subject* |
| =S | *the subject proper* |
| DO= | *preliminary direct object* |
| =DO | *the direct object proper* |
| * | (introducing examples) *ungrammatical/unacceptable example* |

# I. INTRODUCTION

**Common Core English (1.1)**

1.1    This book describes the grammatical structure of present-day standard English. The two most widely recognized spoken standards, American and British English, are grammatically so similar that it seems reasonable to try to describe their "common core," though important differences between American and British English will be pointed out.

**Clause, Phrase, Word (1.2-1.7)**

*The Clause (1.2-1.3)*

1.2    The units of grammatical description are called **structures**. It will be necessary to take account of three structural types: the **clause**, the **phrase** and the **word**. They will be defined in the following. The parts of a structure are referred to as its **constituents.**

1.3    The basic unit of grammatical description is the **clause**. The clause is defined as a structure containing the constituents <u>S</u>ubject, <u>V</u>erbal, <u>C</u>omplement, <u>A</u>dverbial (all or some of them):

<u>The tall undergraduate with the beard</u> <u>was reading</u> <u>the article</u>
                 S                                 V         C
<u>very carefully</u>
     A

This common type of clause, where S precedes V, is called a **declarative** clause. In a declarative clause, neither S nor V can be done without, i.e. they are both **obligatory**. Constituents which can be left out without changing the meaning of the rest of the structure or making it ungrammatical are said to be **optional**. The adverbial is usually optional, but this, as well as the type and number of complements, depends on the type of verbal. In the above example, both C and A are optional:

<u>The tall undergraduate with the beard</u> <u>was reading</u>
                 S                                 V

In the case of S and V, on the other hand, we cannot have one without the other. Such a relationship between constituents is called **interdependence**.

### The Phrase (1.4-1.6)

1.4    When in the preceding we were able to identify the clause constituents, it was because we recognized intuitively that the words *the, tall, undergraduate, with, the, beard* belong together in a way which marks them off as a separate phrase from *was* and *reading*, which in turn form a phrase of their own, etc. We will now define such a **phrase** as a structure containing the constituents **modifier** and **head (H)**, the modifiers falling into **premodifier (PRM)** and **postmodifier (POM)**:

(1)    S:    <u>The</u> <u>tall</u> <u>undergraduate</u> <u>with the beard</u>
             PRM  PRM        H              POM

       V:    <u>was</u> <u>reading</u>
             PRM    H

       C:    <u>the</u> <u>article</u>
             PRM    H

       A:    <u>very</u> <u>carefully</u>
             PRM     H

H is the most important constituent of the phrase; it is possible to rewrite the clause so that each constituent consists of H only:

(2)    <u>Undergraduates</u> <u>read</u> <u>articles</u> <u>carefully</u>
              H           H      H        H
              S           V      C        A

The head is obligatory whereas its modifiers, as we can see, are optional at least in the sense demonstrated by (2). Such a relationship as that between head and modifiers is called **dependence**.

1.5    It is important to distinguish between a constituent and its **realization**. A constituent is like a box whose label says nothing about what is inside it. Although in § 1.4 (1) and (2) the clause structure is the same, the clause constituents are not **realized** in the same way. In § 1.4 (1) they are realized by **complex** phrases (consisting of more than one constituent), while in § 1.4 (2) they are realized by **simple** phrases (consisting of the head only). Clause constituents are typically realized by phrases, and phrase constituents by words, but this typical pattern of constituent realization is often broken, see §§ 1.8-1.9.

1.6    Although the constituents of § 1.4 (1) are all phrases to the extent that they share the PRM-H-POM structure, they are not of the same type. Two of them, *the tall undergraduate with the beard* and *the article*, have a noun as H and are referred to as **noun phrases (NP)**. One, *was reading*, has verbs both as H (the **main verb**) and as PRM (the **auxiliary verb**) and is called a **verb phrase (VP)**. The last type of phrase has either an adjective or an adverb as H — in *very carefully* it is an adverb — and is therefore known as the **adjective/adverb**

**phrase (AP)**. The reason why adjective and adverb phrases are lumped together in this way is that they share the same structure. Thus the adjective phrase corresponding to *very carefully* is *very careful*.

### The Word (1.7)

1.7     Phrase constituents are commonly realized by a **word**. The word, too, is a structure, whose constituents are **root (R)** and **affix**, the latter falling into **prefix (Pf)** and **suffix (Sf)**. Thus, in § 1.4 (1), there are three words we can analyze into word constituents:

$$\underset{\text{Pf} \qquad \text{R}}{\underline{\text{under-graduate}}}$$

$$\underset{\text{R} \quad \text{Sf}}{\underline{\text{read-ing}}}$$

$$\underset{\text{R} \quad \text{Sf} \quad \text{Sf}}{\underline{\text{care-ful-ly}}}$$

For the word parts to be identified as root and affix, each must have a recognizable meaning or general grammatical function of its own. Thus, although neither *reading* nor *carefully* contains suffixes that have meaning in the usual (semantic) sense of the word, they have suffixes with grammatical meaning: *-ing* allows a verb to function as a present participle; *-ful* changes a noun (*care*) into an adjective; and *-ly* changes the adjective into an adverb. On the other hand, it is doubtful whether *gradu-* and *-ate* are felt to make separate contributions to the meaning or function of *graduate*. The smallest unit of language that has a meaning of its own is called a **morpheme**. The study of word structure is often regarded as a special area of grammatical description, called **morphology**, and has not been included in the present book. We shall have little more to say about it except when, occasionally, word structure and other structures are interrelated.

### The Rank Scale — Rankshifting (1.8-1.10)

1.8     It is now time to summarize our **rank scale** of grammatical analysis:

| Rank | Structure | Constituents | Realization |
|------|-----------|--------------|-------------|
| 1 | Clause | S V C A | Phrases |
| 2 | Phrase | PRM H POM | Words |
| 3 | Word | Pf R Sf | Morphemes |

However, before we can show the complete analysis of the example we have been discussing (see § 1.4 (1)), there is still one constituent, the POM *with the beard*, whose realization has yet to be analyzed. As a phrase constituent we would expect it to be realized by a word; instead it is realized by another phrase. When a constituent is realized by a same- or higher-rank structure, we call it **rankshifting**, and we say about *with the beard* that this NP has been **rankshifted**, because instead of realizing a clause constituent as it "ought to" according to the rank scale, it realizes a phrase constituent.

There is one last problem in connection with the analysis of *with the beard*: *with* is not a PRM. In fact, as a preposition (like *at, in, on, by,* etc.), *with* is not part of the NP proper. Instead its function is to show how the NP is related to the larger NP in which *with the beard* is embedded. An NP introduced by a preposition has traditionally been called a **prepositional phrase**.[1] Prepositions share with conjunctions (e.g. *and, but, if, because*) the primary function of "gluing" structures together in this way. The constituent that they realize we call the **junctive (J)**, regardless of whether they function at clause level (*After I had danced with her*) or at phrase level (*After the dance*).

Accordingly, a complete grammatical analysis of our example looks like this:

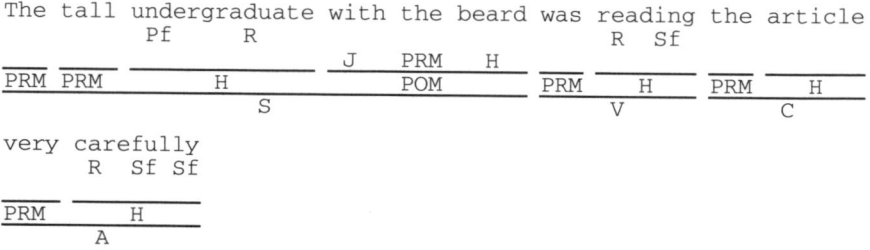

```
The tall undergraduate with the beard was reading the article
         Pf      R                                R   Sf
                                  J    PRM   H
 PRM  PRM        H                     POM        PRM   H    PRM    H
                        S                          V          C

very carefully
      R   Sf Sf

 PRM      H
      A
```

1.9　　Some more examples of rankshifting:

I.a.　*A clause realizing a clause constituent:*

```
He said that he wouldn't come
         J   S      V
 S   V          C
```

```
She wanted to write a book
            V       C
 S     V        C
```

b.　*A clause realizing a phrase constituent:*

```
The man who was a carpenter
        S   V      C
PRM  H        POM
```

```
The lady sitting on the couch
            V       A
PRM  H         POM
```

---

1. In this book it will not be treated as a structural category distinct from the noun phrase.

c. *A clause realizing a word constituent (rare):*

```
Forget-me-nots
  V    C   A
       R      Sf
```

II.a. *A phrase realizing a phrase constituent:*

```
a  ridiculously  low  price
        PRM       H
PRM      PRM            H
```

```
a  boy  your  own  size
        PRM   PRM   H
PRM  H        POM
```

b. *A phrase realizing a word constituent:*

```
The  Mayor  of London's   (limousine)
PRM    H       POM
            R         Sf
```

III. *A word realizing a word constituent:*

```
visit-or-s          use-ful-ness
  R   Sf             R   Sf
  R    Sf            R    Sf
```

1.10    Our analysis of § 1.4 (2) might at first sight appear to be unnecessarily complicated: why maintain that each clause constituent is realized by a phrase and not just a word?

(1)    Undergraduates read articles carefully
            S        V     C      A

The reason is that they can be expanded by phrase constituents:

```
(2)   Few undergraduates here would read  such articles
      PRM       H         POM  PRM   H    PRM    H
              S                  V           C
      very carefully
      PRM      H
            A
```

Consequently we will say that the subject of (1) is realized by a noun phrase whose only constituent is the head, which is realized by the word *under-graduates*. The description of V, C and A will follow the same principle. The realization of clause constituents by one-word phrases is called **simple realization**, see § 1.5.

Another example of simple realization is *Go!*, which is a clause (an imperative clause) consisting of V, which is realized by a verb phrase whose only constituent is H, which is realized by the word *go*. The word *go*, in other words, functions in the same way whether the clause is *go!* or an expanded version:

(3)      You  <u>may  go</u>!
         ___  <u>PRM  H</u>
         S       V

## Subordination and Coordination (1.11)

1.11    Rankshifted clauses are also called **subclauses**. Non-rankshifted clauses are **main clauses**. Thus, in

(1a)    She  promised  <u>that  she  would come</u>
        ___  _____   <u>J    S    V</u>
        S      V              C

(1b)    She  promised  <u>to come</u>
        ___  _____   <u>V</u>
        S      V         C

the main clauses are (1a) *She promised that she would come* and (1b) *She promised to come*, whereas the subclauses are (1a) *that she would come* and (1b) *to come*.

A **sentence** is one or more main clauses, corresponding to units which in written language are bounded by the punctuation mark (.). Thus (2) is a sentence consisting of two main clauses:

(2)      <u>She</u> <u>promised</u> <u>to come</u> <u>and</u> <u>she</u> <u>came</u>
          S       V          C       J     S     V

Main clauses making up a sentence are usually **coordinated** by coordinating junctives, *and*, *but*, *or* (or by commas). The relationship between coordinated items is one of **independence**, cp. §§ 1.3 and 1.4. Not only complete clauses but also clause and phrase constituents can be coordinated, cp. for instance *He took his hat, his coat and his walking stick* (coordinated complements), or *Do you want vanilla, strawberry or chocolate ice cream?* (coordinated premodifiers).

## Form and Function (1.12)

1.12    The **form** of a structure refers to what constituents it consists of, how they are realized and in what order they occur. In § 1.11 above, *that she would come* (1a) and *to come* (1b) are formally different: (1a) is introduced by the junctive *that* and has a subject as well as a complex verbal showing past tense; (1b) has only a verbal in the form of an infinitive introduced by *to*. Their **function** is the same, however: they both function as the complement of *(She) promised*.

Conversely, the phrase *last year* has the same form in (1) and (2) below, but functions differently (as A and POM, respectively):

(1)  <u>Last year</u> <u>his lecture</u> <u>was</u> <u>more interesting</u>
          A              S        V           C

(2)  <u>His</u> <u>lecture</u> <u>last year</u> was more interesting
     PRM     H        POM
     ‾‾‾‾‾‾‾‾‾‾‾‾‾‾‾‾‾‾‾‾‾‾‾    ‾‾‾  ‾‾‾‾‾‾‾‾‾‾‾‾‾‾‾‾
               S              V          C

# II. THE CLAUSE

## THE STRUCTURE OF THE CLAUSE (2.0.1 — 2.7.11)

### Subject and Predicate (2.0.1-2.0.3)

2.0.1  The clause was defined in § 1.3 as a structure which can be analyzed into the constituents S/V/C/A. The clause falls into a number of different types depending on which of (and how) these constituents are actually represented, and in what order, but the point of departure of our description will be the archetypal S/V/C/A structure, the declarative clause:

(1)  <u>Sheila</u> <u>examined</u> <u>the patient</u> <u>yesterday</u>
       S          V              C              A

2.0.2  In § 1.3 we also mentioned the fact that the verbal tends to determine the occurrence of complements and sometimes even adverbials. In example (1) we cannot leave out the complement because the verbal contains the verb *to examine*. In the same way, in example (2), the use of the verb *to put* means that there must be both a complement and an adverbial, while in (3) the verb *to arrive* cannot be followed by a complement.

(2)  Paul put his socks in the drawer
(3)  John has arrived

This means that V/C/A form a substructure of their own; this substructure is called the **predicate**. It is possible to have more than one predicate in the same clause, through coordination. Such predicates may be of different length, but the fact that they can be coordinated proves that they are indeed entities of the same function:

(4)  Kathy *remembered the clown* and *laughed*

2.0.3  In subclauses the predicate sometimes does not contain a verbal, as in (6), compare:

|      |              | Subject     | Predicate          |
|------|--------------|-------------|--------------------|
| (5)  | (I found that) | his action | was foolish (V/C)  |
| (6)  | (I found)      | his action | foolish (C)        |

— just as there are clause types, main clauses (7) as well as subclauses (8), where S is missing:

(7)  Stay with us!
(8)  (I want) to stay with you

We even have **simple clauses** (clauses consisting of only one constituent, cp. § 1.5):

```
(9)    Stay!
(10)   (I want) to stay
```

**The Individual Clause Constituents (2.1-2.5)**

2.1 The **subject** is typically realized by a noun phrase (see Ch. IV). In the common declarative clause the subject precedes, and determines the form of, the verbal. If the subject is a personal pronoun, the pronoun will have the subject form:

(1) *The three little girls from next door* were walking hand in hand

(2) *She* was deeply in love with him

2.2 The **verbal** is always realized by a verb phrase, which consists of a main verb and a maximum of four auxiliary verbs (see Ch. III). The central auxiliaries are *do*, the modal auxiliaries (*can, may, must, shall, will*), *have* and *be. Do, have* and *be* can also function as main verbs.

The first constituent of the verb phrase often occurs in the present or the past tense, e.g. *am/was, says/said*. These forms are called finite, and clauses with finite verb phrases are called **finite clauses**. The other forms of the verb (the infinitive, e.g. *to show*; the present participle, *showing*; the past participle, *shown*) are called nonfinite. If the first constituent of the verb phrase is nonfinite, or if there is no verb phrase at all, the clause is said to be a **nonfinite clause**. In the following examples the main clause is finite, the subclause, nonfinite:

(1) I *want* <u>the patient</u> *to be X-rayed* <u>immediately</u>
  S         S             V         A
  <u>S V</u>              C

(2) You *should have seen* <u>him</u> *kissing* <u>Aunt Mary</u>
                  S    V     C
  <u>S</u>     <u>V</u>             C

(3) He *is having* <u>the house</u> *painted*
                S     V
  <u>S</u>   <u>V</u>         C

(4) I *expect* <u>him home by midnight</u>
          S   A     A
  <u>S V</u>        C

The nature of the main verb determines the structure of the predicate, esp. the number and types of complement, see § 2.6.

2.3.0 **Complements** fall into the following categories:
    (a) subject complement (SC)
    (b) indirect object (IO)
    (c) direct object (DO)
    (d) object complement (OC)

2.3.1     The **subject complement** has either an adjectival phrase or a noun phrase as its
typical realization. The subject complement follows a few main verbs, of which
*be, become* and *seem* are common ones:[1]

```
(1)     Her parents were very rich
(2)     This teacher became a famous actor
```

There is normally number concord between the noun phrase of the subject and
that of the subject complement:

```
(3a)    He seemed such a fool2
(4a)    They seemed such fools
```

— but only if this makes sense in terms of what the subject complement refers
to. There is thus no concord in

```
(5)     Diamonds are a girl's best friend
(6)     The dessert was pancakes
```

2.3.2     **Indirect and direct object**: The direct object is frequently, the indirect object
always,[3] realized by a noun phrase (including those with a pronoun as head):

```
(7)     The old lady gave the little girl/her the ring
                         IO                  DO
```

The direct object is also frequently realized by a clause:

```
(8)     The little girl said she was sorry
                              S    V    C
                                 DO
```

Example (7) indicates the normal positions for these constituents, i.e. after the
verbal, and IO before DO. The order of IO and DO is reversed if IO is realized
by a prepositional phrase (a noun phrase introduced by the junctive *to*):[4]

```
(9)     The old lady gave the ring to the little girl
                         DO              IO
```

---

1. For a special type of subject complement construction, see § 2.3.4, examples (18) and (19).
2. *Look, seem* and *sound* have to be followed by *like* or *to be* in American English, when
governing an indefinite noun phrase. In British English this is also quite common, but not
necessary, in examples like (3a) and (4a).
3. See also § 18.5.3.
4. In British English, *it* or *them* as direct object may precede a pronoun as indirect object
without *to*:
```
        a. He gave it me.
```
The indirect object may also be realized by a noun phrase introduced by *for*:
```
        b. The old lady bought a ring for the little girl (cp. ...bought
           the little girl a ring)
```
However, after most verbs in the relevant contexts, *for...* assumes the meaning of "for the benefit
of...," and would therefore be analyzed as an adverbial rather than as an indirect object; this is
the case in e.g. *The old lady told a story (especially) for the little girl,* which does not mean the same
as *The old lady told the little girl a story.*

Either the indirect or the direct object becomes subject in the corresponding passive clause (S becomes A introduced by *by* or disappears):

(9a)   <u>The little girl</u> <u>was given</u> <u>the ring</u> <u>by the old lady</u>
     S     V   DO    A

(9b)   <u>The ring</u> <u>was given</u> <u>to the little girl</u> <u>(by the old lady)</u>
    S   V    IO      A

The indirect object rarely occurs without the direct object except in passive clauses such as (9b) and after particular verbs (see § 2.6.2), whereas the direct object frequently occurs without the indirect object, as in *Mary sent the ring*, see also (8) above.

2.3.3   **Direct object and object complement**: The distinguishing feature of the DO-OC combination is the fact that the relationship between them corresponds to that between subject and predicate:

(10)   <u>Mary</u> <u>painted</u> <u>the house</u> <u>blue</u>
    S  V   DO   OC

(11)   They chose Peter <u>to represent</u> <u>them</u>
           V    DO
   <u>  </u> <u>  </u> <u>  </u> <u>      </u>
    S   V  DO    OC

In other words, *the house blue* and *Peter to represent them* correspond to *the house became blue* and *Peter was to represent them*.

2.3.4   The reason that the DO and the OC are not analyzed together as one object clause is the fact that the DO is more closely governed by the main-clause verbal than the OC. Thus the OC can often be left out:

(12)   Mary painted the house
(13)   They chose Peter

whereas the predicate of object clauses cannot:

(14)   They found <u>him</u> <u>stupid</u>
        S   SC
   <u>  </u> <u>  </u> <u>     </u>
    S   V    DO

In other words (14) does not include the meaning, *they found him*, but is the same as *they found that he was stupid*.

  Sometimes the OC cannot be left out, either, but it is still possible to see that the main-clause verbal does not govern an object clause:

(15)   <u>His remark</u> <u>made</u> <u>me</u> <u>angry</u>
     S    V  DO  OC

Although I cannot say, *\*His remark made me,*[5] in (15), the meaning is clearly that

---

5. Examples introduced by an asterisk are examples offered as ungrammatical/unacceptable.

his remark did something to me as a result of which I became angry. Other examples where the OC cannot be left out without changing the meaning (16) or causing the utterance to become ungrammatical (17):

```
(16)   Doris called the doctor "Jack"
                         DO       OC
```

```
(17)   The blow knocked Peter unconscious
                        DO       OC
```

In a DO-OC construction only the direct object can become subject of the corresponding passive main clause, in which case the object complement becomes the subject complement (cp. (10) and (11)):

```
(18)   The house was painted blue by Mary
             S        V       SC    A
```

```
(19)   Peter was chosen to represent them
                               V       DO
          S      V          SC
```

2.4.0    **Adverbials** fall into the following categories:
         (a) conjuncts
         (b) disjuncts
         (c) adjuncts

The adverbial is typically realized by adverb phrases, noun phrases and clauses. Noun phrases are often, though not always, prepositional ones (2) where the junctive suggests what type of meaning the A contributes; clauses, too, are often introduced by a junctive or *wh*-word (3), with a similar semantic function, suggesting "place," "time," "cause," "condition," etc.

```
(1)    Jane kissed Frank tenderly
(2)    And on that farm he had a cow
(3)    When the cat is away the mice will play
```

The adverbial differs from other clause constituents in being optional, except in particular clause types (see § 2.6.4), just as it has more options with regard to position in the clause. There is no fixed limit to the number of adverbials which can be introduced into a clause:

```
(4)    (Whether you believe it or not) Jane (certainly) kissed
       Frank (tenderly) (at the party) (last Saturday)
```

The three main types of adverbial, conjunct, disjunct and adjunct, differ according to their degree of integration with the clause: conjuncts and disjuncts are both less integrated with the clause than adjuncts. Frequently therefore they form a separate intonation unit (separated by commas in writing)[6] and are given initial position in the clause, though other positions are not uncommon.

2.4.1 **Conjuncts** are the least integrated category, pointing away from the clause and relating it to the preceding part of the text:

> (5)   I agreed with them that he was incompetent. *Nevertheless* I didn't want to fire him. *Instead* I wanted him promoted to a position where his incompetence would not show. *In other words*, I wanted them to find him a job where he couldn't do any harm

2.4.2 **Disjuncts** represent the speaker's comment on the clause:

> (6)   *Quite frankly*, I think so too ("I'm being frank in saying...")
> (7)   *Preferably* he should leave immediately ("I prefer...")
> (8)   *In all probability*, she will have left a long time ago ("I find it highly probable...")

2.4.3 **Adjuncts** are more closely connected to other clause constituents than conjuncts and disjuncts. One manifestation of this, which can be used as a formal criterion for distinguishing an adjunct, is that the adjunct (as opposed to conjuncts and disjuncts) can be contrasted in interrogative and negative clauses:

> (9)   Will she drive *fast* or will she drive *slowly*?
>        (cp. *Will she drive *furthermore* or will she drive *nevertheless*?)
> (10)  I didn't go there *yesterday* but I am going *today*
>        (cp. *I didn't go there *hopefully*, but I did go *preferably*)

2.4.4 Some adverbials (adjuncts) are so closely connected to the verbal that they are obligatory. The most important clause type with an obligatory adverbial has the verb *to be* as main verb, followed by an adverbial of place or time:

> (11)  He is *in New York*
> (12)  The exam is *tomorrow*

See also §§ 2.6.1-2.6.2 about two other constructions with an obligatory adverbial.

2.5 The **vocative** (Voc) is not really part of the clause structure proper, which is indicated by its independent intonation unit (marked by a comma in writing; see § 2.4.0 n.):

> (1)   *Mark*, I honestly don't think you should do that

---

6. There tend to be distinct patterns in the way the pitch of the voice rises and falls, depending on the meaning. When a particular unit of meaning (e.g. a short clause, a phrase or a word) is given a separate pattern of pitch movement (a separate "tune," or intonation), we refer to it as an intonation unit. The boundary between two intonation units is referred to as an intonation boundary.

(2)    Where did you hide it, *you idiot*?

Voc is always realized by a noun phrase referring to the 2nd person (but cp. § 5.3), and there are few restrictions as to where in the clause it can occur.

### Complementation (2.6.0-2.6.5)

2.6.0    The question of which types of complement, if any, the verbal calls for is often referred to as the question of **complementation**. Here is an overview of the 7 structural types of declarative clause:

1)    *S V*

      $\underset{\text{S}}{\underline{\text{John}}} \ \underset{\text{V}}{\underline{\text{is speaking}}}$

2)    *S V C  (C = SC)*

      $\underset{\text{S}}{\underline{\text{The old man}}} \ \underset{\text{V}}{\underline{\text{is}}} \ \underset{\text{C}}{\underline{\text{happy}}}$        $\underset{\text{S}}{\underline{\text{Kathy}}} \ \underset{\text{V}}{\underline{\text{is}}} \ \underset{\text{C}}{\underline{\text{a plumber}}}$

3)    *S V C  (C = DO)*

      $\underset{\text{S}}{\underline{\text{Mary}}} \ \underset{\text{V}}{\underline{\text{read}}} \ \underset{\text{C}}{\underline{\text{the paper}}}$

4)    *S V C C  (C C = IO DO)*

      $\underset{\text{S}}{\underline{\text{Bill}}} \ \underset{\text{V}}{\underline{\text{gave}}} \ \underset{\text{C}}{\underline{\text{Mary}}} \ \underset{\text{C}}{\underline{\text{a kiss}}}$

5)    *S V C C  (C C = DO OC)*

      $\underset{\text{S}}{\underline{\text{They}}} \ \underset{\text{V}}{\underline{\text{elected}}} \ \underset{\text{C}}{\underline{\text{him}}} \ \underset{\text{C}}{\underline{\text{chairman}}}$        $\underset{\text{S}}{\underline{\text{He}}} \ \underset{\text{V}}{\underline{\text{made}}} \ \underset{\text{C}}{\underline{\text{her}}} \ \underset{\text{C}}{\underline{\text{happy}}}$

6)    *S V A  (A is obligatory)*

      $\underset{\text{S}}{\underline{\text{Henry}}} \ \underset{\text{V}}{\underline{\text{is}}} \ \underset{\text{A}}{\underline{\text{in London}}}$        $\underset{\text{S}}{\underline{\text{Our wedding anniversary}}} \ \underset{\text{V}}{\underline{\text{is}}} \ \underset{\text{A}}{\underline{\text{next week}}}$

7)    *S V C A  (C and A are both obligatory)*

      $\underset{\text{S}}{\underline{\text{I'll}}} \ \underset{\text{V}}{\underline{\text{put}}} \ \underset{\text{C}}{\underline{\text{the milk}}} \ \underset{\text{A}}{\underline{\text{in the refrigerator}}}$

Each of these structural types can be expanded by one or more optional adverbials:

(8)    $\underset{\text{S}}{\underline{\text{John}}} \ \underset{\text{V}}{\underline{\text{laughed}}} \ \underset{\text{A}}{\underline{\text{(very loudly)}}} \ \underset{\text{A}}{\underline{\text{(at my joke)}}} \ \underset{\text{A}}{\underline{\text{(during the lecture)}}}$

This system allows us to distinguish three functional main-verb categories, according to the effect the main verb has on complementation:

(A) **intransitive** verbs, the use of which results in structural type (1)
(B) **transitive** verbs, of which
   - the **monotransitive** ones result in structural type (3) or (7)
   - the **ditransitive** ones result in structural type (4) or (5)
(C) **copula** verbs, the use of which results in structural type (2) or (6).[7]

The same verb can often be used in more than one function, a few even in all three, frequently with a change of meaning in the relationship between subject and verbal (see § 6.4):

```
(9)    The meat smells
           S       V
```

```
(10)   The cook was smelling the soup
           S       V          DO
```

```
(11)   The bread smelt nice
           S       V    SC
```

For verbs with a **clause complement**, see § 2.7 and §§ 3.2-3.4.

To obtain exhaustive information on the transitivity features of the individual verb, it is necessary to consult the dictionary. The following is an overview of the important categories involved.

2.6.1   Where the main verb is **intransitive** the adverbial is normally optional, as in (8) above, but certain intransitives are followed by an obligatory adverbial of place or time:

```
(12)   He was sitting on the veranda
(13)   Byron lived from 1788 to 1824
```

2.6.2   Where the main verb is **monotransitive** the complement is usually the direct object, as in (3) above, but a few verbs which are primarily ditransitive allow for either the direct or indirect object:

```
(14)   I teach the older children French
       S  V          IO              DO
```

```
(15)   I teach the older children
       S  V          IO
```

```
(16)   I teach French
       S  V    DO
```

Other verbs of this type are *ask, tell* (*ask/tell* your teacher, *ask* questions, *tell* stories), *owe, pay* (*owe/pay* the bank, *owe/pay* money).

---

7. Though not all verbs fitting into structural type (6) are copula verbs, see § 2.6.1.

A few monotransitives (e.g. *lack, resemble*) are followed by a DO-like complement which nevertheless cannot become subject in a corresponding passive clause (cp. § 2.3.2):

(17)   They lack water (*Water is lacked by them)

Certain monotransitives take an obligatory adverbial, e.g. *put, set*:

(18)   You should set that dish *in the middle*

2.6.3   **Ditransitive** main verbs are followed either by indirect + direct object (e.g. *give, grant, offer, owe, pay, show, tell*), or direct object + object complement (e.g. *appoint, call, christen, elect, make, name, paint, render*):

(19)   <u>Paula</u> <u>told</u> <u>them</u> <u>a different story</u>
        S     V    IO          DO

(20)   <u>They</u> <u>named</u> <u>him</u> <u>Charles</u>
        S     V     DO    OC

The direct object often occurs without the indirect object (see § 2.3.2), but when certain verbs, e.g. *assure, inform* and *tell*, are followed by a *that*-clause as DO, IO cannot be left out. Compare:

(21)   <u>Paula</u> <u>told</u> <u>a different story</u>
        S     V         DO

(22)   <u>Paula</u> <u>told</u> <u>them</u> <u>that her father had escaped</u>
        S     V    IO          DO

       (not *..told that ..*)

2.6.4   **Copula** main verbs are followed either by a subject complement, i.e. a constituent which characterizes the subject:

(23)   Sheila remained *a quiet girl*
(24)   I am *much stronger than him*

or, if the copula is *be*, by an obligatory adverbial of place[8] or time:

(25)   Peter is *at school*

*Be*, the most important copula verb, is itself empty of lexical meaning. Other copulas have varying degrees of lexical content, such as *become, get, appear, seem, keep, feel, look, smell, taste, sound*:

(26)   John got angry
(27)   This tastes awful

Most of them can also function as transitive or intransitive verbs (see § 2.6).

---

8. In British English, the adverbs *here* and *there* are often left out after *be* in the perfect: *Has the postman been? No, we didn't go to the show yesterday because we'd already been.* This is not possible in American English: *Has the mailman been here? ...we'd already been there.*

2.6.5    The relationship between **transitive** and **intransitive** verbs:
Some verbs are **always intransitive**, e.g. *arrive, rise.*

(28)    Your friend has arrived
(29)    The sun has risen

Some normally intransitive verbs like *die* and *sleep* sometimes take a **cognate object**:

(30)    He *died* the *death* of a hero
(31)    She *laughed* a sad *laugh*

Some verbs are **always transitive**, e.g. *invent, examine*:

(32)    Who invented the steam engine?
(33)    Holmes examined the paper

Many verbs may be used **both transitively and intransitively**, sometimes with little change of meaning:

(34)    He's eating (a steak)
(35)    He smokes (cigars)

Others require in their intransitive use the same type of subject as the object of the corresponding transitive construction; those which are not primarily transitive usually have **causative** meaning when used transitively:

(36)    The door opened/she opened the door (= caused the door to open)
(37)    He marched along/He marched the soldiers to the front (= caused the soldiers to march)

— whereas those which are primarily transitive may acquire a meaning corresponding to the passive when used intransitively, cp.

(38)    They can easily sell his books/His books sell well (= passive: *can be sold*)
(39)    He wound up the clock/The clock winds up at the back (= passive: *is wound up*)

**Verbs with a Clause Object (2.7.0-2.7.11)**

2.7.0    The main verb also determines the (usually several) types of subclause that can function as its direct object. In the following we will give a rough outline of some general categories of the relationship between main verb and direct-object clause.

2.7.1    Verbs whose meaning is related to the expression of **opinion** or **wish** typically govern a *that*-clause, e.g. *admit, argue, believe, claim, demand, deny, find, mean, request, suggest, think, wish* (*that* is often omitted except in formal usage):

(1)     I admit *(that) I had not thought of it*

Many of these verbs govern other types of direct-object clause as well. Some of them, furthermore, require an indirect object besides the *that*-clause, e.g. *convince, satisfy, tell, warn*:

(2)    John convinced *me* that he could do the job

2.7.2    Some of the same verbs, concerning **knowledge** and **doubt**, also govern interrogative clauses, be they *wh*-clauses (finite or nonfinite (infinitive)) or *if*-clauses; e.g. *ask, decide, find out, know, wonder*:

(3)    We don't know *who is responsible*
(4)    We couldn't decide *what to do*
(5)    I wonder *whether/if she would be willing to help*

2.7.3    Verbs of **sense perception** (*feel, hear, notice, see*) enter into three different types of construction:

(6)    I heard him yell for help
(7)    I heard him yelling for help
(8)    I heard that you needed help

The subject of the object clause (*him* in (6-7)) is obligatory. The infinitive is without *to*, except in the passive, see § 3.1. The difference in meaning between an infinitive (6) and an *-ing* clause (7) corresponds to that between non-progressive and progressive, see § 8.2.3. The object clause must be a finite *that*-clause if its main verb is a stative one (*need* in (8), see § 8.1.2).

Two verbs which do not indicate sense perception may govern an infinitive clause without *to* like the one in (6) above, viz. *have* and *know*:

(9)    John had *them build a house*
(10)   I have never known *her (to) tell a lie*

2.7.4    Some verbs can govern a *to*-infinitive clause, which may have a subject, e.g. after *claim, expect, mean, want, wish*. The subject does not appear if it would have been identical with the subject of the main clause:

(11)   I want *to be free* − I want *him to be free*

The subject may also be obligatory, e.g. after *cause, know, require*:

(12)   I know *him to be a coward*

Finally, the *to*-infinitive clause may never have a subject, e.g. after *agree, aim, attempt, consent, decide, decline, demand, deserve, determine, learn, manage, offer, pretend, promise, refuse, threaten*:

(13)   We agreed *to go there together*

2.7.5    In some *to*-infinitive clauses with an obligatory subject, the infinitive is an optional copula, e.g. after *acknowledge, believe, consider, find, hold* (the latter three in the sense of "regard as"), *imagine, proclaim, report, suppose, want*:

```
(14)   They believed him (to be) dead
(15)   I want him (to be) here by tomorrow morning
```

2.7.6   After a few verbs (in particular contexts), the *to*-infinitive clause is introduced
        by the junctive *for* if containing a subject, e.g. after *arrange, plan, telephone*:

```
(16)   She had arranged for the plumber to come around
```

2.7.7   Some verbs govern a present-participle (-*ing*) clause as direct object, e.g. *avoid,
        consider* ("contemplate"), *contemplate, deny, escape, finish, give up, (cannot) help,
        imply, include, keep (on), (don't) mind, postpone, practice* (AE)/*practise* (BE), *put off,
        resent, resist, (cannot) stand, stop, suggest*:

```
(17)   I carefully avoided looking at her
(18)   She gave up trying to please him a long time ago
(19)   I can't help feeling guilty about it
```

The -*ing* clause is usually without a subject, but may sometimes have one,
alternating with a genitive construction (see also §§ 3.1 n., 3.6, 10.3.2):

```
(20)   I resent John('s)/him (his) taking all the credit
```

After a few verbs the subject is obligatory, e.g. after *catch, find, have, leave, send,
set*:

```
(21)   They found him working at his desk
(22)   She soon had them all laughing
```

2.7.8   The -*ing* and the *to*-infinitive clause alternate as direct object after, for instance,
        *begin, cease, continue, dread, forget, intend, neglect, propose, regret, remember*:

```
(23)   He had ceased wondering/to wonder what it was all about
(24)   She continued seeing/to see him whenever she could
```

Some verbs take on a different meaning depending on whether they govern an
-*ing* clause (denoting actualized action) or an infinitive clause (denoting non-
actualized action):

```
(25a)  I forget mentioning it to him
(25b)  I forgot to mention it to him
(26a)  Does he remember locking the door?
(26b)  Does he always remember to lock the door?
(27a)  I regret saying that I don't like you — I didn't mean it
(27b)  I regret to say that I don't like you
(28a)  She tried writing, but he didn't reply
(28b)  She tried to write, but her feelings were too strong for her
```

2.7.9   Prepositions cannot govern *that*- or infinitive clauses, which is why prepositional
        verbs (see § 7.9.2) generally take an -*ing* clause as direct object, cp:

```
(29)   She insisted on a proper wedding (DO = NP)
(30)   She insisted on telling him herself (DO = clause)
```

An exception is the preposition *for* when it introduces an infinitive clause that has a subject (see § 2.7.6 above); thus compare:

```
(31)   I long for him (DO = NP)
(32)   I long for him to come home (DO = clause)
```

where *for* belongs both to the main verb and to the object clause. Another exception is interrogative infinitive clauses:

```
(33)   She is always worrying about what to wear and how to
       get home
```

However, many verbs allow the use of *that*- and infinitive clauses in connection with the deletion of the preposition:

```
(34)   I long to go home (cp. (31))
(35)   She insisted that she wanted to tell him herself (cp. (30))
```

Sometimes it is necessary to let the preposition govern a noun which can then be postmodified by the *that*-clause. Such common "prop" nouns include e.g. *fact, idea, possibility, suggestion*:

```
(36)   Have you allowed for the fact that your new students
       PRM  ___        H         PRM  H          POM→
       V-    S         -V                        DO→

       can't spell
        ←POM
         ←DO
```

```
(37)   I object to the idea that we should pay for it
```

Note that *fact* can only be used if the *that*-clause does refer to something which is a fact.

Finally, a few verbs (e.g. *rely on, see to*) allow the use of *it* as a preliminary object:

```
(38)   You must see (to it) that this never happens again
```

2.7.10  Some verbs can govern a direct-object clause whose verbal is a past participle, e.g. *find, get, have, hear, keep, leave, see, want*; the past-participle clause always has a subject:

```
(39)   Fred got his boss fired
(40)   Al Capone had the man shot
(41)   John wants the job done by Friday
```

2.7.11  Some verbs govern a direct-object/object-complement construction where the object complement is a clause. Thus *let* and *make* take an infinitive clause without *to*, whereas after *help* the infinitive may be with or without *to*:

```
(42)   My parents let/made me write her a letter
(43)   Peter helped (them) do the dishes
```

(44)   I helped *her (to) find her shoes*[9]

A larger group of verbs have a *to*-infinitive clause as OC. Most of these denote "influence," e.g. *advise, allow, ask, encourage, forbid, order, permit, persuade, teach, tell*:

(45)   I allowed Mary to kiss John
```
                         V    DO
       ___ ___ ____ _____
        S   V   DO    OC
```

(46)   I persuaded Peter *to steal the money*

It may be difficult to distinguish verbs of this category from the monotransitive ones of § 2.7.4, e.g. *expect*, cp. (45) with (45a):

(45a)  I expected Mary to kiss John
```
                  S    V   DO
       ___ ___ _____
        S   V         DO
```

However, the meaning of verbs like *allow* always "affects," in particular, the person who would otherwise have been the subject of the subclause, whereas a verb like *expect* can be constructed so as not to single out any particular participant in the event. For instance, *I allowed John to be kissed by Mary* has a different meaning than (45) — the person allowed something is now John, not Mary — in spite of the fact that *Mary to kiss John* (active) and *John to be kissed by Mary* (passive) mean the same. By contrast, *I expected Mary to have kissed John* and *I expected John to have been kissed by Mary* mean the same.

## THE FUNCTIONS OF THE CLAUSE (3.0-3.8.2)

3.0   We distinguish between two main **functional types** of clause: **main clauses**, which are independent in the sense that they are not constituents of a larger structure, and **subclauses**, which are rankshifted (see §§ 1.8-1.9, 1.11). Main clauses can be coordinated (see § 1.11), but as the coordination of main clauses concerns the description of textual units larger than the clause it will not be dealt with here. Subclauses function as constituents of clauses or phrases (in rare cases, even of words, as shown in § 1.9), and it is these functions that we will describe in the following.

Initially, it should be pointed out that there is in principle no limit to the number of times a structure can be rankshifted. In

---

9. The construction without *to* is particularly frequent in American English.

(1)   I heard that he would leave when his car was ready
                                        J      S    V   SC
              J   S      V                        A
      S   V                        DO

*when...ready* has been rankshifted twice, functioning as the adverbial of a clause which is itself the complement of another clause; but the rankshifting could theoretically go on and on (as in *This is the dog that chased the cat that caught the mouse that...*) if it had not, in practice, been limited by the need for comprehensibility.

Rankshifting is often marked by a **junctive** (see § 1.8). Subclauses, furthermore, can also be marked by containing a nonfinite verb phrase (or no verb phrase at all), in which case we call them **nonfinite clauses** (see § 2.2). Finally, rankshifting can be unmarked, as when in informal usage the junctive *that* is optional:

(2)   He knew (that) she would like it


## Subclauses as Subject (3.1)

3.1   Finite subject clauses are introduced by a junctive (*whether* or *that*) or an interrogative pronoun:

(1)   *That she actually did it* came as a complete surprise[10]
(2)   *Whether she liked him* is another question
(3)   *How they did it* was a mystery

Nonfinite (infinitive or present participle) clauses may be with or without a subject of their own; infinitive clauses with a subject (4) are normally introduced by the junctive, *for*:

(4)   (For Sheila) to stop smoking is unthinkable
        J     S       V      DO
              S              V    SC

(5)   *(Me) being a policeman* makes it difficult to cheat[11]

Infinitive clauses functioning as subject are sometimes divided. Clauses of this type can occur with certain alternative copula constructions (e.g. with *seem, appear*), in connection with particular other verbs (e.g. *come to, happen to, tend to*), and in passive clauses with verbs of sense perception. Such clauses are never introduced by *for*:

---

10. This construction alternates with one in which the subordinate clause is POM in a NP realizing the main-clause S: *The fact that he did it* came as a surprise.
11. *Me being a policeman* is informal usage; the more formal construction would employ the genitive form of the pronoun: *My being a policeman*. Cp. §§ 3.6 and 10.3.2.

```
(6)     He appeared to be mad    (cp. He appeared mad)
        S           V    SC           S        V      SC
        S-    V       -S
```

```
(7)     It was seen to be a problem
```

The main characteristic of these is that if the divided subject clause has an object, it can be passivized without changing the meaning of the utterance or making it ungrammatical:[12]

```
(8a)    The President happened to read the document
              S                    V        DO
              S-          V           -S
```

```
(8b)    The document happened to be read by the President
              S                   V          A
              S-          V              -S
```

whereas this kind of passive construction is not possible with a normal direct object realized by an infinitive clause, cp. (9a) and (9b):

```
(9a)    The President expected to read the document
                                 V        DO
              S           V         DO
```

```
(9b)    *The document expected to be read by the President
```

Finally, a divided infinitive clause as subject is found in connection with a copula verb (mostly *be*) followed by adjectives like *bound, certain, likely, sure*:

```
(10)    He was certain to get caught
        S                 V
        S-  V    SC        -S
```

Subject clauses may also occur after a **preliminary subject** (*it*); in finite ones (11) the junctive, *that*, can then be omitted in informal usage:

```
(11)    It was certain (that) he would get caught
                          J    S      V
        S=  V    SC           =S
```

```
(12)    It seems such a waste for a man like him to die so young
(13)    It is a nightmare being married to you
```

*-ing* clauses as subject after a preliminary subject (13) do not contain a subject of their own in written language, though constructions like *It's a nightmare my being stuck here* are not uncommon in speech.

For a special type of subject-clause construction, see § 5.4 on "Cleft Clauses."

---

12. These verbs may cooccur with periphrastic *do* (see § 7.4), which is one reason why we regard them as main verbs rather than auxiliaries premodifying the following verb. Another is the fact that we can change the structure of clauses like (6) and (8), without changing the meaning, to show that the subject of these verbs is a clause:

```
        6a.  It appeared that he was mad
        8c.  It (so) happened that the President read the document
```

## Subclauses as Subject Complement (3.2)

3.2    Finite clauses as subject complement are usually introduced by a junctive (*that,*
*whether, if*), though *that* may be left out in informal style, or they may have an
interrogative pronoun as their first element:

(1)    The fact is (that) her bag was stolen
                    J      S        V
        S    V              SC

(2)    The question is what they will do about it
                         DO    S    V        A
        S        V              SC

(3)    The question is *whether/if she will ever remember*

Nonfinite SC clauses are of the infinitive or present-participle type; the infinitive
clause sometimes has an interrogative pronoun as its first element (5), or it may
have a subject introduced by *for* (7):

(4)    To see her is to love her
        V   DO      V    DO
        S    V     SC

(5)    The problem is where to begin
                        A     V
        S        V    SC

(6)    All I did was *(to) hit him a little*
(7)    The idea is *for Mary to call him on Wednesday*
(8)    Seeing is *believing*

## Subclauses as Direct Object (3.3)

3.3    Finite object clauses are usually introduced by a junctive (*that, whether, if*),
though *that* may be left out in informal style, or they may have an interrogative
pronoun as their first element (for an example with a relative pronoun, see
§ 3.7.1 (8b)):

(1)    She said (that) she was sorry
                  J    S   V   SC
        S    V          DO

(2)    He asked what they gave her
                   DO    S    V   IO
        S    V           DO

(3)    I don't know *whether/if they are coming*

Nonfinite clauses (infinitive, present participle, past participle or no verbal) may
be with or without a subject of their own:

(4)    I want him to come
                S    V
        S  V       DO

(5)    I want <u>to come</u>
                    <u>V</u>
       <u>S</u>  <u>V</u>    <u>DO</u>

(6)    I saw *John kissing Mary*
(7)    Mary resented *kissing John*
(8)    I saw *him beaten in the Derby* last year
(9)    They believed *him (to be) older*

Infinitive clauses may be introduced by an interrogative pronoun:

(10)   I don't know *what to do*

When main clauses with an infinitive-clause object are turned into the passive, only the subject of the infinitive clause is moved in front of the main-clause verbal; cp. (9) and (9a):

(9)    They believed <u>him</u> <u>(to be)</u> <u>older</u>
                              <u>S</u>    <u>V</u>      <u>SC</u>
       <u>S</u>        <u>V</u>          <u>DO</u>

(9a)   <u>He</u> was believed <u>(to be)</u> <u>older</u>
       <u>S</u>                   <u>V</u>      <u>SC</u>
       <u>S-</u>      <u>V</u>            <u>-S</u>

## Subclauses as Object Complement (3.4)

3.4    These are infinitive clauses, see §§ 2.3.3-2.3.4 and 2.7.11:

(1)    Mary let John *kiss her*
(2)    The teacher asked a student *to read aloud*

## Subclauses as Adverbial (3.5.0-3.5.10)

3.5.0  The following is an account of the most important semantic types of adverbial clause.

3.5.1  **Clauses of Time:**
       (A) Finite time clauses are always introduced by junctives like *after, as soon as, before, now (that), until, when, while*, etc.

(1)    I had a cup of coffee *while I waited*

(B) Nonfinite time clauses are often, but not always, introduced by such junctives. They include present-participle (2a-b), past-participle (3a-b) and verbless (4) clauses:

(2a)   Sheila sold her house *before going to Australia*
(2b)   *(After) having talked to him for ten minutes*, she decided
       it was time to leave
(3a)   *Once discovered*, the caverns were soon visited by thousands
       of tourists

```
(3b)    That done, we hurriedly left the house
(4)     When in difficulty, press the red button
```

### 3.5.2 **Clauses of Place** are introduced by *where* and are always finite:

```
(5)     I found my papers where I had left them
```

### 3.5.3 **Conditional Clauses:**

(A) Finite conditional clauses are usually introduced by the junctives *if* and *unless*, less commonly by *on condition (that), providing (that)*, etc. If there is no junctive, the finite verb form *had, should* or *were* precedes the subject (8).

```
(6)     He will help you if you ask him
(7)     He won't help you unless you ask him
(8)     She would have told me, had she been there
```

(B) Nonfinite conditional clauses, introduced by *if* or *unless*, have a past participle or no verbal:[13]

```
(9)     No one is to say anything unless asked
(10)    If in doubt, ask your physician
```

### 3.5.4 **Concessive Clauses** denote a condition fulfilled or a potential cause which does not have the expected effect. They are introduced by *(al-)though, (even) if, even though, while, whereas*. The nonfinite ones have a present participle, a past participle, or no verbal at all, being characteristic mainly of formal written language:

```
(11)    (Even/al-)though he studied like mad, his grades did not
        improve
(12)    Though still working, it's a terribly outdated machine
(13)    Though given every opportunity, he never distinguished
        himself
(14)    His room was comfortable, if small
```

Two special types of concessive clause are introduced by an interrogative junctive or pronoun, viz. *whether...or* clauses, and clauses with an interrogative pronoun followed by *-ever* (or preceded by *no matter*):

```
(15)    I'm going to do it whether you like it or not
(16)    Whatever/no matter what they say, don't let them persuade
        you
```

### 3.5.5 **Causal Clauses:**

(A) Finite clauses denoting cause are introduced by junctives like *as, because, since, considering/seeing (that)*:

```
(17)    I married you because I love you
```

---

13. The present participle in conditional clauses is limited to the idiomatic expressions, *weather permitting* and *God willing* (e.g. *We go for a walk every afternoon, weather permitting*).

(18)  *Seeing that/since she won't tell me the truth*, I'll have to find out for myself

(B) Nonfinite causal clauses, which are usually without junctives, have a present participle, a past participle, or no verbal; they characterize formal (written) usage:

(19)  *Being essentially a man of peace*, he kept quiet and let the others quarrel
(20)  *All her optimism gone*, she now wanted to sell her business
(21)  *Still unhappy*, the child refused to speak

3.5.6  **Purpose Clauses** are most frequently *to*-infinitive clauses, sometimes introduced by *in order* or *so as*:

(22)  He told them the truth *(in order/so as) to prevent gossip*

Finite purpose clauses are introduced by *so that* or, in formal usage, *in order that*, *lest*:

(23)  He died *so that/in order that others might live*
(24)  He closed the door *lest she (should) see what he was doing*

3.5.7  **Consecutive Clauses**, expressing a consequence not necessarily intended, are mostly finite clauses introduced by *so (that)*:

(25)  Nothing more was heard of her, *so that they thought she was dead*

3.5.8.  **Comparative Clauses** are usually introduced by *as, as if, as though*, and may be finite or nonfinite:

(26)  She cooks a chicken just *as/like my mother did*
(27)  She treats me *as if/as though I was a child*
(28)  He remained silent, *as if to demonstrate his dissatisfaction*
      *...as if wondering how to proceed*
      *...as if seized by sudden doubt*
      *...as if in a trance*

In American English, and in nonstandard British English, *like* is frequently used instead of *as if/though* in finite clauses:

(29)  She treats me *like I was a child*

3.5.9  **Subject-Related Clauses** characterize the subject of the main clause, cp. § 4.4.5. They are nonfinite, and are most often without a junctive:

(30)  One of the soldiers, *(with) his rifle trailing behind him*, staggered by
(31)  She gasped, *taken by surprise*
(32)  She died *rich*
(33)  He came out of prison *a changed man*

The types represented by *rich* (32) and *a changed man* (33) are regarded here as verbless clauses containing only a subject complement.[14]

3.5.10  It should be noted, in conclusion, that nonfinite adverbial clauses without a subject usually have an implied subject which is identical with the subject of the main clause:

> (34)   John completed his book *before going to America*
>        (= before he (John) went to America)

Exceptions, though frowned upon by purists, are by no means uncommon. The acceptability of such "dangling participles," however, depends on how easy it is to identify the implicit subject in the context of the main clause:

> (35)   *By not training students to understand spontaneous speech*
>        *in the target language,* they may be handicapped in reaching
>        a high level of proficiency in production (= if we do not
>        train students...we may handicap them...)

### The Subclause as Noun-Phrase Head (3.6)

3.6     *-ing* clauses may be introduced by the genitive form of a noun or pronoun (i.e. the *-'s/-s'* form of a noun, or forms like *my, our, your, her, their, whose*). As the genitive marks the structure of the noun phrase, however (see § 10.3.2), such constructions are regarded as noun phrases with a clause as head:

> (1)     My <u>being</u> <u>a policeman</u> (makes it difficult to cheat)
>                 V        SC
>         ___
>         PRM        H
>
>         (cp. *My position* makes...)
>
> (2)     (I resent) his/John's <u>taking</u> <u>all the credit</u>
>                                      V            DO
>                     _____
>                         PRM       H
>
>         (cp. I resent *his/John's ingratitude*)

See also §§ 2.7.7 and 3.1 n.

### The Subclause as Noun-Phrase Postmodifier (3.7.0-3.7.3)

3.7.0   There are three types of subclause that can function as a noun-phrase

---

14. *Die* is not usually considered a copula verb (see § 2.6.5). However, to the extent that it could be said to have copula function in (32) (cp. *She became rich*), an alternative analysis might be:

> *She died rich.*
> S     V    SC

postmodifier: (1) relative clauses, (2) appositional clauses, and (3) nonfinite clauses.

3.7.1 **Relative Clauses** are finite clauses introduced by a **relative pronoun** (in particular, *who/-m/-se, which, what, that*) or **relative proadverbials** (*where, when, why, how*). These forms function as constituents of the relative clause at the same time as relating it to the noun-phrase head (e.g. *boy* in (1)),[15] which we call the **antecedent** of the relative clause:

(1a)    The boy *who works for Mr. Johnson* is a friend of mine
                 S    V        A
         H              POM
         S                              V         SC

(1b)    The boys *who work for Mr. Johnson* are friends of mine

(2)     The girl *that I mentioned* is visiting us tomorrow
                  DO  S    V
         H            POM
         S                        V      DO    A

(3)     That's the place *where the accident occurred*
                           A        S         V
              H                 POM
         S   V                  SC

(4)     Tell me the reason *why you won't join us*

When the relative pronoun is the subject of the relative clause, as in (1a) and (1b), the form of the relative-clause verbal (*works/work*) is determined by the form of the antecedent (*boy/boys*).

The relative clauses of (1)-(4) are all **defining** relative clauses, necessary for the identification of whatever the head refers to. Relative clauses may also be **nondefining**, in which case they are not necessary for identification but represent an additional piece of information, usually marked by a separate intonation unit/commas (§ 2.4.0 n.); see also § 13.4.3:

(5)     George, *who works for Mr. Johnson*, is a friend of mine
(6)     My younger brother, *whom you just met*, is visiting us tomorrow

The relative clauses of (5) and (6) are analyzed in the same way as (1)-(4), i.e.

---

15. *Wh*-words (*who, what, when, how, where*, etc.) introducing subclauses differ from junctives in that they are constituents (e.g. adverbial or subject) of the subclause:

    a.      (I don't know) *when she arrives*
                            A    S     V
    b.      (The applicant) *who called yesterday*
                            S     V      A

However, they can be said to have a junctive function in so far as they help to identify the function of the subclause, for instance as a direct-object interrogative clause ((a), see 3.3), or as a postmodifying relative clause (b).

as postmodifiers. A (nondefining) relative clause may refer to the whole of the preceding clause, however, in which case the analysis is one of coordination:

(7)    She didn't hear you play, which is a pity
       S      V        DO      S   V   SC

       (= *and this is a pity*)

With other relative clauses (notably those introduced by *what*), the antecedent is included in the meaning of the relative pronoun (e.g. *what* = *that which*). However, we have to analyze them as postmodifiers if the analysis is to explain the difference in meaning between e.g.

(8a)   They only asked what I knew          (interrogative *what*
                      DO   S  V              = "what it was that..")
                           DO

(8b)   They asked only what I knew          (relative *what* = *that which*)
                      DO   S  V
                      ─────────
                      H    POM
                        DO

The relative pronoun may be only part of a relative clause constituent:

(9)    The man *whose house* she bought moved to Iowa
               PRM    H
        ─    ───────  DO     S    V
        H      POM
           S                      V    A

(10)   She told me a ghastly story, *the truth of which is doubtful*
                                     PRM   H    POM
                                              S       V   SC
        ─   ─   ──   ─────────────   H           POM
        S   V   IO                        DO

Finally, if the relative pronoun in a defining relative clause is not the subject, it can be left out, e.g. *that* in (2) above: *The girl (that) I mentioned...*

The use of the relative pronouns and proadverbials is discussed in greater detail in § 18.

3.7.2  **Appositional clauses** are finite postmodifier clauses of the following two types:

(A) The relationship between the antecedent and the appositional clause corresponds to that between a verb and its object clause. The antecedent is thus a noun like *answer, belief, demand, knowledge, suggestion, question,* etc. (cp. §§ 2.7.1-2.7.2):

(1)    The question *of who had committed the crime* was not important (interrogative clause, cp. "they asked *who had committed the crime*")

(2)    The suspicion *that he was lying* worried them greatly (cp. "they suspected *that he was lying*")

Our analysis of appositional clauses introduced by an interrogative pronoun (1) is the same as for relative clauses, i.e. the pronoun is a constituent of the postmodifier clause. Note the junctive *of*, however (see § 10.8.6). Appositional *that*-clauses (2), on the other hand, show up in our analysis (2a) as non-relative because *that* is a junctive, not a constituent of the clause; cp. this analysis with a relative construction (3):

(2a)  The suspicion that he was lying worried them greatly
                      J   S   V
      H                   POM

(3)   The suspicion that he was causing worried them greatly
                      DO  S   V
      H                   POM

Only as a relative pronoun (3) can *that* be replaced by *which* or zero: *The suspicion (which) he was causing...*

(B) The appositional clause may postmodify a "prop" noun like those mentioned in § 2.7.9 (35)-(36), e.g. *chance, fact, idea, news, possibility*:

(4)   His reaction to the news *that she was pregnant* was
      unexpectedly strong
(5)   The possibility *that she actually committed the murder*
      cannot be ignored

In some cases, the relationship between the noun and the appositional clause corresponds to that between a subject complement (containing the same noun or the corresponding adjective) and a subject clause, as in constructions with *fact, possibility*, cp. (5) and (5a):

(5a)  It is possible that she actually committed the murder
                      J   S   A      V        DO
      S= V  SC                      =S

The above examples are all defining appositional clauses. Appositional clauses, like relative clauses (cp. § 3.7.1), may also be nondefining:

(6)   Her answer, *that she didn't love him any more*, drove him to
      despair

3.7.3  **Nonfinite Clauses** (see § 5.10) as noun-phrase postmodifiers have an infinitive, a present-participle or a past-participle verbal:

(1)   This is not the way *(for you) to do it*
(2)   The way *(in which) to get her attention* is by sending her
      flowers
(3)   His desire *to see her* became an obsession
(4)   Their main problem, *how to dig a tunnel under the wall*, was
      a formidable one
(5)   It was a mixture *consisting of oil and vinegar*
(6)   An obituary *written by my friend* appeared last week

The infinitive clause corresponds either to a relative (1-2) or to an appositional (3-4) clause. Thus we note the possible occurrence of a relative pronoun governed by a preposition in (2), and the presence of an interrogative pronoun (*how*) in (4), cp. § 3.7.2 (1). Note also, in examples like (3), that either the first or the second part of the appositional construction could be left out:

```
(3a)   His desire became an obsession
(3b)   To see her became an obsession
```

whereas this would not be possible with the relative construction (2), cp. (2a) and (2b):

```
(2a)   *The way is by sending her flowers
(2b)   *To get her attention is by sending her flowers
```

The infinitive clause is introduced by *for* if it has a subject (1).

The past-participle clause (6) corresponds to the passive, *(which was) written by...*

All of these nonfinite types can be defining as well as nondefining modifiers; compare for instance (3) and (4) above.

### The Subclause as Adjective/Adverb-Phrase Postmodifier (3.8.1-3.8.2)

3.8.1   A clause may realize the postmodifier of an adjective/adverb phrase (AP).[16] This clause postmodifier may **correlate** with either the premodifier (1) or the suffix of comparison in the head (2). Two items are said to correlate (to be correlates) if you cannot have one without the other. When the postmodifier clause is finite, this interdependence is signalled by pairs like *as...as, so...that, (comparative)..than*; when it is nonfinite, by pairs such as *so...as, too...to*:

```
(1)     He is as   tough as they come
                          J    S    V
                   PRM   H      POM
              S  V            SC
```

```
(2)     I like you better than to hurt you like that
                                J     V    DO    A
                         H            POM
              S   V  DO              A
```

```
(3)     Would you be so kind as to lend me £300,000?
(4)     He hid his treasure so carefully that he couldn't find it
        again
(5)     She is more optimistic than he (is)
(6)     This is too good to be true
```

3.8.2   A number of adjectives occur with a clause postmodifier that has **no correlate**.

---

16. The phrase has the same structure whether an adjective or an adverbial is head (see Ch. VI), which is why we refer to it as one type.

Several of these are adjectives denoting a state of mind, e.g. *alarmed, amazed, anxious*:

```
(7)    I'm anxious (for you) to meet him
                     J    S    V    DO
              H           POM
       S V                SC
```

```
(8)    I'm amazed that he passed the exam
                    J   S    V      DO
             H           POM
       S V               SC
```

## THE ORDER OF CLAUSE CONSTITUENTS (4.0-4.4.7)

### Position of the Subject (4.0-4.2.5)

4.0    Typically, the subject precedes the verbal. In the following we shall describe the conditions under which this is not the case.

To do so, we must take a preliminary look at the structure of the verb phrase. The verb phrase has a main verb as H, and a maximum of four auxiliary verbs as PRMs. For the purpose of this chapter we will call the verbal head "V", and the verbal premodifiers, "v". The typical order of subject and verbal, then, is:

S (v v v v) V

If the subject does not precede the whole of the verbal, we have **inversion**. There are two types of inversion, **partial** inversion (§ 4.1) and **full** inversion (§ 4.2).

4.1.0    **Partial inversion** is a type of inversion where only the finite verb (the first verb from the left, in visual terms) is moved to the left of the subject:

```
v S (v v v) V          Have you been drinking?
                        v   S   v     V
                       (cp. You have been drinking)
                            S    v    v      V
```

If the finite verb is the main verb (i.e. if there are no auxiliaries), it is the auxiliary *do* which is introduced to the left of the subject. This is not the case, however, if the main verb is *be* (and *have* in the sense of "possess," in conservative British English),[17] in which case the main verb itself is moved to the left of the subject:

```
                  Do you smoke?        (cp. You smoke)
(but:)            Are you happy?       (cp. You are happy)
```

Partial inversion is made obligatory by particular grammatical contexts, see §§ 4.1.1-4.1.7. We treat inversion of the type exemplified by *Are you happy?* under partial inversion (although it is in fact the whole of the verbal which is moved here, cp. § 4.2.0) because this type is obligatory in the same grammatical contexts as partial inversion generally.

4.1.1    Partial inversion is used in interrogative main clauses whose subject is not an interrogative pronoun, and in tag questions (where the main verb is understood, see (3)):

```
(1)      Will you help me?
(2)      Where do you live?
(3)      (You're leaving), aren't you?
                             v       S
```

Interrogative subclauses do not have inversion, see § 5.2.4.

4.1.2    It is also used if the clause is introduced by a negative or restrictive constituent:

```
(4)      Not a single mistake did she make
          A         DO          v    S   V
```

```
(5)      Only then did I realize how wrong I was
```

though not if this constituent is a disjunct or conjunct (7), or a focus adjunct (see § 4.4.5) preceding a disjunct (6) or subject (8):

```
(6)      Not surprisingly, she refused to comment on her colleague's
         performance
(7)      He badly wanted to leave, only he couldn't
(8)      Only John failed the exam[18]
```

4.1.3    Partial inversion occurs in elliptic clauses (i.e. clauses where the rest of the predicate is understood) after *neither, nor* and *so*; the meaning is "the same goes for...":

---

17. *Have* in American English, and increasingly in British English, is treated in all contexts as a normal main verb, with *do*-inversion: *I don't have any money; does he have any money?*
    When *have* means "possess," the most widely used form in British English is *have got*: *I haven't got any money; has he got any money?*
    In conservative British English, *have* in the sense of "possess" is constructed without *do*: *I haven't any money; has he any money?*
    When *have* does not mean "possess" British English too treats it like a normal main verb: *I didn't have any breakfast; did you have a good holiday?*
    18. Observe also that *only* is not restrictive when it means "as recently as," i.e. it does not cause inversion in the type, *Only two weeks ago I saw him walking down the street.*

```
(9)   I don't like it, and neither does my wife
(10)  I like it very much, and so does my wife
```

4.1.4 Partial inversion also occurs if the clause is introduced by an adverbial or complement containing an expression of degree. This construction is found mainly in literary style:

```
(11)  So arrogantly did he behave that he managed to turn everyone
      against him
(12)  Well do I remember the day when she first came to this town
(13)  Many a morning had they spent fishing together in the bay
```

4.1.5 Furthermore, partial inversion occurs in conditional clauses without *if*. Such clauses always contain *had, should* or *were* as the finite verb. This construction is more common in written than in spoken language:

```
(14)  He would not have been so honest, had he been sober
(15)  Should you want any help, let me know
(16)  You would be shocked, were I to repeat what she said
```

4.1.6 Partial inversion occurs in negative imperative clauses which have a subject:

```
(17)  Don't you dare touch me again!
```

4.1.7 Finally, it occurs when *may* expresses "wish":

```
(18)  May we live to see the day!
```

4.2.0 **Full Inversion** means that the whole of the verbal is moved to the left of the subject, including the main verb.

```
(v v v v) V S          In the swing was sitting the most
                       beautiful girl I had ever seen
```

Full inversion never involves the use of auxiliary *do*, nor is it usually obligatory (though see § 4.2.2). Instead, it may be chosen for stylistic reasons as a manifestation of the "end-weight" principle that long and important constituents tend to appear in clause-final position: the subject is usually long and weighty (it is never a pronoun), as compared with the verbal, which is less charged with meaning and often simple.

4.2.1 Full inversion is frequently found after (or in the middle of) a "direct speech" object:

```
(1)   "I saw his car outside her house," explained the boy
           DO                              V        S
```

```
(2)   "I don't know," answered my sister, "but I can find out"
```

though it is just as common for the subject to precede the verbal:

```
(3)   "I saw his car outside her house," the boy explained
(4)   "I don't know," my sister answered, "but I can find out"
```

Inversion also occurs when *so* replaces initial direct speech governed by *say* or *think*:

(5)     <u>And</u> <u>so</u> <u>say</u> <u>all of us</u>
        J   DO   V      S

(6)     *So* thought all the others

Before the direct-speech object inversion occurs only in newspaper style:

(7)     Said stunning twenty-eight-year old ex-Bunny Julie: "I never
        want to see him again."

4.2.2   Full inversion is used in clauses without a complement which are introduced
        by an adverbial. In spoken language this adverbial must be realized by a short
        adverb of place or time (8)-(9), or by an imitative word (10):

(8)     <u>Here</u> <u>comes</u> <u>the bus</u>     (cp. *Here it comes*)
        A     V      S

(9)     Now is the time to think about it
(10)    Bang went the gun

In literary language there are fewer restrictions on the length and type of the
initial adverbial, though most often it is one of place (the inversion may be
obligatory, as in (12a) and (12b)) or, less frequently, time (11):

(11)    In that decade began the Industrial Revolution
(12a)   Against one wall was a sofa covered with horsehair
(12b)   Outside the window stood a flagpole

4.2.3   Full inversion, furthermore, is used in clauses introduced by an emphatic subject
        complement:

(13)    <u>Far more effective</u> <u>would be</u> <u>a complete reshuffle of the</u>
              SC             V         S→

        <u>government</u>
          ←S

4.2.4   In formal style inversion may occur optionally in clauses introduced by *as* and
        *than*:

(14)    The Liberals voted against, as did the Socialists and the
        Communists
(15)    The Conservatives were more optimistic than were the
        Liberals and the Socialists

In (14), the main verb of the *as*-clause is missing. Because inversion is optional,
we regard the occurrence of the auxiliary *do* in this type, not as an instance of
partial inversion, but as an exception to the rule that *do* as an auxiliary is never
involved in full inversion.

4.2.5   A special type of full inversion, where the present participle of the main verb

(+ an object or adverbial) is followed by the progressive auxiliary (see § 7.7) and, finally, a long and weighty subject, is quite frequent in literary style and journalese:

```
(16)   Coming down the hill was the most dilapidated car
         H                    PRM
         ‾‾‾‾‾‾             ‾‾‾‾‾
         V-         A        -V                           S→
         ‾‾     ‾‾‾‾‾‾‾   ‾‾‾   ‾‾‾‾‾‾‾‾‾‾‾‾‾‾‾‾‾‾‾‾‾‾‾‾‾
       I had ever seen
       ‾‾‾‾‾‾‾‾‾‾‾‾‾‾
             ←S
```

**Position of the Complement (4.3.0-4.3.3)**

4.3.0   The position of the complement is normally after the verbal. In the following we shall look at cases where the complement precedes subject and verbal.

4.3.1   In interrogative main and subclauses the complement has initial position if it contains an interrogative pronoun:

(1)     *Who(m)* did she contact?
        DO      V-   S    -V

(2)     *Whose books* are these?
(3)     I asked him *what* the thieves had stolen

4.3.2   Likewise, in relative clauses the complement has initial position if it contains a relative pronoun:

(4)     Is the man *whom* you observed present in this courtroom?
(5)     That's the student *whose books* you stole
(6)     He looks like a fool, *which* he is

4.3.3   Initial position (fronting) is optional, and determined by stylistic considerations, when the purpose is to give the complement special emphasis:

```
(7)     A lot of good that will do me
        ‾‾‾‾‾‾‾‾‾ ‾‾‾‾ ‾‾‾‾ ‾‾ ‾‾
           DO      S    V    IO
```

(8)     *Quite a party* we had last night
(9)     *Not a single mistake* did he make (cp. § 4.1.2)

Sometimes fronting lends contrastive emphasis to the complements of two different clauses:

(10)    *Difficult* it may have been; *impossible* it was not

The subject complement, finally, may have initial position in concessive clauses signalled by the junctives, *as* and *though*:

```
(11)  Unfortunate as it is, it is not a disaster¹⁹
(12)  Ridiculous though it seemed, somebody had stolen his socks
         SC         J   S   V
                 ───────────────       ──────────  ──────  ─────────────
                       A                    S         V          DO
```

and in nonfinite clauses without a verbal if the subject is a long and weighty one:

```
(13)  (She found)
       S    V

      treacherous any suggestion that they call off the strike
      ───────────                          S
          SC      ──────────────────────────────────────────────
                                    DO
```

In the same way the object complement may precede the direct object if the latter is long and weighty:

```
(14)  (An accident had rendered)
          S             V

      helpless the only person who might have saved them
      ──────── ─────────────────────────────────────────
        OC                      DO
```

### Position of the Adverbial (4.4.0-4.4.7)

4.4.0    The adverbial has three stylistically neutral positions: initial, verb-neighbor and final. It depends mainly on the length (§§ 4.4.1-4.4.2) and type (§§ 4.4.3-4.4.5) of the adverbial, which of the three positions it can occur in.
    **Initial position** (I-pos) is before subject and verbal:

```
(1)   In Britain at that time this problem was still being debated
      ───────── ────────────
          A          A
```

According to this definition, both adverbials in (1) are in I-pos.
    **Final position** (F-pos) is after subject, verbal and complement (if there is any):

```
(2)   He spoke well at the debate this morning
                ──── ───────────── ────────────
                 A         A             A
```

All three adverbials in (2) are in final position.
    **Verb-neighbor position** (V-pos) depends on the structure of the verb phrase:
    (A) If the verb phrase is **simple**, V-pos is before the verb phrase except if the verb is *be*:

```
(3)   I never lie to you
(4)   She is always truthful
```

V-pos is before *be*, however, if *be* is stressed:

```
(5)   I never 'was very good at telling lies
```

---

19. In American English the construction is usually also introduced by *as*: *As unfortunate as it is...*

(B) If the verb phrase is **complex**, V-pos for adverbials that are **not** degree or manner adverbials is after the first auxiliary:

(6)    The child has *obviously* been maltreated

except if the auxiliary is stressed, or if it includes the contraction, *-n't*, in which case the adverbial occurs before the auxiliary:

(7)    I *always* 'did like Tom better than Jim
(8)    The child *obviously* hasn't been maltreated

In American English the adverbial frequently occurs before the auxiliary even when these conditions are not met.

If the adverbial is one of degree or manner, V-pos is immediately before the main verb:

(9)    His conduct has evidently been *thoroughly* vindicated
(10)   She has nevertheless been *kindly* received

(C) V-pos may be between verbal and object only if the adverbial is short and the complement very long and heavy:

(11)   He examined *carefully* each of the three documents that he had been given

(D) In *to*-infinitive clauses, V-pos is often between *to* and the verb except in very formal language; grammarians call this the "split infinitive":

(12)   This time I want to *really* enjoy myself

4.4.1   **Long adverbials**, i.e. adverbials realized by clauses or complex phrases, as well as compilation of adverbials (15)-(16), normally occur only in I- or F-pos, regardless of their type:

(13)   He asked her to dance with him *when the party was almost over*
(14)   *After the party*, they went to his place for a drink
(15)   *At the contest this morning* her alacrity was positively disgusting
(16)   She fought back *vigorously at the contest this morning*

Only in newspaper language is it common, for clauses beginning with a name, to have long adverbials of time and place occur in V-pos (so as to allow the important information given **about** the name to occur last):

(17)   Britain's Prime Minister, Mrs. Margaret Thatcher, *yesterday at a meeting with union leaders attending a Labour Conference in London* announced her intention of standing firm against a demand by British miners that...

4.4.2   **Short adverbials** (realized by simple phrases or short complex ones) can occur in all three positions (I-, V- and F-pos), depending on their type:

```
(18)   Yesterday I didn't know you as well as I do now
(19)   I had quite simply forgotten all about it
(20)   He explained matters to his wife upstairs
```

A compilation of adverbials in the same V-pos "slot" is not common except where one of them is *not*:

```
(21)   She had not really thought all that much about it
```

4.4.3   **Conjuncts** typically occur in I-pos, as we would expect in view of the fact that they relate the clause to what has gone before, see §§ 2.6.0-2.6.1. In fact, words like *altogether, besides, first(ly), second(ly)* etc., *hence, likewise, only, similarly*, when they function as conjuncts, rarely occur in any other position:

```
(22)   I'm hiring you because of your impressive qualifications.
       Besides, you have an honest face.
```

Some conjuncts can occur in other positions as well, and a few words are found regularly in other positions, e.g. *anyhow, anyway, then* and *though*:

```
(23)   He wasn't invited, but he came anyway
(24)   This problem, then, is our main worry
(25)   I very much felt like hitting her. I didn't do it, though
```

Conjuncts are usually separated from the rest of the clause by intonation boundaries (indicated by commas in writing; see § 2.4.0 n.), especially when they are not in I-pos.

4.4.4   **Disjuncts** fall into two categories: modal disjuncts and style disjuncts. **Style disjuncts**, through which speakers characterize the way they are expressing themselves, generally occur in I-pos and are separated from the rest of the clause by a comma or an intonation boundary (see § 2.4.0 n.):

```
(26)   Frankly, I don't know if I can trust you
(27)   Honestly, that's all the money they gave me
```

**Modal disjuncts** convey the speaker's attitude to, or belief concerning, the rest of the clause. They are most often placed in I-pos, but may also occur in V-pos. If they are given F-pos, which is rare, they are always separated from the rest of the clause by a comma or an intonation boundary:

```
(28)   Hopefully, it will be a while before he visits us again
(29)   She will probably never see me again
(30)   He will agree to see you again, naturally
```

4.4.5   **Adjuncts** fall into at least 16 different semantic types. However, 7 of these are always realized by clauses (adjunct clauses have been dealt with in § 3.5), which means that they can occur in either I-pos or F-pos, but not normally in V-pos:

conditional, concessive, causal, purpose, consecutive, comparative and subject-related adjuncts. The 9 types which can be realized by shorter forms than clauses, showing greater positional variety, are: time, frequency, place, degree, manner, viewpoint, subject, focus and formula adjuncts.

**Time** adjuncts are in I-pos or F-pos, though a few (*now*, *then*, *recently*) can also occur in V-pos:

```
(31)   Tomorrow I'll mow the lawn
(32)   I'll mow the lawn tomorrow
(33)   She has now moved to New York
```

**Frequency adjuncts** (e.g. *always, frequently, never, often, rarely, usually*) are typically in V-pos:

```
(34)   He has never been to Norway
(35)   I have often seen him at her house
```

but in I-pos or F-pos if the adjunct is longer:

```
(36)   As a rule it is very quiet here during the day
(37)   I have seen him at her house on several occasions
```

**Place adjuncts** are typically in F-pos; though I-pos is sometimes possible, especially when there are other adverbials in F-pos as in (40):

```
(38)   I put my cup on the table
(39)   Dinner was served in the kitchen
(40)   In the kitchen the landlord and his wife were arguing
       noisily
```

**Degree adjuncts** say to what extent the content of the verb is true. Most of them take V-pos, but some occur in F-pos:

```
(41)   You hardly know him
(42)   I very much enjoyed your speech/I enjoyed your speech very
       much
(43)   We don't mind in the slightest
```

**Manner adjuncts** normally belong in F-pos:

```
(44)   She worked hard
(45)   He had treated her badly
```

V-pos is sometimes possible, especially when the verb phrase is in the passive, in which case the manner adjunct is usually placed immediately before the main verb:

```
(46)   She had been badly treated
```

**Viewpoint adjuncts** indicate that the content of the clause is true from a particular point of view. They are thus semantically related to disjuncts, which is reflected in the fact that they typically have I-pos (though V- and F-pos are also possible) and are separated from the rest of the clause by a comma or an intonation boundary (see § 2.4.0 n.):

(47)     *Financially*, this is undoubtedly a sound investment. *From a political point of view*, however, the transaction is unwise

**Subject adjuncts** characterize the subject with regard to the action of the verb. They occur in I- or V-pos (whereas if the same adverbial can occur in F-pos, it tends to become a manner adjuncts, see § 4.4.7)

(48)     *With considerable strength*, he pushed the door open (He was strong)
(49)     She *deliberately* misled us (She was being deliberate)

**Focus adjuncts** are called thus because they put focus on the most important (most heavily stressed) element of the message, usually by occurring immediately before or after it:

(50)     *Only* 'Kate works on Saturdays/Kate *only* 'works on Saturdays/Kate works *only* on 'Saturdays/Kate works on 'Saturdays *only*
(51)     *Even* 'Peter will give you one/Peter will *even* 'give you one

Other common forms with this function include e.g. *alone, also, exactly, in particular, not, too.*
**Formula adjuncts** are part of politeness formulas and comprise a small group of adverbs, e.g. *cordially, humbly, kindly, please.* Their position is V-pos except *please*, which also occurs in I- and F-pos:

(52)     We *cordially* invite you to our party
(53)     Would you open the window, *please*?/Would you *please* open...?

4.4.6    The normal **order of adverbials** in I-pos is as follows:

[conjunct, disjunct or viewpoint adjunct], place adjunct, time adjunct

though normally there are no more than two adverbials in I-pos, of which at least one is a place or time adverbial:

(54)     *However, in America* no one took this problem seriously

In F-pos it is not unusual to find three adverbials, of which the typical order is:
manner, place, time

(55)     She played *beautifully at the concert last night*

As for more than one adverbial in V-pos, see § 4.4.2

4.4.7    The same adverbial may change meanings according to position. The most important tendency here is for many non-manner adverbials (disjuncts, and viewpoint, subject and formula adjuncts) to become manner adjuncts in those positions which are characteristic of manner adjuncts (§ 4.4.5):

(56a) *Naturally*, we have fertilized our vegetables with horse manure
(modal disjunct)

(56b) We have fertilized our vegetables *naturally*, with horse manure
(manner adjunct)

(57a) Our vegetables have *naturally* been fertilized with horse manure
(modal disjunct)

(57b) Our vegetables have been *naturally* fertilized, with horse manure
(manner adjunct)

## CLAUSE TYPES (5.0-5.10)

### Form vs. Interactional Function (5.0)

5.0    There are three main types of clause: **declarative**, **interrogative**, and **imperative** clauses, to be defined below. Each type can be used for many different communicative purposes (see also § 9.15.0). In terms of the interaction between speaker and addressee, the direct form/purpose correspondences are:

declarative clause  — **statement**       *The school was built in 1970*
interrogative clause — **question**        *What time is it?*
imperative clause   — **order**           *Open the door!*

However, speakers often want to be less than direct, for reasons of politeness or some other special reason. Thus the direct form/purpose correspondences are frequently broken, as when a question is asked by means of a declarative clause (1), or when an order is issued in the form of an interrogative clause (2):

(1)    You say your husband is out of town?
(2)    Will you open the door, please?

In (1) the special reason for breaking the direct form/purpose correspondence could be a wish not to sound too interested, as if the speaker is not really asking. In (2) the speaker pretends, by way of sounding polite, that "no" would be an acceptable answer.[20] Statistically speaking, orders and requests are in fact more often expressed through interrogative than through imperative clauses.

The act of making a statement, asking a question or giving an order is called a **speech act**.

After the basic clause types (§§ 5.1-5.3), we shall go on to describe several different sets of features which combine with each or some of them, to produce **cleft, negative, passive** and **elliptic** clauses (§§ 5.4-5.7). Likewise we shall touch on **clause/predicate substitution** (§§ 5.8-5.9) and **nonfinite clauses** (§ 5.10).

### Declarative Clauses (5.1)

5.1    A declarative clause is an SVCA structure which, unlike interrogative and imperative clauses, has no special characteristics. Variations like those described in § 2.6 are not distinct enough to count as separate clause types in the way the interrogative or the imperative clause is. As our examples so far have almost exclusively been declarative clauses, this clause type will not need special exemplification here.

### Interrogative Clauses (5.2.0-5.2.4)

5.2.0    The main characteristics of interrogative clauses are **partial inversion** (see § 4.1.1) and/or the presence of **interrogative words** (*wh*-words like *who, what,* etc). The two main types of interrogative clause are *yes/no*-interrogatives and *wh*-interrogatives.

5.2.1    *Yes/no* **interrogative clauses** always have partial inversion, but do not contain interrogative words. Questions formulated as *yes/no*-interrogatives concern the truth value of the whole clause and are answerable by *yes* or *no*:

```
(1)    Have you written the letter yet?
(2)    Are all the women here as cheerful as you are?
(3)    Do you live near the school?
```

A special kind of *yes/no*-interrogative is the so-called **tag question**, which is added on to other clause types, usually by way of requesting confirmation of their content. After declarative clauses, the tag question consists of the auxiliary verb and the subject (in the form of a pronoun) of the declarative clause. If the latter has no auxiliary, *do* is used in the tag (5); if *be* is the main verb, the inversion, as usual, does not require an auxiliary (6):

```
(4)    You haven't written the letter yet, have you?
```

20. Note that the "question mark" indicates a questioning *intonation* in types like (1), whereas in (2) it is the conventional indicator of a particular *syntactic* construction, i.e. the interrogative clause.

(5)    You live near the school, don't you?
(6)    Not all the women here are as cheerful as you, are they?

Positive declarative clauses are followed by negative tags, as in (5). Negative declarative clauses are followed by positive tags, as in (4) and (6).

A special type of tag question, usually expressing curiosity or surprise, is positive although it follows a positive declarative clause:

(7)    So you are marrying him after all, are you?

5.2.2   **Wh-interrogative clauses** are introduced by an interrogative (*wh-*) word: *who, whom, whose, what, which, why, where, when* or *how*. They ask for information concerning a particular clause constituent (or part of it); they take partial inversion except where the *wh*-word is the subject:

(8)    Who stole my pencil?
       ‾S‾

(9)    Who did you give it to?
       ‾H‾                 ‾J‾
       IO-                 -IO

(10)   Which of them would you choose?
       ‾‾‾‾‾‾‾‾‾‾
            DO

(11)   What are they?
       ‾‾‾‾
        SC

(12)   What did they elect him?
       ‾‾‾‾
        OC

(13)   How do I know I can trust you?
       ‾‾‾
        A

5.2.3   The *wh*-word of the interrogative main clause may in fact be a constituent, not of the main clause itself, but of a divided subclause:

(14)   What did you expect her to say?
       ‾‾‾‾                ‾‾‾ ‾‾‾‾‾‾
        DO                  S    V
       DO-   V-   S    -V    -DO

When the *wh*-word is governed by a junctive, the junctive often has to occur in final position, whereas obligatory initial position for the junctive is less common:

(15)   *What* did you want to do that *for*?
(16)   *On whose behalf* are you acting?

Most often this problem is one of style:

(17)   *Who* should I address the request to?
(18)   *To whom* should I address the request? (formal/literary)

5.2.4   Interrogative subclauses are introduced by an interrogative word, but do not
        have inversion. **Yes/no-interrogative subclauses** are introduced by the junctives
        *whether* or *if*:

(19)    He inquired *whether his wife had checked in*
                (cp. *Has my wife checked in?*)
(20)    She asked me *if I would read the letter aloud to her*
                (cp. *Will you read the letter aloud to me (please)?*)

**Wh-interrogative subclauses** are introduced by the same *wh*-word as the
corresponding main clause:

(21)    He asked me *what they looked like*
                (cp. *What do they look like?*)
(22)    I don't know *how much cash I would need*
                (cp. *How much cash would I need?*)

**Imperative Clauses (5.3)**

5.3     An imperative clause is typically used to get the addressee to carry out an
        action, i.e. it is an order or a request. As the understood subject is always the
        addressee, the imperative clause usually does not contain an explicit subject:

(1)     Sit down!
(2)     Get out of here!

A 2nd person subject is sometimes used for emphasis, however, just as a 2nd
or 3rd person subject may occur if the addressee has to be found among several
people present. Because it is unusual for subjects to be optional like this, the
imperative "subject" is regarded by some grammarians as a vocative (see § 2.5):

(3)     Now *you* listen to me, and *you* listen carefully!
(4)     *Somebody* shut the door!  (cp. Shut the door, *somebody*!)

The verbal is usually simple, containing the basic form of a main verb (see *shut*,
not *shuts*, in (4)). The auxiliary *do*, however, is used in negative and emphatic
imperative clauses, even in combination with *be*:

(5)     *Don't* listen to him!
(6)     *Don't* be such a fool!
(7)     *Do* be more careful from now on!

*Get* as passive auxiliary, furthermore, is not uncommon:

(8)     Don't *get* run over by a car!

Note that *do* cooccurs with another auxiliary, in (8), which is not possible
outside imperative clauses.
        Tag questions after imperative clauses most often have the form, *will you?*
After the type beginning with *let's*, however, the tag is, *shall we?*

(9)     Listen, *will you?*
(10)    Let's do it tomorrow, *shall we?*

When an imperative clause is linked to a main clause by *and*, it functions as a conditional clause:

```
(11)   Ask no questions and you'll be told no lies
```

See also § 7.3.7.

### Cleft Clauses (5.4.1-5.4.2)

5.4.1   "Cleft" clauses are called thus because they represent the splitting of a main clause into two clauses, one embedded in the other. Cleft clauses are used to emphasize a particular constituent. One type turns the original clause into the subject of a new clause, replacing the constituent in question by *what* (or *the one who*, if a person is meant), so that the constituent can be moved to end-weight position as the subject complement; compare:

```
(1)    Sheila fixed the car yesterday
```

with:

```
(1a)   The one who fixed the car yesterday was Sheila
                S      V      DO        A
       PRM  H              POM
                            S                      V    SC
```

```
(1b)   What Sheila fixed yesterday was the car
        DO    S     V       A
        H           POM
                    S                 V    SC
```

For the analysis of (1b), see § 3.7.1.

If (a larger part of) the predicate of the original clause is emphasized, it is replaced by *what + do*, and the new subject complement becomes a nonfinite clause:

```
(1c)   What Sheila did yesterday was fix the car
```

5.4.2   The other type of cleft clause uses *it* as preliminary subject to turn the original clause (see (1) in § 5.4.1) into one where the emphasized constituent becomes the subject complement (or obligatory adverbial), while the rest of the original clause becomes the real subject, introduced by *who, which, that*:

```
(1d)   It was Sheila who fixed the car yesterday
       S=  V    SC              =S
```

```
(1e)   Was it yesterday (that) Sheila fixed the car?
        V  S=    A                   =S
```

Note the difference between the "regular" preliminary-subject construction (see § 3.1) and a cleft clause: The subject clause of the regular preliminary-subject construction (2a) is present also in the version without a preliminary subject (2b):

(2a)   <u>It</u> <u>is</u> <u>a shame</u> <u>*that she has lost*</u>
     S=  V   SC         =S

(2b)   <u>*That she has lost*</u> <u>is</u> <u>a shame</u>
         S          V   SC

The subject clause of the cleft construction (3), on the other hand, comes about by "cleaving" a main clause that does not contain such a subclause (e.g. *She has lost a bracelet*):

(3)   <u>It</u> <u>is</u> <u>a bracelet</u> <u>*that she has lost*</u>
    S=  V    SC         =S

    cp. *That she has lost* is a bracelet

### NOT-Clauses (5.5)

5.5   The common way of negating a clause (be it declarative, interrogative or imperative) is by turning it into a *not*-clause, either by inserting the form *not* as a separate adverb after the first auxiliary, or by using the negative form of the auxiliary (containing a contracted form of *not*: -*n't*). What makes this a distinct clause subtype is the fact that the structure, v *not* (v) V, is obligatory: if the verbal is simple, the auxiliary *do* has to be used:

(1)   I can*not* (can't) see the house from here[21]
(2)   They do *not* (don't) know the difference
(3)   Does it *not* (Doesn't it) bother you?
(4)   Do *not* (Don't) try to contact them!

unless, in declarative and interrogative clauses, the main verb is *be*:

(5)   He is*n't* happy about it

In imperative clauses *do* is **always** necessary with *not*:

(6)   Don't be such a spoil-sport!
(7)   Don't be taken in by their facile promises!

The contracted form of auxiliary + *not* (*doesn't, won't, haven't, aren't* etc.) is characteristic of spoken, or informal written, language. Note that *am not* is not contracted, but replaced by *aren't*, in questions (*I'm good at this, aren't I?*).

---

21. Note that *cannot* is written as one word.

**Passive Clauses (5.6)**

5.6     Passive clauses (be they declarative, interrogative or, in rare cases, imperative (see § 5.5 (7)) differ from active clauses in that

(A) the direct or indirect object of the active clause becomes the subject of the passive clause;

(B) a form of *be* is inserted immediately before the main verb, the main verb being a past participle;

(C) the subject of the active clause is left out, or is turned into an adverbial introduced by *by*.

```
(1)   I'm being kept in the dark (cp. they're keeping me in the
      dark)
(2)   Was the ticket paid for by your employer? (cp. Did your
      employer pay for the ticket?)
(3)   Mary soon gained the children's affection, whereas Peter was
      laughed at (cp. ...whereas the children laughed at Peter)
```

Passive clauses are used when what would have been the subject of the active clause is unknown or considered unimportant (1), or if it is so important that it deserves end-weight position (2), or if the active-clause object is needed in initial position (3).

**Elliptic Clauses (5.7.0-5.7.3)**

5.7.0   Just as pronouns are used to avoid repetition of preceding noun phrases (*"A fat old man with a wooden leg* had entered; *he* held a pistol in his left hand"), ellipsis, which means omission, is the feature used when one does not want to repeat all the constituents of a previous clause.

Two criteria have to be fulfilled for the omission to constitute what we call ellipsis:

(I)  It must be possible to identify exactly what has been omitted.

(II) It must be possible to insert the missing constituents without the clause becoming ungrammatical.

```
(1)   A:  You haven't done your homework
      B:  Yes, I have (done my homework)
```

Criteria (I) and (II) are not fulfilled in examples (2) and (3) respectively, which is why we do not consider them elliptic:

```
(2)   Why do soldiers learn to kill (other soldiers, other people,
      human beings)?
(3)   They want me to come, and I want to come
      (not *I want me to come)
```

5.7.1   The most common type of elliptic clause is the one exemplified by (1) in § 5.7.0, consisting of subject + finite auxiliary (+ *not*, if the clause was positive in the previous utterance, cp. (4)). If the previous verbal did not have an auxiliary, *do* is used[22] — except if the main verb is *be*, in which case *be* occurs in the elliptic clause:

(4)  A:  Have you done your homework yet?
     B:  No, I *haven't*
(5)  A:  I don't think he even tried
     B:  Oh yes, he *did*
(6)  A:  I think she is very bright
     B:  She *is*

5.7.2   *Wh*-interrogative clauses are frequently responded to by an elliptic clause containing only the constituent asked about:

(7)  A:  Who gave it to you?
     B:  *Shirley*                                                  (S)
(8)  A:  What did you get for your birthday?
     B:  *A book on World War I*                                    (DO)
(9)  A:  What will you do now?
     B:  *Look for a new job*                                  (Predicate)

5.7.3   A *wh*-word may constitute an elliptic interrogative clause:

(10)  A:  Bill gave it to someone
      B:  *Who?*
(11)  A:  I'm going to America
      B:  *When?*
(12)  A:  I'm not going anyway
      B:  *Why not?*

*Why* after a negative clause (12) is often followed by *not*. *How* has to be accompanied by the auxiliary *could* in expressions of reproach or disagreement (13); in similar expressions with *why*, *why* is followed by *should(n't)*:

(13)  A:  She sold the house
      B:  *How could* she!

(14)  A:  They didn't pay me anything
      B:  *Why should* they?

## Predicate Substitution (5.8.0-5.8.2)

5.8.0   Predicate substitution serves the same purpose as ellipsis (avoiding repetition), and so has the same kind of effect on the clause structure (abbreviation). The predicate substitutes are *so* and *it*. They occur together with an auxiliary verb echoing the previous clause, or the auxiliary verb *do*.

5.8.1   *So* substitutes for (part of) a predicate that is true also of another subject:

---

22. In British English *do* is sometimes used as a substitution form (pro-form, see § 5.9.2 n.) after the auxiliary in such clauses: *I never mention it, but I should do; I don't know if he did it, but he may have done*. In American English only ellipsis is possible: *...but I should; ...but he may have.*

```
(1)    A:    Chris is staying at the hotel
       B:       So     is Martin
             (V- + A)  -V   S
```

*So* in (1) refers to the part of the predicate consisting of main verb (*staying*) and adverbial (*at the hotel*). This type has partial inversion. In case of negation, after a negative clause, there is no predicate substitute, the elliptic clause being introduced by *nor* or *neither* as adverbial (corresponding to *not...*, *either*):

```
(2)    A:    Joan doesn't smoke
       B:    Nor/neither do I   (i.e. I do not smoke, either)
                A      V  S
```

5.8.2    Both *so* and *it* are predicate substitutes in combination with *do* as main verb. *It* tends to have more concrete/narrow/literal reference than *so*:

```
(3)    A:    Do you often let her know you love her?
       B:    I haven't done so in a long time
             S     V      DO      A
```

```
(4)    A:    Do you make love often?
       B:    We haven't done it in a long time
             S      V      DO      A
```

which explains the difference between (B) and (C):

```
(5)    A:    I mow my lawn twice a week
       B:    Don't expect 'me to do so (presumably: "mow my lawn
             twice a week")
       C:    Don't expect 'me to do it (i.e. "mow your lawn twice
             a week")
```

In other words, *it* covers the meaning of the preceding clause more literally.

### Clause Substitution (5.9.0-5.9.3)

5.9.0    Even whole clauses can be replaced by pro-forms[23] when incorporated into other clauses. In the following we will mention the most typical constructions of this kind, though only some of them could be said to constitute distinct clause types.

5.9.1    **Subject and object clauses** are often substituted by demonstrative pronouns (*this/that*), the relative pronoun *which*, and the personal pronoun *it*:

```
(1)    A:    John failed the exam again
       B:    I already knew that
       C:    I didn't, but it was to be expected
```

---

23. Substitute forms are generally known as **pro-forms**. The most important group are the pro*nouns*, whose typical function, as the name indicates, is to replace noun phrases.

(2)    *It* is a shame they won't help him (*it* as preliminary
       subject, see § 3.1)
(3)    Larry was in love with Gale, *which* Susan didn't seem to mind

5.9.2  *So* in connection with preliminary-subject *it* replaces the subject proper in:

(4)    A:   She doesn't like you
       B:   *So* it seems/it seems *so*

*So* replaces the object clause of certain verbs expressing opinion, wish or
perception. With some of them, depending on the speaker, the position of *so*
tends to be fixed, whether final (after verbs of opinion or wish) or initial (after
verbs of perception):

(5)    A:   Do you think she will accept?
       B:   I hope *so*
(6)    A:   He has been to Australia
       B:   *So* I gather

*So* often occurs after the verbs *say* and *tell*:

(7)    I know the Earth is round because my Daddy told me *so*
(8)    The economy is a mess; even the Prime Minister says *so*

With some of these verbs the expression *as much* can be used in a similar way:

(9)    The universities need more money; the government's own
       report says *so/as much*
(10)   We know he was there on Friday night; he's already admitted
       *as much*

In cases where initial and final *so* alternate, the choice of initial *so* allows the
verb to be in final position, where the added emphasis often implies that its
object (the clause represented by *so*) is not necessarily true:

(11)   His wife has never been unfaithful, or *so* he thinks

Final *so* after a past-tense verb, on the other hand, often expresses what was to
be expected:

(12)   A:   It was Joan who stole that money
       B:   I thought *so*

5.9.3  Certain verbs of opinion (e.g. *believe, expect*) which regularly take *it* as an
object-clause substitute may instead, in the simple present tense after a first
person subject, be followed by *so*, to express the speaker's uncertainty about the
truth of his/her statement (see "Speaker Belief and Attitude," esp. § 9.12).
Compare:

(13)   A:   Had you heard that she had committed suicide?
       B:   Yes, and I believed *it* (i.e. that she had committed
            suicide)
       B:   Yes, I believe *so* (i.e. that I had heard...)

**Nonfinite Clauses (5.10)**

5.10 Nonfinite clauses are characterized by having no verbal, or a verbal in which the first verb from the left is either an infinitive (e.g. *(to) show*), a present participle (e.g. *showing*), or a past participle (e.g. *shown*). If the nonfinite clause has a subject, this is usually in the object form when pronominalized:

```
(1)    They expect him to leave immediately
(2)    She heard them yell for help
(3)    He tried to avoid spilling coffee on the rug
(4)    I'll see you beaten/fired yet!
```

Nonfinite clauses are mostly subclauses, as in (1)-(4). Nonfinite main clauses do occur, however:

```
(5)    George an informer? That's a little hard to believe!
(6)    Me apologize to him? It's out of the question!
(7)    To imagine that anybody could have believed such nonsense!
```

# THE SEMANTICS OF THE CLAUSE (6.0-6.4.2)

6.0 We shall, finally, look at some of the most general semantic characteristics of the clause. These concern the relationship between subject and predicate, on the one hand, and that between verbal and the rest of the constituents, on the other.

**Predication vs. Attribution (6.1)**

6.1 There are basically two ways in which we can link nouns (e.g. *incident*) to whatever we want to say about them (e.g. *unfortunate*). One is called **predication**, and is characteristic of the clause:

```
(1)    The incident is unfortunate
       Subject      Predicate
```

The other is called **attribution**, which characterizes the phrase:

```
(2)    The unfortunate incident
       PRM     PRM         H
```

The predication **establishes** the relationship between *incident* and *unfortunate*, which is why, when a clause is reacted to, it is generally the predication that the reaction is aimed at:

```
(3)    The incident is unfortunate
       - No, it is not (unfortunate)
```

whereas attributive relations are seen as **already established**, indeed often (especially in definite noun phrases) as **presupposed**:

```
(4)     The unfortunate incident occurred yesterday
        - No, it did not (occur yesterday)
```

i.e. the negative reaction in (4) is to whether the incident occurred yesterday, not to whether the incident is to be regarded as unfortunate.

### Theme/Rheme (6.2)

6.2     The first element of the clause, that which I am going to say something about, is called the **theme** by some grammarians. That which is said about the theme is called the **rheme**. Typically, as in § 6.1 (1), the theme coincides with the subject, the rheme with the predicate. This, however, is by no means always the case:

```
(1)     Tomorrow I'm going to see my lawyer
(2)     When are you going to see the dentist?
(3)     Are you sick?
(4)     Because I like you, I'll help you once more
```

In (1) I'm saying something about tomorrow; in (2) I'm asking about the time of the action; in (3) the theme, through the fronting of the finite verb, is the truth value of the predication; in (4) the theme is the cause of the action.

   If no theme is needed, a special construction can be used in which the subject (which may be preliminary (6)) is realized by a "slot-filler" empty of meaning (*it* or *there*, cp. §§ 15.4.4, 17.5.2), e.g.

```
(5)     It is raining
(6)     There are two men at the door
          S=    V    =S      A
```

In spite of such examples, the theme/rheme distinction can still be regarded as basic to the subject/predicate relationship.

### Given/New (6.3)

6.3     Another basic distinction, which interacts with theme/rheme, is that between "given" and "new." **Given** elements are those which have already been introduced earlier on (like *she* in (2)), and which are now referred to again because something **new** is said about them:

```
(1)     The road was being watched by an old woman
(2)     She could see a boy riding a bicycle
(3)     The boy (he) was no more than five
(4)     The bicycle (it) was old and rusty
```

Typically, as in (1)-(4), subject, theme and "given" coincide. Any one of the "new" elements, e.g. *a boy* or *a bicycle* in (2), can become "given" in the next clause, see (3) and (4); "given" status is signalled by the definite article or pronouns. As with theme/rheme, the given/new distinction does not **always** coincide with subject/predicate:

```
(5)   A:   Where is the bicycle?
      B:   A little boy stole it
```

In (B), the "given" element is *it* (hence the pronominal form), but it is a "new" element, *a little boy*, which is both subject and theme. Still, we would naturally expect *it* (*the bicycle*) to become the theme of (B), cp. *it was stolen by a little boy*, and when instead we find a "new" element in thematic position we experience it as a shift in focus.

We conclude that it is typical of the grammatical subject/predicate relationship to convey, in semantic terms, both the theme/rheme and the "given"/"new" distinction, and that these correspondences are only broken when there are special reasons for it in terms of the structure of textual units larger than the clause.


### Case Roles (6.4.0-6.4.2)

6.4.0   Another way of describing the semantic relationship between clause constituents is to regard the verbal as the central constituent. If, for instance, the verbal denotes an event, it is possible to view the other constituents as representing participants and things (**actants**) with specific roles in that event. Such semantic roles are often called **case roles**:

*EVENT: kill*

```
(1)   Beth killed her husband with a sledgehammer yesterday
       S     V      DO            A                  A
```

| ACTANTS: | | CASE ROLES: |
|---|---|---|
| a person who acts: | *Beth* (S) | Agentive |
| a thing or person that is affected: | *her husband* (DO) | Afficative |
| a tool: | *a sledgehammer* (A) | Instrumentative |
| a time: | *yesterday* (A) | Temporative |

*EVENT: build*

```
(2)    Charlie built Doris a house in the country
         S     V     IO    DO        A
```

| ACTANTS: | | CASE ROLES: |
|---|---|---|
| a person who acts: | *Charlie* (S) | Agentive |
| a thing which is created (a result): | *a house* (DO) | Efficative |
| a person who receives: | *Doris* (IO) | Dative |
| a place: | *in the country* (A) | Locative |

6.4.1   Examples (1) and (2) above show us the typical correspondences between clause
constituents and case roles:

| | |
|---|---|
| Subject | Agentive |
| Direct object | Afficative |
| | Efficative |
| Indirect object | Dative |
| Adverbial | Instrumentative |
| | Temporative |
| | Locative |

However, the pattern is easily broken, especially as regards the various case
roles that can be found as subject; cp.

```
(3a)   John opened the door (S = Agentive)
(3b)   The door opened (S = Afficative)
```

Some verbs form pairs according to their ability to construct like (3a) or (3b),
e.g. *fell/fall, lay/lie, raise/rise, set/sit*:

```
(4a)   John is felling the tree (S = Agentive, DO = Afficative)
(4b)   The tree is falling (S = Afficative)
(5a)   He set her down gently on the sofa (S = Agentive, DO =
       Afficative)
(5b)   A large bed sat squarely in the middle of the room (S = Af-
       ficative)
```

More generally it is the passive construction which is used to place the
afficative, efficative or dative in subject position:

```
(6)    The door was opened by John (S = Afficative, A = Agentive)
(7)    The house was built by Charlie (S = Efficative, A =
       Agentive)
(8)    Doris was given a pen (S = Dative, DO = Afficative)
```

at the same time as the agentive may either be emphasized, by being placed
last, or suppressed; cp. the relative effect on the reader of (9a)-(9c), based on an
authentic example (version (9c)):

```
(9a)   Yesterday an Israeli guard shot an Israeli girl walking
       through a Palestinian village
(9b)   Yesterday an Israeli girl walking through a Palestinian
       village was shot by an Israeli guard
(9c)   Yesterday an Israeli girl was shot walking through a
       Palestinian village
```

Other case roles besides those mentioned so far can become subject, though not
through the passive, but in connection with particular verbs:

```
(10)   This key opens all the doors of the building
       (S = Instrumentative)
```

(11)  The 14th century saw the rise of the Middle Class
      *(S = Temporative)*[24]
(12)  Hyde Park Corner witnessed a most peculiar exhibition of
      rhetorical talent yesterday *(S = Locative)*

6.4.2   Except for (11) and (12) above, whose form is special (formal), we have exemplified case roles and role/constituent correspondences through uncomplicated
clauses expressing a straightforward event. Case-role analyses of other types of
clause can be much more difficult, and will not be attempted here. Only one
more case role, which is not related to events, will be demonstrated because it
is frequently used by grammarians. It is called **experiencer** to denote the role
of the subject in relation to verbs of perception and cognition ("private" verbs,
see § 8.1.2):

(13)  He felt a stab in his left arm
(14)  She remembered him

Four common perceptual verbs form pairs according to whether their subject is
the experiencer or the agentive (*see/look at, hear/listen to*), cp.

(15)  He heard you *(S = Experiencer)*
      but he won't listen *(S = Agentive)*

---

24. The verbs used with this type are *see* and *find*.

# III. THE VERB PHRASE

## Introduction (7.0)

7.0 The constituents of the verb phrase can be realized only by verbs. The verbs realizing its premodifiers (the auxiliary verbs) constitute a **closed set**. By this we mean a small group of forms with a grammatical function which does not easily acquire new members. The verbs realizing the head of the verb phrase (the main verbs), on the other hand, belong to an **open class**, by which we mean a large group of lexical items which easily acquires new members.

The verb phrase is the only structure in our system which only has one function: that of realizing the verbal constituent of the clause. Conversely, the verbal is the only constituent which can only be realized by one type of structure, namely a verb phrase. We say that there is a one-to-one relationship between verb phrase and verbal.

The form of the verb phrase determines the functional possibilities of the clause whose verbal constituent it is, but this aspect has already been dealt with in § 2.7 and § 3, *passim*. Consequently, we shall have no more to say about the function of the verb phrase in this chapter.


## THE STRUCTURE OF THE VERB PHRASE (7.1-7.9.4)


### The Forms of the Verb (7.1)

7.1 Before looking at the structure of the verb phrase, let us look briefly at the forms of the verb. The verb has a maximum of five forms:[25]

| | |
|---|---|
| -Ø (zero) | *show* |
| -s | *shows* |
| -(e)d | *showed* |
| -ing | *showing* |
| -(e)n | *shown* |

When grammarians refer to these forms, however, they traditionally use names which are defined not only in terms of the **form** itself, but also in terms of how it happens to be used, i.e. its actual **function**.

Thus *show* is called the **present tense** when it represents agreement (concord) with the subject:

---

25. The verb *to be* has eight.

```
(1)     They (she) always show(s) me the pictures
```

It is called the **infinitive** when, as the first verb form in a subclause (perhaps introduced by the infinitive marker *to*), it does not represent agreement (concord) with any subject (2); and when it succeeds a modal auxiliary (*may* in (3)):

```
(2)     I want to show you something
(3)     I may show it to you some day
```

With most verbs (e.g. *ask, gather, haunt, play*) the -(e)d form has to cover both the functions of *showed* and the functions of *shown*. If the -(e)d form functions like *showed* (indicating past time or hypothesis) it is called the **past tense**:

```
(4a)    I showed you the pictures yesterday
(4b)    I played with him all day yesterday

(5a)    If I showed them to you, would you promise not to tell
        anyone?
(5b)    If he played today, it might make his leg injury worse
```

If the -(e)d form functions like *shown* and other verbal -(e)n forms, we call it the **past participle**. In other words, an -(e)d form is considered a past participle when it succeeds a form of *have* (6b) or *be* (7b); when, as the first verb form in a subclause, it has a meaning corresponding to such a construction with *have* (8b) or *be* (9b); and when it functions as a premodifier in the noun phrase (10b). Compare:

```
(6a)    They have shown me the pictures
(6b)    They have played well today

(7a)    The obituary was written by his friend
(7b)    He was asked to come

(8a)    (The mouse lived on) crumbs fallen from the table
                                        ‾‾‾‾‾‾ ‾‾‾‾‾‾‾‾‾‾‾‾‾‾
                                           V         A
                               ‾‾‾‾‾‾‾‾‾‾‾‾‾‾‾‾‾‾‾‾‾‾‾‾‾‾‾‾‾‾‾‾
                                    H              POM
        (i.e. ...which had fallen...)

(8b)    He addressed the crowd gathered in the square
        (i.e. ...who had gathered...)

(9a)    (It was) an obituary written by his friend
                               ‾‾‾‾‾‾‾ ‾‾‾‾‾‾‾‾‾‾‾‾‾
                                  V          A
               ‾‾ ‾‾‾‾‾‾‾‾ ‾‾‾‾‾‾‾‾‾‾‾‾‾‾‾‾‾‾‾‾‾‾‾‾‾‾
               PRM    H              POM
        (i.e. ...which was written by...)

(9b)    I couldn't answer the questions asked by the students
        (i.e. ...which were asked by...)

(10a)   This is the oldest known version of the epic
(10b)   They live in a haunted castle
```

The *-ing* form, on the other hand, has the same functions for all verbs (though not all verbs have an *-ing* form). The traditional name for this form is the **present participle**.

In other words:

**The present tense** is a verb form (e.g. *walk(s), cut(s), sing(s)*) which functions like *show(s)* in (1) above with regard to subject-verb concord.[26]

**The past tense** is a verb form (e.g. *walked, cut, sang*) which functions like *showed* in expressing either past time ((4a) and (4b)) or non-factuality ((5a) and (5b); see § 9.1.1).

**The infinitive** is the -Ø form of the verb (e.g. *walk, cut, sing*) in syntactic surroundings like *show* in (2) and (3) above.

**The past participle** is a verb form (e.g. *walked, cut, sung*) which functions like the verbal *-(e)n* forms, as in (6a)-(10b) above.

**The present participle** is a verb form ending in *-ing*.

## The VP Premodifiers: a Structural Overview (7.2)

7.2     The verb phrase consists of a maximum of four premodifiers (auxiliary verbs) and a head (main verb). Our example contains all four premodifiers, but it should be noted that verb phrases containing two nonfinite forms of *to be* are few and far between:

(1)     The house *would have been being renovated* at this moment if we'd had the money

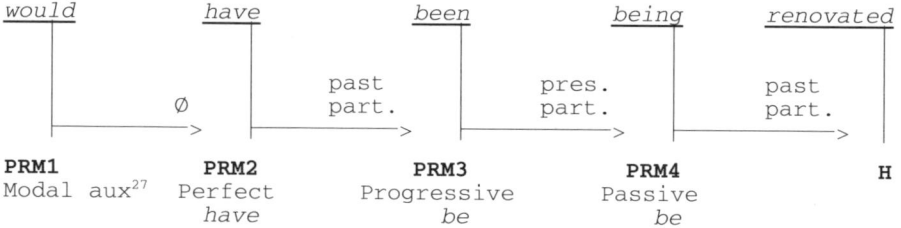

| PRM1 | PRM2 | PRM3 | PRM4 | H |
|------|------|------|------|---|
| Modal aux[27] | Perfect have | Progressive be | Passive be | |

One more auxiliary, *do*, fits into PRM1 in several ways, but as it is a purely syntactic device, which does not share the semantic functions of the modal auxiliaries, and which does not (except in imperative clauses) cooccur with any other auxiliary, we shall regard it as special and refer to it as **periphrastic *do***.

The system can be summarized as follows:
(a)     If there are any auxiliaries, they always precede the main verb.
(b)     The question of finiteness (§ 7.3.0) is decided in the first verb from the left (which is the main verb if there are no auxiliaries). For instance if the VP has tense conjugation (cp. *will/would*), or if it is nonfinite, this shows up in the first verb from the left.

---

26. Only the verb *to be* also shows subject-verb concord in the past tense: *I was/you were* etc. The modal auxiliaries, on the other hand, do not show subject-verb concord at all.
27. The central modal auxiliaries are *can, may, must, shall, will*.

(c)     If there are more auxiliaries than one, their relative order is as indicated
        in (1).

(d)     The type of auxiliary/PRM determines whether the following verb is an
        infinitive, past participle or present participle, but **not what verb** it is.

The four PRM's represent the following **grammatical categories**:

PRM1: Mode
PRM2: Perfect Aspect
PRM3: Progressive Aspect
PRM4: Voice

Thus a verb phrase is either (1) **modal** or **nonmodal**, (2) **perfect** or **nonperfect**,
(3) **progressive** or **nonprogressive**, (4) **active** or **passive**, depending on whether
the PRM in question is present or absent. Although the absence of a PRM is just
as important for the meaning of the verb phrase as the presence of it (as we
shall see later), we will as a rule describe the structure of the verb phrase in
terms of what PRM's are present, besides indicating the form of the first verb
from the left; verb phrases containing *do* as an auxiliary will be referred to as
**periphrastic**:

(2)     He *will have gone* by then          (*present-tense modal, perfect VP*)
           PRM1 PRM2   H

(3)     She *should have* the letter         (*past-tense modal VP*)
              PRM1     H

(4)     *Have* you *been drinking?*          (*present-tense perfect, progressive VP*)
        PRM2       PRM3    H

(5)     I *could  be  dreaming*              (*past-tense modal, progressive VP*)
          PRM1   PRM3   H

(6)     She *had  been arrested*             (*past-tense perfect, passive VP*)
            PRM2 PRM4    H

(7)     She  *is   being arrested*           (*present-tense progressive, passive VP*)
             PRM3   PRM4      H

(8)     He wants
        *to be told* now                     (*infinitive passive VP*)
        PRM4   H

(9)     She denies
        *having been* rude                    (*present-participle perfect VP*)
           PRM2   H

(10)    *Did* you *do* all that?             (*past-tense periphrastic VP*)
        PRM1       H

Note that our delimitation of auxiliaries, in (1), prevents us from making the
mistake of regarding *want* in (8) and *denies* in (9) as additional premodifiers to
*told* and *been*, respectively. They must be main verbs, in other words, each of

them constituting a verbal that governs a nonfinite clause.

Observe, further, that three highly frequent verbs — *have, be, do* — can function as main verbs besides being auxiliaries, see (3), (9), (10).

**The First Verb from the Left (7.3.0-7.3.7)**

*Finiteness (7.3.0)*

7.3.0    The **finiteness** of a verb phrase is signalled in the first verb from the left.

If the verb phrase is **finite**, the first verb from the left is called the **finite verb**. The form of the finite verb (or the relationship between the form of the finite verb and the form of the subject) reflects three grammatical categories: **tense** (see § 7.3.1), **concord** (§ 7.3.2) and **mood** (§ 7.3.3).

If the verb phrase is **nonfinite**, the first verb from the left is an infinitive, a present participle, or a past participle, see § 7.1. Nonfinite verb phrases are primarily important in terms of the functional possibilities of the clause in which they occur (see § 2.7 and § 3), and will not receive further treatment here.

*Tense (7.3.1)*

7.3.1    English has two tenses, **present tense** and **past tense**. These are purely formal categories, referring to contrasts like *is/was, bend(s)/bent, swim(s)/swam, walk(s)/walked, will/would*, and should not be confused with the semantic categories of past, present, future (etc.) **time**.

Most verbs have two forms (*-Ø* or *-s*) in the present tense. *Be* has more than two, whereas modal auxiliaries only have one.

In the past tense only *be* has more than one form (*was* and *were*), whereas the regular-verb ending is *-ed*.

The semantics of the tenses will be discussed in § 8, *passim*.

*Concord (7.3.2)*

7.3.2    In the indicative (see § 7.3.3) there is concord between the subject and a present-tense verb in terms of **number** and **person**: the verb is an *-s* form if the subject is the third person singular, and a *-Ø* form in all other cases (e.g. (1) below). All verbs show concord in the present tense except the modal auxiliaries (2). *Be* has a more complicated pattern (3)-(6), showing concord also in the past tense (indicative):

**Present tense**                                              **Past tense**

*am*    <==   1st person singular        ⌐            ==>   *was*

*is*    <==   3rd person singular                     ==>   *were*

*are*   <==   2nd person and the
              whole of the plural

Examples:

(1)    I (she) *sing(s)* rather well
                   H

(2)    I (she) *can* swim
              PRM1   H

(3)    I  *am*  seeing her tomorrow
          PRM3    H

(4)    You/they *are* rejected
                 PRM4    H

(5)    He *was* disgusting
           H

(6)    We *were* only dreaming
          PRM3          H

**Noun-phrase subjects** generally determine the concord through their explicit
indication of number in the head of the noun phrase:

(7)    The student(s) *was (were)* studying very hard

If there is no explicit indication of number, concord is determined by whether
in the given context the subject refers to one or more entities:

(8)    The sheep *was/were* kept in a pen behind the house

The form of the verb may conflict with the number indication of the subject,
because concord is determined by content rather than form:

(9)    Five months *is* a long time
(10)   Phonetics *is* an interesting subject
(11)   *Dubliners is* a collection of short stories by James Joyce
(12)   The majority of the students *have* already passed their exams
(13)   My family *are* heavy drinkers[28]

With **arithmetical problems**, American English usually uses singular concord,
whereas there is some alternation between singular and plural concord in
British English:

---

28. American English would prefer: *The members of my family are...*, to avoid the formal
disagreement between a singular subject and a plural verb, cp. § 12.5.9.

```
(14)   Nine and/plus five is fourteen   (AE & BE)
(15)   Nine and five are fourteen   (BE)
(16)   Ten fives are fifty   (this whole expression is BE only)
```

**Coordinated noun phrases** usually require plural concord, as in (17), but not if they are felt to constitute one concept, as in (18):

```
(17)   Peter and Mary are university students
(18)   Whisky and soda is the only drink they make
```

After coordination by means of *or*, and *(n)either - (n)or*, concord is sometimes determined by the number of the last noun phrase:

```
(19)   Neither the twins nor their mother was/were present
(20)   Neither Jane nor I are (am) able to be there
(21)   Either John or his brothers are responsible
```

**Indefinite and interrogative pronouns** generally require a verb in the 3rd person singular, except when there is an explicit indication of number (25):

```
(22)   Nobody knows the trouble I've seen
(23)   Everyone was there
(24)   Who is responsible?
(25)   Who are the people responsible?
(26)   What is the matter?
```

though singular and plural are both possible if the noun phrase contains a plural postmodifier:

```
(27)   None of them is/are coming
(28)   Either of them is (are) suitable   (usually singular)
```

*Which* has either singular or plural concord depending on the content:

```
(29)   He looked at the books and asked me which was/were best
```

**Relative pronouns** are neutral with regard to concord, but there is concord between the finite verb and the antecedent of the relative clause (see § 3.7.1):

```
(30)   It is hardly fair that those who are rich are given money,
       whereas I, who am poor, have to pay
```

The **preliminary subjects** *it* and *there* differ with regard to concord: *it* is automatically followed by the 3rd person singular form of the verb, regardless of the number of the real subject:

```
(31)   It is the Johnsons
```

whereas the verb form after *there* is determined by the real subject except in very colloquial language (34):

```
(32)   There is a man at the door
(33)   There are so many things I want to do
(34)   There's a man and a woman at the door
```

**Clauses as subject** take a 3rd person singular verb form:

```
(35)   Seeing her parents suffer was unbearable
```

(36)   To marry six wives *has* always been my ambition

This rule can also be used to explain the following apparent anomaly:

(37)   More jobs *means* greater affluence
       ("creating more jobs...")
          V        DO
              S

though (37) could also be explained in terms of noun phrase structure (i.e. "the *fact* of there being more jobs..."). See also §§ 12 and 15, regarding number and person.

### *Mood (7.3.3-7.3.7)*

7.3.3   English has three moods: the **indicative**, the **subjunctive** and the **imperative**. The vast majority of finite verb phrases in this book so far have been in the indicative, and the three moods are best described in terms of how the subjunctive and the imperative differ from the indicative. As some of these categories cannot be defined without reference to context, we will, for practical reasons, deal with both form and usage here. Initially, then, we can say that whereas there is in principle no limit to the meanings that can be conveyed by the indicative, there are well-defined restrictions on the meanings and uses of the imperative and the subjunctive.

7.3.4   The use of the **subjunctive** is one of the few areas of English grammar where there are really conspicuous differences between American and British English. Formally, the subjunctive differs from the indicative in lacking subject-verb concord. This means that the formal difference between indicative and subjunctive shows up only in the 3rd person singular present tense (*he plays* vs. *he play*). The past tense does not show mood distinctions, having only one form (*you/he played*). The verb *be* is an exception, the subjunctive having the form *be* throughout the present tense (contrasting with *am/are/is*), and *were* throughout the past tense (contrasting with *was* in the 1st and 3rd persons):

|  |  | Indicative | Subjunctive |
|---|---|---|---|
| Present tense |  | *am* |  |
| of | *to be* | *is* | *be* |
|  |  | *are* |  |
|  |  | *play* |  |
|  | other verbs | *plays* | *play* |
| Past tense |  | *was* | *were* |
| of | *to be* | *were* |  |

```
(1)    It's important that they be warned immediately
(2)    We recommend that she stay with us a little while longer
(3)    If I were married I wouldn't want children
```

Semantically, the subjunctive conveys the speaker's **attitude** or **belief** regarding the clause (see further § 9 on modality), saying that the speaker regards its content as either desirable (§ 7.3.5) or hypothetical (§ 7.3.6). Roughly speaking, the type expressing **desirability** (e.g. (1) and (2) above) is highly frequent in all styles of American English; in British English, other constructions are preferred (see below), the subjunctive being confined mostly to formal (often legal) language. The type expressing **hypothesis,** on the other hand, is more common in British than in American English, though still found primarily in formal written language. *Were* in the type exemplified by (3) is common even in informal style, in British English, whereas informal American English prefers *was.*

7.3.5    The present subjunctive, typical of American English, expresses **desirability** when governed by particular verbs which indicate that the speaker wants something to be done, or by adjectives or nouns of similar meaning. Thus in (1) and (2) above the subjunctive is governed by *important* and *recommend,* respectively. The subjunctive is also used when such forms report the wish of somebody else, as in (4)-(7) below.

This type of subjunctive also has syntactic manifestations, as it occurs unchanged in past-tense contexts, and does not require the use of *do* in negations:

```
(4)    He demanded that they release the hostages
(5)    Their suggestion is that we not leave until tomorrow
```

Of these, (4) is possible (though not common) in British English, whereas (5) does not occur. Rather than the subjunctive, British English typically prefers a construction with *should* or other alternatives:

```
(6)    He demanded that they should release the hostages
(7)    Their suggestion is that we don't leave until tomorrow
```

Both varieties of English share the use of certain idioms in which the desirability meaning of the present subjunctive is also found:

```
(8)    God bless you! Long live the Queen!
(9)    Be that as it may.../Suffice it to say...
```

7.3.6    The only common use of the subjunctive to express **hypothesis** (in British and formal American English) is the use of the past-tense subjunctive of *be* in conditional, concessive, comparative and object clauses, when the hypothesis is non-factual or contrary-to-fact:

```
(10)   If I were your age I would travel and see the world
(11)   They would pass that resolution whether I were there or not
(12)   He acts as if he were mad
(13)   I wish she were here
```

The present subjunctive (in conditional and concessive clauses) to indicate uncertainty is rare and confined to highly formal language; the form is usually *be*:

```
(14)    If this be thought a feasible solution, we implore the
        committee to act accordingly
(15)    Whatever be the reason for his crime, it can never be
        forgiven
```

7.3.7  Formally, the **imperative** verb phrase differs from the indicative in the following way: the finite verb is always a -Ø form, i.e. there is no concord between the verb phrase and the subject (which is usually absent); *do* is the only commonly occurring auxiliary, though other auxiliaries do occur for special effect and in a few idioms; *do* may cooccur with another auxiliary (*be* or *get*), and with *be* as main verb:

```
(16)    Don't tell me!
(17)    Be seen reading the Times, if you want people to believe
        you're an important businessman
(18)    Give him the money and have done with it!
(19)    Don't be taken in by their smiles
(20)    Don't get run over by a car
(21)    Don't be a fool!
```

In terms of meaning, as these examples demonstrate, the imperative shares with the subjunctive the expression of speaker attitude (desirability): the speaker wants something to be done. The understood subject of the imperative is always the 2nd person. When the subject is made explicit, this often gives the imperative a patronizing ring:

```
(22)    You be a good little boy and do what you're told
(23)    Don't you worry — nothing will happen!
```

The subject comes **after** the finite verb in *don't you* (23) and a few idiomatic expressions like *mind you*:

```
(24)    I have no objection, mind you, but I really don't see the
        point
```

Imperatives with *let's* are negated without use of *do* in formal style:

```
(25)    Let's not worry about that now (formal)
(26)    Don't let's worry about that now (informal)
```

For more details on the imperative, see § 5.3.

**Periphrastic *do* (7.4)**

7.4  Periphrastic *do* has three, finite, forms: *do, does, did*. It does not cooccur with any other auxiliary, or with the verb *to be*, except in imperative clauses (see §§ 4.1.0, 7.3.7). It is followed by a verb in the infinitive without *to*. Its main functions are:

(A) to make partial inversion possible where there is no other auxiliary to move to the left of the subject, most importantly in interrogative main clauses without an interrogative pronoun as subject (see §§ 4.1.0-4.1.6):

(1)    *Do* you *like* my new hat? Where *did* you *buy* that dress?

(B) to introduce *not* in clauses where there is no other auxiliary:

(2)    He *does* not *know* her address; she *did*n't *stop* eating; *don't make* me laugh!

(C) for emphasis:

(3)    He really *does* try hard! But I *did* lock the door! *Do* be careful![29]

### PRM1: The Modal Auxiliaries (7.5.1-7.5.2)

7.5.1    The **central modal auxiliaries** are *can/could, may/might, shall/should, will/would, must*. These verbs can only function as auxiliaries. As they have only finite forms (a present- and a past-tense form, except *must*, which has only one form), it follows that they have to occur as the first constituent of the verb phrase. They do not show subject-verb concord or mood contrasts. They are followed by an infinitive without *to* (-Ø form):

(1)    She *could* have phoned
(2)    You *must* be dreaming
(3)    He *will* be executed

7.5.2    The **marginal modal auxiliaries** include several idiomatic expressions which are difficult to describe satisfactorily: *be (to), be about (to), be going (to), have got (to), have (to), had better, had/would rather/ sooner, ought (to), used (to), dare, need*. These are **marginal** modals because none of them shares **all** the characteristics of the central modals: several of them are followed by a *to*-infinitive; *have (got) to* and *be (about/going) to* show subject-verb concord; *had better* and *had rather* (etc.) have one, complex, form; *need* and *dare* can function as main verbs. Three of them are included although they may be preceded by other auxiliaries (which is against the basic criterion of a modal auxiliary): *be about to, be going to*[30] and *have to*.[31]

---

29. Emphatic *do* in polite requests is more common in British than in American English, where *please* is preferred: *Please be careful!*

30. Before *be going to*, a modal disjunct is usually preferable to an auxiliary : She is *probably going* to help me.

31. *Have (to)* even cooccurs with periphrastic *do*, which in other cases we have regarded as a criterion of main-verb status (see also § 7.4). We include *have (to)* among the marginal modal auxiliaries because it is often used interchangeably with *must* and *have got (to)* (though see also §§ 9.7.1-9.7.2), and in deference to tradition.

Another traditional marginal modal, *(be) able (to)*, alternates with *can* (see § 9.5.2 n.), but as *able (to)* is hardly different from *capable (of)* and *willing (to)*, we choose to analyze this as a postmodified adjective functioning as subject complement: He was *(un)able to talk*. See also § 21.2.6 (adjectives with an obligatory postmodifier) and § 22.1.2.

Like the rest of these forms, they often express meanings similar to those conveyed by the central modals.

Examples:

(4)   I *have (got)* to go now
(5)   She *is going* to help me
(6)   They *were* to see her immediately
(7)   You *had better* talk to her yourself
(8)   *I'd rather* talk to her myself

*Used to* alternates between modal-auxiliary status (no periphrastic *do*) and main-verb status (use of periphrastic *do*) in interrogative and negative clauses; only the main-verb construction is possible in American English:

(9a)   She used not <u>to like</u> that   (formal BE)
        PRM       H
    S   V-    A    -V     DO

(9b)   She didn't use <u>to like</u> that   (AE and BE)
        PRM    H      V    DO
    S     V        DO

*Ought to* behaves in a similar way, but the main-verb construction of this verb is considered nonstandard:[32]

10a)   You *ought not* to have done that   (*ought* is a modal auxiliary)
10b)   You *didn't ought* to have done that   (*ought* is a main verb)

*Dare* and *need* occur as modal auxiliaries only in interrogative and negative clauses, and only in British English:[33]

(11)   He *needn't* say anything about it   (Cp. *need* as main verb: "He *does not need* to say..."/"He *needs* the benefit of an education")
(12)   *Dare* I ask what the purpose is of all this? (Cp. "*Did* he dare to ask...")

*Dare* has the past-tense form *dared* also as a modal auxiliary:

(13)   He *dared* not ask her again

The form *dare* (as well as *must* and *need*) can be used with past-time reference in reported speech:

(14)   He said he *daren't* ask her again
(15)   They said she *needn't* bother

The semantics of the modal auxiliaries will be dealt with in § 9, *passim*.

---

32. For informal interrogative and negative clauses American English uses *should* instead of *ought*.

33. In American English they are treated as modal auxiliaries only in set phrases like *Need I say more*, and *I dare say...*

**PRM2: Perfect *have* (7.6)**

7.6    Perfect *have* has four forms, corresponding to the form system of the regular
       verbs. It is followed by a verb in the past participle. Perfect *have* can be the first
       verb from the left in the VP, in which case its form may represent any finite or
       nonfinite category, or it may follow a modal auxiliary, in which case its form
       is an infinitive without *to*:

```
(1)    She has lost all her money, but I have won some
(2)    He had believed in her
(3)    They denied having seen her before
(4)    You must have been out of your mind
```

The semantics of the perfect will be discussed in §§ 8.2.2, 8.3.1-8.3.2.


**PRM3: Progressive *be* (7.7)**

7.7    Each of the eight forms of the verb *be* except *being* can function as progressive
       auxiliary. It is followed by a verb in the present participle. Progressive *be* can
       be the first verb from the left in the VP, in which case its form may represent
       any finite or nonfinite category, or it may follow a modal auxiliary and/or
       perfect *have*, in which case its form is nonfinite:

```
(1)    I'm writing a letter, and Mary is mowing the lawn
(2)    If I were facing a crisis like this, I'd be terrified
(3)    She seems to be crying a lot these days
(4)    You should be enjoying yourself
(5)    He had been enjoying himself
```

Various aspects of the semantics of the progressive will be dealt with in §§ 8.2.3,
8.3.2, 8.4.2, 8.5.1-8.5.2, 8.6.


**PRM4: Passive *be* (7.8)**

7.8    Each of the eight forms of the verb *be* can function as passive auxiliary. It is
       followed by the past participle of the main verb. Passive *be* can be the first verb
       from the left in the VP, in which case its form may represent any finite or non-
       finite category, or it may follow any of the other PRM's, in which case its form
       is nonfinite:

```
(1)    You are both fired!
(2)    The window was broken by a burglar
(3)    He must avoid being seen with her
(4)    You should have been given a prize
(5)    That problem is being taken care of
```

See also §§ 5.6 and 6.4.1 on the use of the passive.

**Head: Complex Main Verbs (7.9.0-7.9.4)**

7.9.0   Whereas the number of different verbs which can occur as verb-phrase premodifiers (auxiliary verbs) is limited to those that have been introduced in the course of § 7, almost any verb can occur as head (main verb), although the meaning of the head may restrict the choice of premodifiers, see § 8.1.0 ff.

Main verbs are either simple or complex. **Complex main verbs** derive from verbs which so frequently govern a particular type of adverbial or complement that (a part of) that adverbial or complement becomes part of the verb:

(1)     Our water supply has *run out*
(2)     His lawyer *looked into* the case
(3)     *Take care!*

The most general characteristic of a complex main verb is that the original verb has changed or lost its meaning: *run* is not likely, in (1), to have the same independent meaning as in *There was a hole in the barrel so all the water ran out; looked* in (2) could mean "took a look (into the box)," or it could combine with *into* to mean "investigated"; and *take* in (3) does not have the meaning of *take* in *Take an aspirin!* These differences can be captured by grammatical analysis, cp.

(1a)    There is a hole in the barrel — the water has run out
                                          S              V    A

(1b)    Our water supply has run out
             S                V

(2a)    His lawyer looked into the case
             S        V        A

(2b)    His lawyer looked into the case
             S        V          DO

(3a)    Take the aspirin that I gave you!
         V          DO

(3b)    Take care that you don't fall
         V          DO

There are three types of complex verb: phrasal verbs (1b), prepositional verbs (2b), and object verbs (3b).

*Phrasal verbs (7.9.1)*

7.9.1   Phrasal verbs are verbs which have merged with a small adverb, and which therefore have to be distinguished from verbs that are followed by such an adverb functioning as adverbial, cp. § 7.9.0 (1a) and (1b).[34] Phrasal verbs can be both **intransitive**:

---

34. Firmly established phrasal verbs tend to form nouns with the stress on the first syllable: *'coverup, 'feedback, 'giveaway, 'handout, 'pinup, 'takeoff, 'takeover.*

(4)     <u>Peter</u> <u>is showing</u> <u>off</u>  (cp. <u>Peter</u> <u>is falling</u> <u>off</u>)
         S      V             S       V    A

(5)     <u>The buffoon</u> <u>threw up</u>  (cp. <u>The balloon</u> <u>went</u> <u>up</u>)
            S        V              S      V   A

(6)     <u>Won't</u> <u>you</u> <u>give in</u>?  (cp. <u>Won't</u> <u>you</u> <u>come in</u>?)
         V-    S   -V          V-   S   -V  A

and **transitive**:

(7)     <u>He</u> <u>took down</u> <u>her address</u>
        S     V        DO

(8)     <u>The cartoonist</u> <u>brought out</u> <u>her most dominant characteristics</u>
              S          V               DO

(9)     <u>Doris</u> <u>put up</u> <u>the money</u>
         S    V      DO

Transitive phrasal verbs allow the complement to come between their two elements. This is compulsory when the complement is a pronoun:

(7a)    <u>He</u> <u>took</u> <u>it (her address)</u> <u>down</u>
        S  V-        DO       -V

        (cp. <u>He</u> <u>took</u> <u>the flag</u> <u>down</u>)
             S   V    DO   A

(8a)    (The cartoonist found her most dominant characteristics and)

        <u>brought</u> <u>them</u> <u>out</u> <u>brilliantly</u>
          V-    DO  -V    A

        (cp. <u>He</u> <u>brought</u> <u>the hostages</u> <u>out</u>)
             S   V     DO   A

(9a)    <u>Doris</u> <u>put</u> <u>it (the money)</u> <u>up</u>
         S   V-     DO     -V

        (cp. <u>Doris</u> <u>put</u> <u>her feet</u> <u>up</u>)
              S   V   DO   A

Transitive phrasal verbs can be turned into the passive like most transitive verbs:

(10)    Her address *was taken down*
(11)    The money *was put up* by Doris

### *Prepositional verbs (7.9.2)*

7.9.2   Prepositional verbs are verbs which have attracted the preposition of an ensuing noun phrase, and which therefore have to be distinguished from verbs that are followed by a prepositional phrase functioning as adverbial, cp. § 7.9.0 (2a) and (2b). A few more examples:

(12)    <u>They</u> <u>turned to</u> <u>their master</u> <u>for guidance</u>
         S    V       DO      A

        (cp. <u>They</u> <u>came</u> <u>to their master</u> <u>for guidance</u>)
              S   V     A        A

```
(13)   (He was cunning but) she saw through him
                            S      V        DO

       (cp. (The window is so dirty) you can't see through it)
                                      S     V       A
```

```
(14)   I can't live on my present salary
       S      V         DO

       (cp. I live on Long Island)
            S    V       A
```

Among the words which can function as junctives are quite a few which may also be adverbials, e.g. *along, down, in, off, on, over, through*. It is possible, however, to distinguish a prepositional verb from a phrasal verb. For one thing, whereas phrasal verbs can be either transitive or intransitive, prepositional verbs are always transitive (see (12)-(14)). For another, whereas phrasal verbs can be divided by their complement, as in (7a)-(9a), the complement of a prepositional verb has to occur after the preposition, cp.

```
(15)   She looked over her notes − she looked them over
(16)   Let's go over the details once more − *Let's go them over
```

though it is sometimes possible to change a prepositional verb into a phrasal verb by moving the complement (with a change of meaning!):

```
(17)   He turned on his wife in anger   (prepositional verb)
(18)   He turned her on   (phrasal verb)
```

Like other transitive verbs, prepositional verbs can normally be turned into the passive:

```
(19)   The master was turned to for guidance
(20)   The children will be looked after by their grandmother
```

### Object verbs (7.9.3)

7.9.3  Object verbs are verbs which have merged with a following noun, and which therefore have to be distinguished from verbs that govern a noun functioning as complement, cp. § 7.9.0 (3a) and (3b). The object verb, because it incorporates its original object, is nearly always intransitive (though cp. (3b)). A few more examples:

```
(21)   The meeting took place at the local school
           S          V           A
```

```
(22)   She tends bar/shop in Cedar Crest
        S      V           A

       (AE, cp. AE & BE bartender)
```

```
(23)   He must make amends for what he has done!
        S      V             A
```

In a few cases, the original object can no longer be used independently, e.g. *amends* in (23).

### Complex prepositional verbs (7.9.4)

7.9.4    Both phrasal and object verbs may combine with a following preposition to form a complex prepositional verb.

Phrasal verb + preposition:

```
(24)   We have run out of water
(25)   I won't put up with your insolence much longer
(26)   She was looked up to by the whole gang
```

Object verb + preposition:

```
(27)   They lost track of him over the years
(28)   She gave birth to a little girl
(29)   He was taken care of by all of us
```

## TIME PERSPECTIVE (8.0-8.8.5)

### Introduction (8.0)

8.0    The structure of the verb phrase reflects the speaker's need to make choices along two semantic dimensions: (a) time perspective and (b) speaker belief and attitude. In our overview of what the verb phrase contributes to the expression of such meanings, it will also be necessary, to some extent, to involve forms from outside the verb phrase with which it interacts.

Initially, as the range of possible meanings along the two dimensions is restricted somewhat by the semantics of the particular main verb, let us look at the main verb in terms of semantic categories.

### Semantic Main-Verb Categories (8.1.0-8.1.7)

8.1.0    Main verbs can be categorized semantically in many different ways according to the purpose of the description. The categories needed to group verbs according to their complementation (see § 2.6) are not necessarily the same as those needed to group them in terms of how they combine with auxiliary verbs. As it is the latter question which is our main concern in this chapter, it is also this question which determines the following semantic categorization.

A main verb is categorized according to its **typical use**. Thus when a verb is referred to as e.g. dynamic (§ 8.1) or inconclusive (§§ 8.1.4-8.1.7), this label characterizes its predominant, but not necessarily only, function.

8.1.1    The meaning of a main verb may be more, or less, easy to conceive of as an on-going process or temporary condition. It so happens that the progressive aspect is used to indicate an ongoing process or temporary condition, which means that we can use the progressive to distinguish between verbs that can be associated with this meaning and verbs which cannot:

```
(1)    They are playing in the courtyard
(2)    I'm staying right here
(3)    She is dying
(4)    Who is knocking?
(5)    *That book is belonging to me
(6)    *He is resembling his father
(7)    *I'm knowing that song by heart
(8)    *Are you seeing what I mean?
```

Verbs like *play, stay, die, knock*, which can take the progressive, are called **dynamic verbs**, whereas those like *belong, resemble, know, see*, which do not normally take the progressive, are called **stative verbs**. The distinction between dynamic and stative verbs is usually considered the basic semantic distinction of the main verbs. Often the same verb can be used either dynamically or statively, cp. (8) above with a context in which *see* is dynamic:

```
(8a)   You are seeing things!
```

and compare examples like the following:

```
(9)    Ireland lies west of England
(9a)   The ship is lying in the port of Liverpool
(10)   Bob lives in Phoenix (more or less permanently)
(10a)  Bob is living in Phoenix (for the time being)
```

8.1.2    **Stative verbs** fall into two groups: relational and private verbs.

    **Relational verbs** indicate a relation between things and/or persons, e.g. *belong, contain, concern, cost, differ, equal, fit, include, involve, lack, measure, own, resemble, weigh*.

    **Private verbs** are called thus because the truth of their meaning can be known only by the experiencer (see § 6.4.2):

```
(11)   I love classical music
(12)   Sally reminds Peter of her mother
```

Private verbs also include e.g. *believe, doubt, forgive, imagine, know, like, notice, recognize, regard as, remember, think, understand*, as well as the verbs of sense perception, *feel, hear, see, smell, taste*.[35]

    The modal auxiliary *can* often makes explicit the stative use of some private

---

35. The difference between *listen to* and *hear*, and between *look at* and *see*, which we have already touched upon in connection with case roles (§ 6.4), is also one of dynamic vs. stative: *He didn't hear what you said because he wasn't listening.*

verbs, e.g. *imagine, remember, understand,* and the verbs of sense perception; cp.
dynamic (a) and stative (b) use:

```
(13a)  He remembered to close the window!
(13b)  He could remember closing the window (besides: He remembered
       closing...)
(14a)  She smelled the perfume before buying it
(14b)  He could smell the perfume
```

See also § 9.5.2.


8.1.3    **Dynamic verbs** can be divided into activity verbs, transitional verbs and
momentary verbs.

   **Activity verbs** are verbs like *ask, drink, eat, help, listen to, look at, read, remind*
*(remind somebody to...,* cp. (12)) *say, talk, try, work,* etc.

   **Transitional verbs** mark the transition from one state of affairs to another;
the transition may happen at a point in time, e.g. *arrive, break, die, land, leave,
open,* or it may happen more or less gradually, e.g. *change, melt, widen.*

   **Momentary verbs** refer to events of very short duration, e.g. *hit, jump, kick,
knock, nod, tap.*


8.1.4    Dynamic verbs, furthermore, fall into two groups: those which are **conclusive**, and those which are **inconclusive**, according to whether the natural
conclusion of the action is part of the meaning of the clause. Compare:

```
(15)   Bill crossed the street (in 10 seconds) (conclusive)
(16)   Bill listened to Joan (for 10 seconds) (inconclusive)
```

(15) implies "Bill reached the other side," which is why it is possible to measure
how long it **took**, cp. the adverbial *in 10 seconds.* In (16) there is no such natural
conclusion implicit in the meaning of *listened to,* which is why it makes sense
to indicate for how long the activity went on *(for 10 seconds).* In fact, the
possibility of using an adverbial of duration introduced by *for* can be used as
a criterion of an inconclusive(ly used) verb.

   Transitional and momentary verbs are by definition conclusive, whereas most
activity verbs can be either or, according to the context:[36]

```
(17)   Bill chopped the wood in two hours (conclusive)
(17a)  Bill chopped wood for two hours (inconclusive)
(18)   Joan read the paper in two hours (conclusive)
(18a)  Joan read the paper for two hours (inconclusive)
```

However, a number of activity verbs are primarily inconclusive, such as *fight,*

---

36. In other words, transitional and momentary verbs cease to have transitional/momentary
meaning if they are constructed as inconclusive, see §§ 8.5.2 and 8.6. Some activity verbs form
pairs according to the conclusive/inconclusive distinction, cp. *fall asleep/sleep, find/look for,
lose/lack, work out/work at.*

*hold, listen, quarrel, struggle, talk, try, wear, work.*

The distinction between conclusive and inconclusive is not relevant with stative verbs.

8.1.5    In § 8.1.1 we defined dynamic(ally used) verbs with reference to their ability to take the progressive aspect. The question, however, whether a dynamic verb does in fact take the progressive is to some extent linked to the conclusive/inconclusive distinction: one of the basic uses of the progressive is to make a verb inconclusive in a context where it would otherwise have been conclusive. Compare the following, and see further §§ 8.2.3, 8.5.2 and 8.6:

```
(19)   Bill crossed the street
(19a)  Bill was crossing the street
(20)   Joan died
(20a)  Joan was dying
(21)   Peter knocked on the door
(21a)  Peter was knocking on the door
```

8.1.6    Furthermore, ambiguity of structure as exemplified below cannot occur with inconclusive verbs, but only with certain conclusive ones:

```
(22a)  The ticket was used (immediately)
       ‾‾‾S‾‾‾ ‾‾V‾‾

(22b)  The ticket was used (so I had to buy another)
       ‾‾‾S‾‾‾ ‾V‾ ‾SC‾

(23a)  The window was broken (by the burglar)
       ‾‾‾S‾‾‾ ‾‾V‾‾

(23b)  The window was broken (so we couldn't keep the wind out)
       ‾‾‾S‾‾‾ ‾V‾ ‾SC‾
```

where *used* and *broken* are main verbs in a passive verb phrase in the (a) examples, but subject complement in the (b) examples (corresponding to their meaning as noun-phrase premodifiers, cp. *a used ticket, a broken window*).

8.1.7    The following diagram sums up our semantic categorization of main verbs:

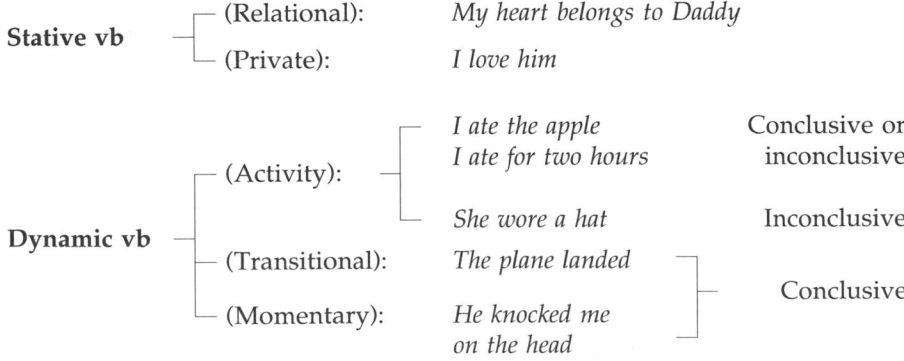

**Tense and Time, Aspect and Perspective (8.2.1-8.2.3)**

*Tense and time (8.2.1)*

8.2.1   The first verb from the left in the verb phrase often tells us whether the speaker views the action as belonging to the present or the past; in the following examples, this verb happens to be the only one (the main verb):

```
(1)     Neil scores a goal
(2)     Neil scored a goal
```

In other words, in (1) **present time** is expressed by the **present tense** form of the verb, in (2) **past time** is expressed by the **past tense** form of the verb. Referring to **future time** requires the use of some other time marker such as the auxiliary verb *will*:

```
(3)     Neil will score a goal
```

The relationship between time and verb form is not quite as simple, however, as these examples might lead us to suppose — in fact, this is why we need both terms, "time" and "tense" — because time is sometimes expressed through other means than tense forms, just as the tense forms can have several different meanings; cp.

```
(4)     If Neil scored a goal tomorrow (this would considerably
        improve his chances of becoming captain)
```

In (4), time (future) is expressed by the adverb *tomorrow*, whereas the past-tense form of *score* (together with *would* in the main clause) expresses non-reality (hypothesis), not past time.

The past tense, in fact, has these two basic meanings, "past time" and "non-reality." A possible common denominator for these two meanings is the concept of "remoteness": the past tense says that the event is remote, whether in terms of time or in terms of reality.

Because of this complex relationship between form and meaning, we shall also have to distinguish, in the following, between "aspect" (a linguistic form) and "perspective" (the meaning with which the form is typically associated).

*Perfect aspect and relational perspective (8.2.2)*

8.2.2   If I want to indicate that an action precedes the point in time that I am talking about, I can use the **perfect aspect** auxiliary, *have*, as in:

```
(5)     Neil has scored a goal — now we're in the lead!
```

where the action (Neil scoring a goal) must have taken place before the clause is uttered, which is the time I am talking about ("now"). In other words, (5) differs from (2) above in that the action, though occurring in the past, is viewed as relevant to the speaker's present situation:

```
(2x)  Neil scored a goal (on that occasion)
(5x)  Neil has scored a goal (we're in the lead)
```

Thus in (5) we say that the action has been given **relational perspective**.

### *Progressive aspect and situational perspective (8.2.3)*

8.2.3   Furthermore, an event can be viewed either as a whole, or in situational perspective. If I view it as a whole, I ignore any aspect of process or duration. This is the natural perspective when the event is referred to as one in a series of events:

```
(6)   This morning I got up at seven. I took a quick shower,
      brushed my teeth and had breakfast. Then I...
```

or when an event is repeated at regular intervals:

```
(7)   I wash my car every Sunday
```

I give a bird's eye view of the event, as it were, without getting close to the actual action. However, an event can also be viewed in a situational perspective, in which case the speaker focuses on the action as an ongoing process without beginning or end. Typically a situational perspective is chosen when the speaker wants to describe things as they are at a particular moment in time, i.e. the various processes that are going on:

```
(8)   It was an ordinary morning. I was finishing breakfast by
      myself, the children were getting ready for school, and my
      wife was backing the car out. Suddenly...
```

Here we are brought **into** the situation, and are made to feel almost as if we are experiencing the situation ourselves. The effect is achieved formally by means of the **progressive** auxiliary, i.e. a form of *be* followed by a verb ending in *-ing*, though sometimes it is signalled by the *-ing* form alone, cp.:

```
(9a)  She crossed the street — I saw her cross the street
(9b)  She was crossing the street — I saw her crossing the street
```

Note that in a situational perspective, the event is not necessarily concluded later (see § 8.1.4). Thus example (9b) could be the background of another event viewed as a whole, *...when she got hit by a car*, whereas (9a) implies that she reached the other side of the street safely. Furthermore, an event seen in a situational perspective is going on for a limited period of time, cp.

```
(10a) Harry is talking too fast (perhaps he is nervous)
(10b) Harry talks too fast (this is a permanent characteristic)
(11a) Joe is being naive (he is currently behaving in such a way)
(11b) Joe is naive (a permanent state)
```

The distinction between viewing the event as a whole and in a situational perspective **is** only relevant with **events**. A state cannot be viewed as a whole, because it is not conceived of as having a beginning and an end; nor can it be seen in a situational perspective, because it refers to a "general truth" which cannot characterize any particular situation as opposed to other situations. Hence states cannot be referred to by means of the progressive aspect (see also § 8.1.1):

```
(12)   Blood is thicker than water
(13)   London stands on the Thames
(14)   I believe in Santa Claus
```

Try, for instance, to make (13) part of a situational context: *The sun was shining, the birds were singing, and *London was standing on the Thames.*

## Past Time (8.3.1-8.3.2)

### *Absolute past time (8.3.1)*

8.3.1    Typically an event is placed in absolute past time by means of the **past tense**:

```
(1)    Hitler attacked Poland in 1939
```

I am placing the event (*..attack..*) at the time in the past that I am talking about (1939). If on a **time line** I call the point where the **event** takes place, *E*, and the time that I am talking about (**referring** to), *R*, the two points coincide to the left of the point when I **utter** the sentence, *U*:

$$E/R \qquad U$$

*past* <== —————|—————|————————— ==> *future*

The reference point (*R*) does not have to be explicitly indicated by an adverbial. Thus the events of (2) and (3) are also placed in absolute past time, though the adverbial of (2) indicates duration, not absolute time, and (3) contains no adverbial at all:[37]

```
(2)    My uncle stayed at the Savoy for two weeks
(3)    I decided to give Peter the book
```

When the clause is tenseless (nonfinite), or when the past tense of a modal auxiliary would have a different meaning, **perfect aspect** *have* is used to place the event in absolute past time:

```
(4)    Having seen a doctor yesterday, he now feels much better
       (= Because he saw a doctor yesterday...)
```

---

37. After a past-tense form in the main clause, the subclause is generally also in the past tense, even if it does not have past-time reference:
```
       a.   I haven't seen him — in fact I didn't know he was still alive
```
though sometimes the sense of present relevance is so strong that the present tense may prevail:
```
       b.   He knew that nitric acid dissolves/dissolved zinc
```

```
(5)     He may have seen a doctor yesterday
        (= It is possible that he saw a doctor yesterday)
```

In (5) the past tense of *may* would have indicated tentativeness, perhaps a polite suggestion, but not past time: *He might see a doctor*.

Finally, events clearly placed in absolute past time by the adverbials may be rendered particularly lively by the use of the **present tense** (the so-called "historic present"). This feature occurs only in spoken narrative, often of personal experiences:

```
(6)     Yesterday I'm in the supermarket when this woman comes up
        to me and accuses me of stealing her purse
```

### Relational past time (8.3.2)

8.3.2    I may want to place the event, or the start of the event, in the past **in relation to the reference point** (the time talked about), regardless of whether the reference point is in the past, the present or the future. Relational perspective is achieved by means of perfect aspect *have*, see § 8.2.2.

**(A)  The reference point is the time of utterance:**

$$
\begin{array}{ccc}
 & E & R/U \\
past \;\texttt{<==} & \underline{\quad\;|\quad\quad\quad|\quad\quad} & \texttt{==>}\; future
\end{array}
$$

i.e. a past event or state of affairs is seen as relevant to a reference point which coincides with the time of utterance, through the use of the **present perfect**:

```
(7)     I've brought my car  (I can take you to the station)
(8)     They have quarrelled (that is why they are not talking to
        each other)
(9)     He has lived here for ten years  (he still lives here)
(10)    She has owned the house since 1970  (she still owns it)
```

With dynamic verbs (most often conclusive, as in (7), though *quarrelled* in (8) is inconclusive), this construction denotes the present result of a past event. With stative verbs, it refers to a state of affairs lasting up till the present time, as in (9) and (10). To express an **event** lasting up till the present time, the present perfect alone is not enough,[38] cp.

```
(11)    He has written a book since May
```

Note that (11) would mean that the book was completed some time **before** the speaker's present. However, if **progressive aspect** *be* is added, the effect is achieved through the increased focus on the process itself, and the implication that it is not necessarily completed (see § 8.2.3):

```
(12)    He has been writing a book since May
```

---

38. Unless iterative meaning is meant, see § 8.6

Because of its focus on a possibly incomplete process, the progressive may represent a different context than when the perfect alone is used:

```
(13a)  I've cleaned the car (look how beautiful it is!)
(13b)  I've been cleaning the car (that's why I'm so dirty)
(14a)  Who has drunk my beer? (my glass is empty)   (BE)
(14b)  Who has been drinking my beer? (some of it is gone)
```

The American version of a sentence like (14a) would usually be, *Who drank my beer?*: In American English there is a strong tendency to use the past tense for recently completed events, where British English uses the present perfect (see also §§ 8.7.2, 8.7.6):

```
(15)   A man came barging into the room: "They shot Kennedy!"
(16)   I didn't see Kathy this morning
(AE:  (16) could be said in the afternoon or in the morning)
(BE:  (16) could be said in the afternoon only)
```

Very different contexts can be indicated by choosing either the present perfect or the past tense:

```
(17a)  Bill has been a chain smoker all his life (he is still
       alive)
(17b)  Bill was a chain smoker all his life (he is now dead)
(18a)  I've seen that film (so I won't go again)
(18b)  I saw that film (and, yes, it was very good)
(19a)  I've been to the dentist this morning (BE: said before noon)
(19b)  I went to the dentist this morning (BE: said in the
       afternoon)
```

The adverbials found in these examples (*all his life, this morning*) can thus be combined with both the present perfect and the past tense. However, adverbials of absolute past time (e.g. *yesterday, last week, in 1960*) naturally tend to occur only with the past tense. Some adverbials are in themselves indicators of relational perspective and so go together with the present perfect, e.g. *so far* and *since five o'clock*, and *now* combines with the present perfect as well as with the present tense.[39] See also §§ 8.7.0-8.7.6.

**Nonfinite forms of perfect** *have* may make a past event relevant to the time of speaking, or to a point in the past, depending on the context, cp. (20) and (21):

```
(20)   Having seen a doctor yesterday, I now feel much better
       (= Because I saw a doctor yesterday...)

(21)   Having bought a new car, they now have no money left
       (= Because they have bought a new car...)
```

---

39. With verbs of "communication" such as *hear, see, notice, understand, learn, say, tell*, the present tense of the main verb can denote relational perspective:
```
        I hear (Mary tells me) you have been ill = I have heard... (Mary
        has told me...)
```

**(B)  The reference point is in the past:**

```
              E     R     U
past  <==    ———⌐————⌐————⌐———      ==> future
```

— an event or state of affairs can be placed in the past in relation to a past reference point, by means of the **past perfect**:

(22)   She *had finished* the book by ten o'clock last night

Here the past point of reference is represented by the adverbial, *by ten o'clock last night*, in relation to which the event is in the past. Often the reference point is represented by another event, as in:

(23)   When they *had baked* the cake, they *ate* it

where the eating coincides with the reference point, in relation to which the baking is in the past:

```
              E/R    U
past  <==    ———⌐————⌐———      ==> future
                ..ate..
```

```
              E     R     U
past  <==    ———⌐————⌐————⌐———      ==> future
          ..had baked..
```

In reported speech, it depends on the context whether the past perfect simply places a past event (*E*) before the reported speech-event, or whether *E* is understood to be relevant to the reported speech-event in a way corresponding to the use of the present perfect, cp.

(24)   He said he *had visited* his mother the day before
       (= He said, "I *visited* my mother yesterday")

(25)   She told me she *had bought* a new car
       (= She said, "I *have bought* a new car")

**(C)  The reference point is in the future:**

```
              U     E     R
past  <==    ———⌐————⌐————⌐———      ==> future
```

— an event can be placed in the past in relation to a future point of reference by means of **perfect aspect** *have*, as in:

(26)   She *will have accomplished* the task by this time tomorrow
(27)   Wait till she *has finished*

Thus in (26) the adverbial, *by this time tomorrow*, represents the future reference point in relation to which *...have accomplished...* is in the past.[40]

## Present Time (8.4.0-8.4.2)

8.4.0    An event or state of affairs may be placed at the time of utterance, which is also the time being talked about (the reference point):

$$E/U/R$$

*past* <==   ——————————————   ==> *future*

```
(1)    I hear an owl
(2)    Mary lives in Japan
```

### Absolute present time (8.4.1)

8.4.1    The speaker may use the **present tense** of the main verb to indicate that an event happens at the point of utterance, as in (1) above. This is possible if the utterance represents:

— *simultaneous commentary*

(the verb is usually dynamic with conclusive meaning, but *hear* in (1) is stative, and *stir* in (4) is inconclusive):

```
(3)    Here they come now!
(4)    I now add a little milk and stir the mix gently with a spoon
(5)    Harry discovers her letter on the mantelpiece, reads it, and
       throws himself on the bed (stage direction)
```

— *an action which is defined by a present-tense verb:*

```
(6)    I (hereby) declare this meeting closed  (= a declaration)
(7)    I (hereby) promise to marry you (= a promise)
```

The latter type of utterance is further characterized by having a 1st-person subject, and by the possibility of adding *hereby*, as in (6) and (7). Verbs which allow this construction, e.g. *appoint, declare, demand, forbid, promise, recommend, request* are called **performative** verbs (these are by definition conclusive).

### Extended present time (8.4.2)

8.4.2    "Present time" may also refer to a time span which includes the time of speaking, but which extends into the past as well as into the future; this is the case when we use the present tense of verbs denoting a state of affairs (stative verbs), cp. also (2) above:

---

40. Past time in relation to future-in-the-past (cp. § 8.5.2 (B)) is found only in (perhaps implied) reported speech: *By seven he would have accomplished the task (they thought).*

```
(8)     Peter is in the kitchen
(9)     Sheila owns a house
(10)    Ireland lies west of England
```

The time span may be vastly different, as in these three examples, but in each case the present tense places the content of the clause within the speaker's perceived present-time horizon.

The present tense of dynamic verbs, when used in this way, acquires the meaning of something that happens regularly (see further § 8.6):

```
(11)    John walks to work
```

though dynamic verbs can of course be combined with the progressive aspect (see § 8.2.3) to denote something that is going on right now:

```
(12)    What are you reading?
```

where *What do you read?* would be a question about reading habits.

With modal auxiliaries, which are usually neutral in regard to time (see § 9.1.1), present time is signalled by the **absence of the perfect**, or the presence of the **progressive** (only dynamic verbs):

```
(13)    Peter must be in the kitchen
(14)    It may rain a lot in that part of the country
(15)    Neil might be scoring a goal at this very minute
```

**Future Time (8.5.1-8.5.2)**

*Absolute future time (8.5.1)*

8.5.1   An event or state of affairs may be placed in future time, which is also the time being talked about (the reference point):

$$\text{past} <== \quad \overset{\displaystyle \text{U} \qquad \text{E/R}}{\underset{}{\rule{0pt}{0pt}}} \quad ==> \textit{future}$$

```
(1)     I'll call him next week
```

Thus in (1) the event, ..*call*.., is placed at a future reference point represented by the adverbial, *next week*. Future events are events which have not yet taken place, and so they are by definition non-factual. In some cases, however, they can be represented as factual by means of the **present tense** of the main verb:

```
(2)     Kathy arrives tomorrow
(3)     I get back on Friday
```

We would say (2) or (3) to indicate fact according to an itinerary; this is only possible with dynamic verbs accompanied by a time adverbial. If, on the other hand, we use the more general way of referring to the future, the **modal auxiliary** *will* (*shall*):

(4)    Kathy *will arrive* tomorrow
(5)    I'*ll get* back on Friday

these utterances become more subjective **predictions**. In other words, referring to the future usually involves the indication of varying degrees of belief that the event will come true. When in this chapter we talk about "future time reference", what we really mean is "prediction with a high degree of certainty," whereas "uncertain" predictions will be dealt with in § 9 (e.g. §§ 9.1.5, 9.3-9.6), such as

(6)    I *may get* back on Friday

Expressions describing what the speaker wants to happen are obviously interpreted as referring to the future

(7)    You *must get* back on Friday
(8)    I *want* you *to give* these books to Peter

These, too, will be dealt with in § 9 (e.g. § 9.1.7, 9.7-9.10).

Because modal auxiliaries are frequently ambiguous, the **progressive** may follow to indicate that the **only** function of the modal is to place the event in the future, cp.

(9)    He *won't come* to the party ("doesn't want to" and/or future)
(10)   He *won't be coming* to the party (future)

*Will* does not occur in adverbial subclauses of time and condition, where the present tense of the main verb is used instead:

(11)   I'll tell you if/when he *comes* ("if/when that event takes
       place")

### *Relational future time (8.5.2)*

8.5.2    An event may be placed in the future **in relation to the reference point** (the time talked about), regardless of whether the reference point is in the present, the past or the future:

**(A)  The reference point is the time of utterance:**
Like a past event (cp. 8.3.2 A), a future event too can be viewed in terms of its relevance to the time of utterance:

$$\begin{array}{ccc} & \text{U/R} & \text{E} \\ & | & | \\ \textit{past} <== & \text{———————————} & ==> \textit{future} \end{array}$$

This can be achieved, for instance, by means of the verbs *be going to, be about to, be to,* and by the progressive. With *be going to* the event is seen as the future result of a present cause or intention, but the main thing is the implication that there are present indications of what will happen in the, often near, future:

— *Present cause*

(12)   It's *going* to rain (I see some dark clouds)
(13)   Mary *is going* to have a baby (she is pregnant)

— *Present intention*

(14)   She *is going* to sue for a divorce
(15)   What *are* you *going* to do tomorrow?

**Be about to** is almost synonymous with *be going to*, but implies that the future event is imminent:

(16)   Tim *is about* to say something, so don't interrupt!

**Be to** marks a future event which is the result of a present arrangement between the speaker and somebody else:

(17)   I'm *to* leave for Holland in the morning

The **progressive**, too, can indicate a present plan for the future, but it does not have to be the result of an agreement with somebody else:

(18)   I'm *leaving* for Holland in the morning

However, *be to* and the progressive have almost identical meanings in examples like:

(19)   I'm *to see* my boss in the morning (he has asked me to see him)
(20)   I'm *seeing* my boss in the morning (I have an appointment)

With verbs denoting the transition from one state of affairs to another (**transitional verbs**, see also §§ 8.1.3-8.1.5), e.g. *land, kill, change, melt*, the progressive comes to describe the process leading up to (the completion of) the transition:

(21)   The plane *is landing* (but it has not landed yet)
(22)   His job *is killing* him (but he is not dead yet)
(23)   The wind *is changing* from north to east (at the moment it is blowing from the north east)
(24)   The ice *is melting* (but it has not melted completely)

#### (B) The reference point is in the past:
An event can be placed in the future in relation to a past reference point:

```
             R       E         U
past  <==   ―――――――――――――――――     ==> future
```

This can be achieved by the past tense of the above verb forms. Their respective meanings do not change, cp.

```
(25)   Her brother found out she was going to have a baby
(26)   Tim was about to say something, when he was interrupted
(27)   The secretary told me I was to leave for Holland the next
       morning
(28)   I went to bed early since I was leaving for Holland the next
       morning
(29)   The safety belts were fastened — the plane was landing
```

### (C) The reference point is in the future:

Placing the event in the future in relation to a future reference point -

$$
\text{past} \iff \;\; \underset{\text{U} \quad\quad \text{R} \quad\quad \text{E}}{|\!\!-\!\!-\!\!-\!\!-\!\!-\!\!|-\!\!-\!\!-\!\!-\!\!-\!\!|} \;\; \implies \textit{future}
$$

is not nearly as common as (A) and (B) above, though it does happen with *be about to* and the progressive:

```
(30)   When Tim is about to speak, poke him in the ribs
(31)   I don't want to go out Thursday night, because I'll be
       leaving for Australia the following morning
```

### Iterative Events (8.6)

8.6      An event may be seen as something that repeats itself regularly, i.e. as an iterative event. This is the most common meaning when a dynamic verb is in the **present tense**, but the meaning is retained in the past tense depending on the context:

```
(1)    I generally have lunch at 1 o'clock (In those days I
       generally had...)
(2)    I buy my shirts at Harrods (In those days I bought...)
(3)    John works at a clothing factory — i.e. he works there every
       day (In those days John worked...)
```

If an event repeats itself regularly **within a limited period of time**, the **progressive aspect** may be used, cp.:

```
(4a)   I'm driving to work until my bicycle has been repaired
(4b)   I (always) drive to work
(5a)   Joan is teaching grammar this semester
(5b)   Joan teaches grammar (she is a grammar teacher)
```

The progressive may describe what is going on every time another event occurs:

```
(6)    He is usually working when I see him
```

Together with a frequency adverbial like *always, continually*, etc. the progressive can mark a process that repeats itself too often, i.e. every time you look, you can count on it that this particular process will be going on:

```
(7)    I'm always getting colds
(8)    He was for ever getting into trouble
```

Some events cannot be viewed as "ongoing" because they have no duration. If they are rendered by the progressive it can only denote the repetition of them (**momentary verbs**, e.g. *knock, jump, shoot*, see §§ 8.1.3-8.1.5), cp.

```
(9)    He was shooting at the can, but missing (several shots)
(10)   He shot at the can, but missed (one or several shots)
```

Finally, events placed in relational past time by means of the **perfect aspect** may be iterative in the sense of something that repeats itself for a period up till the point of reference (cp. 8.3.2 A):

```
(11)   I've always watched football on Saturday afternoons
(12)   The news had been broadcast at ten o'clock for as long as
       she could remember
```

### Time Adjuncts (8.7.0-8.7.6)

8.7.0   As will have become apparent from the preceding, adverbials of time play an important part in specifying the time reference of the verb phrase. We have already drawn a distinction between time and frequency adjuncts in terms of their position in the clause (§ 4.4.5). From the point of view of how they interact with the verb phrase to place the content of the clause in a time perspective, however, it will be necessary briefly to refine upon this categorization. In the following, therefore, we shall distinguish between adjuncts of **absolute and relative time location** (§§ 8.7.1-8.7.2), **absolute and relative duration** (§§ 8.7.3-8.7.4) and **definite and indefinite frequency** (8.7.5-8.7.6).

*Adjuncts of time location (8.7.1-8.7.2)*

8.7.1   **Absolute time location:** An event can be located absolutely in time by means of adjuncts like those in the following examples,

```
(1)    Charlie died a month ago
(2)    Last week I visited the Lake District
(3)    Sheila paid him yesterday
(4)    She is working in the field today
(5)    Today she even smiled at me
(6)    Are you going to that party tonight?
(7)    I leave for Japan tomorrow
(8)    Sheila arrives next week
```

Note that the event may happen at a point **within** the specified time period, cp. (4) and (5).

8.7.2   **Relative time location:** The adjunct can also place the event in relation to the time of another event, cp. (1)-(8) with

```
(1x)   (She told me) Charlie had died a month before
(2x)   (On March 14 I went to Lancaster.) The previous week I had
       visited the Lake District
(3x)   (I paid him the day we left.) Sheila paid him the day before
```

(4x)  (I'll see her Friday.) She'll be working in the field *that day*

(6x)  Would he be going to the party *that evening* (she wondered)

(7x)  (I retire on the fifth of June and) I leave for Japan *the day after*

(8x)  (Paul will get here around the second and) Sheila arrives *the following week*

In American English the adverbs *already, still* and *yet* often combine with the past tense where British English would require the present perfect (see also §§ 8.3.2 (A), 8.7.6):

(9a)   I already *read* that book   (AE)
(9b)   I *have* already *read* that book   (BE & AE)
10a)   I *didn't pay* for this book yet   (AE)
10b)   I *haven't paid* for this book yet   (BE & AE)

### Adjuncts of duration (8.7.3-8.7.4)

8.7.3   **Absolute duration:** The duration of an event ("How long...") may be measured in absolute terms, rather than in relation to when it begins or ends (cp. 8.7.4),

(11)   I'm staying with them *for two weeks*
(12)   He learned more *during those two weeks* than he had *in a lifetime*
(13)   He is *temporarily* out of a job
(14)   She has *always* lived there

Note that the adjunct in (11) does not help us determine whether the event is in present or future time.

8.7.4   **Relative duration:** The duration of an event may be measured in relation to the time when it began; the adjunct is frequently introduced by *since*, the event being rendered in the perfect aspect (see § 8.2.2),

(15)   I've been staying with them *since last Thursday*
(16)   I hadn't seen her *since she visited me in October*
(17)   He has been quite busy *lately*
(18)   She has *recently* been working for a law firm

### Adjuncts of frequency (8.7.5-8.7.6)

8.7.5   **Definite frequency:** The frequency of an event ("How often...") may be measured by the period of time which elapses between each occurrence, or by the number of times it occurs:

(19)   We have classes *every other day*
(20)   *Twice a year* I spend a week in Paris
(21)   I have kissed her *once* (only)

Note that as a time adjunct, *once* (cp. (21)) would take the past tense, not the present perfect: *I once kissed her.*

8.7.6 **Indefinite frequency:** The frequency indication may be vaguer or more subjective, as in

(22)   We *usually* take a walk in the afternoon
(23)   He was *always* making a fool of himself
(24)   They have *often* visited him in prison
(25)   She is *never* there when she is needed

In American English the adverbs *always* and *(n)ever* tend to combine with the past tense in contexts where British English would require the present perfect (see also §§ 8.3.2 (A), 8.7.2):

(26a)  I never *went* to Italy  (AE)
(26b)  I *have* never *been* to Italy   (BE)

**Overview of some Form/Meaning Relationships (8.8.1-8.8.5)**

*The tenses (8.8.1-8.8.2)*

8.8.1  **Present tense:**
A.  The event happens at the point of utterance (§ 8.4.1)

I *hear* an owl
I now *add* a little milk and *stir* the mix gently with a spoon
I (hereby) *declare* this meeting closed

B.  Extended present time (§ 8.4.2)
1)  State of affairs (stative verbs)

Sheila *owns* a house

2)  Iterative event (dynamic verbs; also § 8.6)

John *walks* to work

C.  Future time (with obligatory time adverbial, § 8.5.1)

Kathy *arrives* tomorrow

D.  Past time (in spoken narrative: § 8.3.1)

Yesterday I'*m* in the supermarket when this woman *comes* up
to me and *accuses* me of stealing her purse

E.  Relational perspective (verbs of "communication": § 8.3.2 n.)

I *hear* you have been ill

8.8.2  **Past tense** (basic meaning: "remoteness" § 8.2.1)
A.  Absolute past time (§ 8.3.1)

Hitler *attacked* Poland in 1939
She *stayed* at the Savoy for two weeks
John *worked* at a clothing factory

B.  Present or future time (in subclause: expressed by past tense because main-clause verb is in past tense; § 8.3.1 n.)

> I haven't seen him — in fact I didn't know he *was* still
> alive
> I didn't know she *was* coming tomorrow

C.  AE: relational perspective (§§ 8.3.2, 8.7.2, 8.7.6)

> I already *read* that book
> I never *went* to Italy

D.  Remoteness in terms of reality (e.g. § 8.2.1)

> If Neil *scored* a goal tomorrow, this *would* considerably
> improve his chances of becoming captain
> I wish you *were* here
> *Would* you pass the wine, please? (conventional expression
> of politeness, §§ 9.2.4, 9.10.3, 9.15.2)

### *The perfect aspect (8.8.3-8.8.4)*

8.8.3  **Present perfect:**

A.  Past event viewed as the cause of a present situation (dynamic verbs; § 8.3.2 A)

> I'*ve brought* my car (I can take you to the station)
> They *have quarrelled* (that's why they are not talking to
> each other)

B.  Event that repeats itself for a period up till the present time (dynamic verbs; § 8.6)

> I'*ve* always *watched* football on Saturday afternoons

C.  State of affairs lasting up till the present time (stative verbs; § 8.3.2 A)

> He *has lived* here for ten years
> She *has owned* the house since 1970

8.8.4  **Past perfect:**

A.  An event or state of affairs placed in the past in relation to a past reference point (§ 8.3.2 B)

> She *had finished* the book by ten o'clock last night

B.  Non-reality in the past (§ 9.6.3):

> If you *had helped* me, I would have helped you

*The progressive aspect (8.8.5)*

8.8.5    A.  Ongoing process, not necessarily completed (§§ 8.1.5, 8.2.3, 8.3.2)
        1)  The ongoing process forming the background of another event

Bill *was crossing* the street when he got run over by a car

        2)  Two or more processes viewed as parallel and simultaneous

Joan *was watching* TV while Tom *was playing* with the children

        3)  After the perfect: event lasting up till present time

Who has *been drinking* my beer? (cp. BE: Who has drunk my beer)

        4)  Event which repeats itself too often:

I'm always *getting* colds (§ 8.6)

B.  Ongoing process or temporary condition, as opposed to iterative process or general condition (§§ 8.4.2, 8.6):

Tom *is reading* The Times (cp. Tom *reads* The Times)
Joan *is writing* a letter (cp. Joan *writes* for a living)
Harry *is talking* too fast (§ 8.2.3; cp. Harry *talks* too fast)
They *are living* with his parents (§ 8.1.1; cp. They *live* with his parents)

C.  Iterative event (momentary verbs; § 8.6)

He *was shooting* at the can but *missing*

D.  Process leading up to a transition (transitional verbs; § 8.5.2)

The plane *is landing*

E.  With modals:
        1)  present time (§ 8.4.2)

He might *be scoring* a goal (at this very minute)

        2)  future time (§ 8.5.1)

He won't *be coming* to the party

F.  Relational future time (§ 8.5.2)

I'm *leaving* for Holland in the morning

**SPEAKER BELIEF AND ATTITUDE (9.1.0-9.16.5)**

### Introduction (9.1.0-9.1.8)

9.1.0   We saw in § 8 that the verb phrase is central in placing the clause in a time perspective, although the verbal interacts with other clause constituents and with the context in doing so. The situation is much the same with regard to the expression of speaker belief and attitude. At the core of this general area of meaning we find the category of **modality**, which is especially frequent in a particular class of auxiliary verbs, the modal auxiliaries (see §§ 7.5.1-7.5.2), though it is also to be found in other forms, verbs as well as nonverbs.

### *Definition of modality (9.1.1)*

9.1.1   Semantically it is possible to regard various categories of the verb-phrase premodifier as modifying the whole rest of the clause rather than just the main verb. Tense, for instance, is often a way of placing the main content of the clause, the **proposition**, in time:

(1)     Neil did his homework

        = [Neil + do + his homework] + [past tense]
                **proposition**                **happened in the past**

Sometimes, and typically when the first verb is a modal auxiliary, a tense distinction does not represent a **time** distinction (see *might* and *should* in (2) and (4), which do not place the proposition in the past). In fact, the modal-auxiliary forms usually express a different type of meaning:

(2)     Neil *might* do his homework
(3)     Neil *will* do his homework
(4)     Neil *should* do his homework
(5)     Neil *must* do his homework

This meaning system is the system of **modality**. In (2) and (3) the form in italics says how **probable** the speaker **believes** the proposition to be in terms of whether or not it will come true (in (3) the probability is viewed as **very** high). In (4) and (5), on the other hand, the italicized form expresses the speaker's **attitude**, i.e. to what extent the fulfillment of what the proposition says is regarded as **desirable**. As one would expect with expressions of probability and wish, they often place the proposition in the future.

### Same form, different meaning (9.1.2)

9.1.2   The same form may mean one thing in one context, and something else in another. We saw in § 8 that the present tense did not always express present time (e.g. *She arrives tomorrow*). Often a past-tense form denotes past time (*She arrived yesterday*), but sometimes it does not (*If she arrived tomorrow we could meet her at the station*). Modal auxiliaries typically convey modality as defined in § 9.1.1, but some of them can have other meanings as well, cp.

(6)   Neil *can* climb the wall in 30 seconds

where *can* ("is able to") is part of the proposition, the utterance being a statement of fact. In other cases the same modal can denote **either** probability **or** desirability, depending on the context; thus the statement that *I'm always forgetting my credit cards* might warrant either of the following comments:

(7)   You *must* be careless (probability)
(8)   You *must* be careful (desirability)

### Same meaning, different form (9.1.3)

9.1.3   Although belief and attitude are regularly expressed in the verb phrase, including the main verb, they can also be conveyed through other means, for instance through adjectives, adverbs and nouns; compare e.g.

(9)    Sheila *may* not send the letter
(10)   *Perhaps* Sheila won't send the letter
(11)   *Possibly* Sheila won't send the letter
(12)   It is *possible* that Sheila won't send the letter
(13)   There is a *possibility* that Sheila won't send the letter

Although (9)-(13) can all express the same degree of probability, it does not follow that they would be used interchangeably, see §§ 9.2-9.14.

### Probability and desirability signals (9.1.4-9.1.8)

9.1.4   Speaker belief and attitude (modality) is expressed through the following linguistic categories: the **imperative**, the **subjunctive**, **modal auxiliary verbs**, the **past tense** without past-time reference, **tag questions**, **hedges** (see below), and certain semantic classes of **main verbs**, **adjectives**, **adverbs** and **nouns**. Features such as stress and intonation, too, play a part in conveying modality in spoken language. Although the term "modal" has traditionally been used only about the modal auxiliaries (and therefore in § 7.2 we have used it about a verb phrase that contains a modal auxiliary in PRM1), it will be used here in reference to any grammatical category which expresses modality. Most expressions of modality can be (roughly) related to a particular area on either of two semantic scales: the **scale of probability** (§ 9.1.5) and the **scale of desirability** (§ 9.1.7).

9.1.5    The **scale of probability** ranges from fact (formally unmarked) to contrary-to-fact; the right-hand column represents arbitrarily chosen examples:

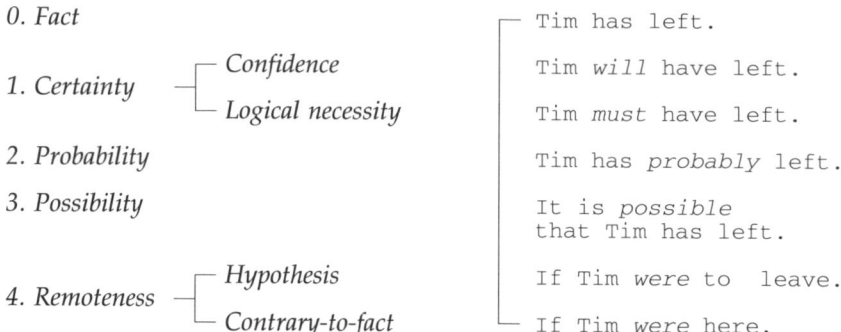

*0. Fact*                                                    Tim has left.

*1. Certainty* ─┬─ *Confidence*                 Tim *will* have left.
                └─ *Logical necessity*          Tim *must* have left.

*2. Probability*                                Tim has *probably* left.

*3. Possibility*                                It is *possible*
                                                that Tim has left.

*4. Remoteness* ─┬─ *Hypothesis*                If Tim *were* to  leave.
                 └─ *Contrary-to-fact*          If Tim *were* here.

Note that you are only taking the truth of the proposition as certain if you do not say anything about how certain you are. In other words, you only assert factuality (*it's a fact that..*) when you feel the factuality of the proposition has been questioned.

9.1.6    Various forms can be used to avoid sounding categorical and to signal noncommitment. They are thus related to speaker belief without clearly belonging to the scale of probability. They include **tag questions** (see § 5.2.1), which often invite confirmation of the speaker's opinion:

(14)    The way terrorism has spread is frightening, *isn't it?*
(15)    They show violence on TV, *don't they?*

and a mixed bag of forms often referred to as **hedges** (or "downtoners"), e.g. *actually, really, kind/sort of, or something (like that), tend (to)*:

(16)    I don't *really* see what you mean
(17)    I *kind of* knew this would happen
(18)    The age limit is sixteen *or something*, isn't it?
(19)    I *tend* to agree

9.1.7    The **scale of desirability** ranges from non-involvement (formally unmarked) to command:

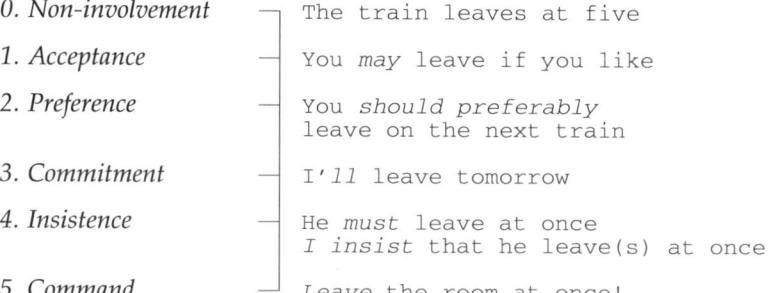

*0. Non-involvement* ─┐    The train leaves at five

*1. Acceptance* ──────┤    You *may* leave if you like

*2. Preference* ──────┤    You *should preferably*
                          leave on the next train

*3. Commitment* ──────┤    I'*ll* leave tomorrow

*4. Insistence* ──────┤    He *must* leave at once
                          I *insist* that he leave(s) at once

*5. Command* ─────────┘    *Leave* the room at once!

9.1.8   Another type of meaning, closely related to modality "desirability," is primarily conveyed by adverbs and adjectives (though other constructions do occur, cp. (24) below). This we will call **presuppositional attitude**:

(20)   *Surprisingly*, John didn't mention it

i.e. the speaker presupposes (regards it as a fact) that "John didn't mention it," and *surprisingly* expresses the speaker's reaction to this fact. Compare expressions of desirability and probability, which by definition (see 9.1.1) do not presuppose the truth of the proposition, e.g.

(21)   *I'm sure* John didn't mention it
(22)   *Hopefully*, John didn't mention it

In (21) "John didn't mention it" is **asserted**, not presupposed, *I'm sure* saying to what extent the speaker regards the assertion as true; in (22) the truth of the proposition is obviously not known.

Expressions of presuppositional attitude include *fortunate/-ly*, *wise/-ly*, *amusing/-ly*, *pity*, *shame*, among others:

(23)   It's *fortunate* that we bought some beer
(24)   It's *a pity* John didn't mention it

**Modal Auxiliaries: Implicitness and Subjectivity (9.2.1-9.2.6)**

9.2.1   The meanings of the modal auxiliaries are less explicit than those of the other probability and desirability signals, i.e. they depend to a large extent on the context. It is thus possible for each of the central modal auxiliaries to be used either as a probability or a desirability signal depending on the context, see (7) and (8) in 9.1.2. The modal auxiliaries imply purely subjective belief or attitude, as opposed to the **apparent** objectivity of the modal adjectives and their derivatives, see § 9.11.

The central modal auxiliaries are *can/could, may/might, must, shall/ should* and *will/would*. In terms of meaning, however, *can* and *will* are frequently neither probability nor desirability signals, see below. The marginal modals that can be either probability or desirability signals are *be (to), have got (to), had better, had/would rather/sooner, need* and *ought*.

9.2.2   In declarative clauses modal auxiliaries normally express the **speaker's** belief or attitude, whereas in interrogative clauses it is the belief or attitude of the **next** speaker, i.e. the person **addressed**, which is elicited:

(1)   *Will* John be coming? = *Do you think* John will be coming
(2)   *Shall* I help you? = *Do you want me to* help you?

9.2.3   Probability and desirability signals express speaker belief or attitude *at the moment of speaking*. The past tense, therefore, does not refer to past time, but is in itself a probability signal, as in:

```
(3)    George might write the letter
```

i.e. "there is that possibility (*may*), though it is only slight (*might*)."

9.2.4   Only in reported speech, i.e. when a past utterance is reported, can the past tense have past-time reference. Thus,

```
(4)    George said he might write the letter
```

could mean: *He said, "I may write the letter,"* though also: *He said, "I might write the letter."*

9.2.5   It follows from what we have said in §§ 9.2.3-9.2.4 that, if the modal auxiliary is a probability signal, the past tense is usually not available if we need to place the proposition in the past. This has to be done by means of the perfect aspect auxiliary, *have*:

```
(5)    George may have written the letter
```

for which there are thus two possible meanings: *It is possible that George wrote the letter*, and *It is possible that George has written the letter*.

However, if in the present tense the modal auxiliary is not a probability signal, the past tense may be used to refer to past time:

```
(6)    George can swim   (fact = he knows how to)
(7)    George could swim when he was five   (fact = he knew how to)
```

9.2.6   It is possible to mitigate requests by reference to the grammatical subject's **ability** (8) or **will** (9), as well as to **necessity imposed by the situation** (10):

```
(8)    Can/could you reach the ash-tray?
(9)    Will/would you pass the salt?
(10)   You don't have to shout
```

*Could* (8) and *would* (9) indicate that the "question" is hypothetical, making the request particularly tentative (i.e. (8) = "Could you reach the ash tray if I asked you to?").

**Modal Auxiliaries and Probability (9.3.1-9.6.3)**

*Confidence (9.3.1-9.3.6)*

9.3.1   The speaker is confident the proposition will come true. The usual form is *will* (*'ll, won't*), but in formal British English *shall* is sometimes used after a first person subject:

```
(1)    You'll understand better if I tell you the whole story
(2)    George will be fifty next year
(3)    I shall see her at the conference
```

These examples are typical in containing an adverbial expression of condition or future time.

9.3.2    As *shall* and *will* can also convey attitude, they are sometimes ambiguous unless used with the progressive; thus

(4)    I *won't* discuss it with him till after the meeting

could be either a prediction or a commitment ("I promise not to...") whereas with the progressive it can only be a prediction:

(5)    I *won't be* discuss*ing* it with him till after the meeting

For other ways of expressing future time, see §§ 8.5.1-8.5.2.

9.3.3    The past tense expresses either confidence felt in the past ("future in the past" (6)); or it is used, not to express time, but to indicate that the proposition is only a hypothesis (7), perhaps even to the extent of being contrary-to-fact (8):

(6)    I had no doubt I *would*/*should* see her at the conference
       (*should* in this type is only used in BE)
(7)    If he *should* arrive early, give him a drink
       (*should* in conditions)
(8)    She *would* be furious if she knew

In (6), *would*/*should* as past-tense forms cohere with *had no doubt* in placing this feeling in past time, in relation to which the proposition predicted (*I + see her at the conference*) is in the future. In (7), the function of *should* is to say that the proposition (*he + arrive early*) is by no means certain to happen. In (8), *would* indicates that "she" will **not** be furious, being the correlate of the past-tense form *knew* in the conditional clause: "she" does **not** know.

9.3.4    In making an assumption about the *present*, one can show confidence by means of *will*:

(9)    The exam *will* be over by now — it's 12 o'clock

*Must* can be used with a similar meaning (see § 9.4), but the assumption is based on deduction from facts available:

(10)   The exam *must* be over — the students are leaving the
       building

The past tense form *should* (and *ought to*) can be used to indicate that the assumption (based on logical deduction, see § 9.4.3) may be false:

(11)   He *should* (*ought to*) be home by now — unless he has stopped
       for a drink

9.3.5    *Will* can express confidence that something will happen every time in a given situation, i.e. that it is a habit:

```
(12)    He will talk for hours every time the subject is brought up
```

The past tense *would*, which has past-time reference in this sense, should be compared with *used to*, which can have a similar meaning, but which tends to focus on contrast with the present:

```
(13)    Churchill would smoke twenty cigars or more a day
(14)    I used to smoke forty cigarettes a day — now I smoke eighty
```

9.3.6    Finally, *will* can express confidence in what will happen every time the particular *qualities* of the grammatical subject are put to the test:

```
(15)    Lava will float on water
(16)    This lecture-room will seat 300 people
```

If *will* is strongly stressed it denotes inevitability, in comments on events:

```
(17)    People 'will criticize a new approach
(18)    John 'would make a mess of things    (i.e. it was to be
        expected)
```

### Logical necessity (9.4.1-9.4.3)

9.4.1    The speaker concludes, in terms of logical necessity, that the proposition is true:

```
(1)·    Paul must have left early to be here already
(2)     It must have been a wonderful experience
```

This use of *must* is usually not found in interrogative clauses and, in British English, negative clauses. For interrogative clauses a number of alternative formulations are available, such as the adverb *necessarily*. If you conclude that something is **not** the case, the form to be used is *cannot*:

```
(3)     Is the report necessarily true?
(4)     The report can't be true
```

If the negative conclusion is less certain, American English tends to use (uncontracted) *must not*, cp. § 9.5.1:

```
(5)     She must not have done what she claims to have done    (AE)
```

9.4.2    If the conclusion is that something is **not necessarily** the case, various expressions can be used:

```
(6)     The report needn't necessarily be true (BE, see § 7.5.2)/is
        not necessarily true
(7)     The report doesn't have to be true
```

Compare:

```
(8)     The report may not be true
```

which simply indicates possibility without any suggestion of logical necessity.

Note the logical relationship in meaning between (6), "it is *not* necessary that X" and (8), "it is possible that *not* X".

9.4.3   Note also that the use of *should* and *ought* implies logical deduction (see also § 9.3.4):

(9)   I gave him enough money, so he *should* be all right
(10)   It *shouldn't* cost much if we do it ourselves

### Possibility (9.5.1-9.5.2)

9.5.1   The speaker finds it possible that the proposition will/will not prove true:

(1)   The report *may* be true
(2)   Kate *may* have forgotten about the meeting
(3)   It *may* not be too late

*May* does not occur in interrogative clauses in this sense, but is replaced by other expressions such as *do you think* (4) or, occasionally, by *can* (5):

(4)   *Do you think* it is true?
(5)   *Can* she have forgotten about the meeting?

The past-tense forms *might* and *could* ("remote possibility," see § 9.6.1) are inter-changeable in positive statements and interrogatives, except that *could* tends to express a stronger (i.e. less remote) possibility than *might*:

(6)   The report *might/could* be true
(7)   *Might/could* the report be true?
(8)   The report *might* not be true

*Can* in the sense of **denial** of possibility replaces *must* ("logical necessity") in negative clauses, though in American English *must* is frequently used in this sense (see also § 9.4.1):

(9)   It *cannot* be true   (The negative version of *It must be true*)
(10)   High interest rates *must not* be discouraging shoppers very much (AE)

The possibility of using *can* ("possibility") to convey the same type of meaning as *must* ("necessity") has to do with the fact that *not* negates the modality in the case of *can*, whereas it negates the proposition in the case of *must*. In other words, "*not* possible that X" means the same as "necessary that *not* X."

9.5.2   *Can*, on the other hand, is not a modality signal when it denotes a possibility which depends on qualities within the grammatical subject:

```
(11)  We can all swim  ("ability")⁴¹
(12)  Even experts can make mistakes  ("theoretical possibility")
```

or when it makes explicit the stative use of verbs of sense perception and certain other private verbs like *imagine, remember, understand* (see § 8.1.2):

```
(13)  He couldn't taste the garlic in the soup (cp. He tasted the
      soup before serving it)
```

### Remoteness (9.6.1-9.6.3)

9.6.1   Remoteness (see § 8.2.1) in terms of reality is the most common general meaning of the past-tense form of a modal auxiliary, but usually it is added to a more specific meaning that depends on the individual modal (see also § 9.2.3). Compare:

```
(1)   I can do this  (ability)
      if you will help me  (willingness)

(2)   I could do this  (ability + remoteness)
      if you would help me  (willingness + remoteness)
```

9.6.2   Unlike other past-tense forms, *were (to)*⁴² (past tense of the marginal modal *be (to)*) is used for the sole purpose of marking remoteness. *Should*, too, can be used in this way (see also § 9.3.3). In comparison with the past tense of the main verb (3a), the modal auxiliary makes the proposition even more remote:

```
(3a)  If she walked in on us now, we would have a lot to explain
(3b)  If she were to walk in on us now, we would have a lot to
      explain
(4a)  If you change your mind, let me know
(4b)  If you should change your mind, let me know
```

9.6.3   **Non-reality in the past** is expressed by adding perfect *have* to the past-tense form of the modal auxiliary. In connection with a conditional clause, the latter has the past perfect:

```
(5)   You might have told me
(6)   If you had helped me, I would have helped you  (but you
      didn't, so I didn't)
```

---

41. *Be able (to)* is used to make up for "ability"-*can*'s lack of nonfinite forms:
```
      a. They have not been able to decipher the message yet
      b. Being unable to decipher the message, they still do not know
         what happened to the ship
```
It is also used in the sense of "manage":
```
      c. The boat capsized, but fortunately we were able/managed to swim
         ashore.
```

42. Or *was to* informally, in the first and third person singular (*were to* being the subjunctive).

### Modal Auxiliaries and Desirability (9.7.1-9.10.3)

*Insistence (9.7.1-9.7.3)*

9.7.1   This area on the scale of desirability (§ 9.1.7) is represented by *must* in the sense of necessity imposed by the speaker:

```
(1)    You really must be careful
(2)    You must not tell him
```

*Not* in (2) negates the proposition, not the necessity (i.e. "I find it necessary that *not* X"). To negate the necessity ("I do *not* find it necessary that X), the form to be used is *need* or *have*:

```
(3)    You needn't come if you don't want to   (British English)
(4)    You don't need/have to come if you don't want to
```

*Must* (and *needn't*) can refer to past time only in reported speech. If a past-tense form is needed for mitigation, *should* ("preference," see § 9.9.1) is used instead of *must*, cp. § 9.9.1.

9.7.2   If the necessity is imposed by external circumstances, especially in the case of **general** necessity (6), *have (to)* is used instead of *must*:

```
(5)    We have to pay the fine within 10 days
(6)    In my country you have to go to school on Saturdays
```

*Have got to* with stress on *'got* has the same meaning as *must*:

```
(7)    You've 'got to help me
```

Otherwise it tends to correspond to *have to*, though it is not generally used in the sense of "general necessity," cp. (6).

9.7.3   The speaker may want to play down his/her own authority by using *be (to)* in reference to what has been "arranged" (cp. § 8.5.2):

```
(8)    You're not to see him again!
```

*Commitment (9.8.1-9.8.2)*

9.8.1   An utterance may commit the speaker to an action. If the action is viewed by the addressee as something positive, the utterance is interpreted as a promise. If the action is viewed as something negative, the utterance is interpreted as a threat. The exact shade of meaning is determined by the context:

```
(1)    I will see that he gets the message
(2)    I will beat you up if you tell anybody
(3)    Be patient. You shall/will have the whole story tomorrow
```

In American English *shall* is rare outside very formal styles (both *shall* and *will* are in any case often contracted to *'ll*, in American as well as British English).

9.8.2   *Will/shall* express either the **speaker's** commitment or willingness, as in (1)-(3), or that of the **grammatical subject** ((5) and (6)):

```
(5)     The student just won't do his homework
(6)     Take a seat, please — Mr. Smith will see you in a moment
```

**Preference (9.9.1-9.9.3)**

9.9.1   This category expresses what the speaker feels is preferable. It is represented, first of all, by *should*:

```
(1)     You should be more polite to her
(2)     He should visit the dentist more regularly
```

*Should* expresses what the speaker thinks desirable either from a moral or a pragmatic standpoint, but where the speaker does not have the authority to insist upon it. Thus *should* substitutes for the missing past tense of *must* "insistence," adding remoteness ("I don't have the authority to insist"), often for reasons of politeness.

In British English *ought* is used in much the same way as *should*, except that the evaluation expressed by *ought* tends, by implication, to be objective rather than representing the speaker's subjective views, cp.

```
(3)     You ought to see a doctor (high blood pressure can be very
        dangerous)
(4)     You should see a doctor  (if you are so worried about that
        bruise)
```

In American English *ought* is not very common outside formal written language, *should* being used instead.

9.9.2   In British English, the present tense, *shall*, is often used in questions representing offers, and in requests for instructions (in both cases asking about the next speaker's preference):

```
(5)     Shall I hold the door for you?   (offer)
(6)     Shall I bring the wine list, Madam?
        (request for instructions)
```

In American English *shall* is not very common outside very formal styles (see § 9.8.1). In questions like (6) American English may use *should*, but other constructions are also available. The alternative constructions are also common in British English:

```
(7)     Would you like me to hold the door for you?
(8)     Should I/would you like me to bring the wine list?
```

9.9.3 The marginal modal auxiliary *had better* expresses what the speaker regards as preferable:[43]

(9)    He*'d better* tell her now

*'d rather* expresses speaker preference only when used in the 1st person (*'d* is usually taken to stand for *would*), otherwise it refers to the grammatical subject; cp. (9) and (10):

(10)   He*'d rather* tell her now

*Acceptance (9.10.1-9.10.3)*

9.10.1 The speaker has nothing **against** the proposition. Both *may* and *can* are used in this sense, to give or ask for permission:

(1)    You *may* borrow it, if you like
(2)    You *can* go now

Expressions of permission may be used as an indirect (e.g. polite) way of giving orders, in fact (2) allows for this interpretation. *May* in permissions is somewhat formal, especially when *may not* in permission **denied** is used instead of *must not* ("insistence that *not* X"), cp.

(3)    The patient *mustn't* get out of bed
(4)    This book *may not* be introduced into the U.S.A.

9.10.2 Apart from the question of formality, *can* is used instead of *may* when the permission has already been given, perhaps by a third party:

(5)    What are the library rules like at your university? *Can* students take books out of the university library?

In this sense of "standing permission" the past tense *could* can refer to past time:

(6)    In those days there were all sorts of restrictions; for one thing, students *could* not take books out of the university library

whereas reference to the **giving** of permission requires the use of *be allowed*:

(7)    Yesterday afternoon we *were allowed* to go swimming because it was so hot

9.10.3 The past-tense forms *might* and *could* to ask for the next speaker's permission

---

43. An expression of speaker preference which we have not given a separate entry because it is very formal/rare is *may* in wishes: *May all her troubles be little ones!*

are normally used only in polite questions, implying that the possibility of rejection is not being ruled out:

(8)    *Might/Could* I make a suggestion?

**Modal Adverbs and Adjectives: "Objectivity" (9.11)**

9.11    As we saw in the preceding paragraphs, the meanings of the modal auxiliaries depend to a great extent on the context. Another characteristic, in comparison with other probability and desirability signals, is that the various shades of speaker belief or attitude which they express tend to be implicitly subjective. By contrast, modal adverbs and, in particular, modal adjectives are sometimes chosen so as to give the impression that what the speaker is saying is based on objective evidence or criteria:

(1)    The socialists will *probably* lose ground in today's election
(2)    The holder of this post should *ideally* be single
(3)    The socialists are almost *certain* to lose ground in today's election
(4)    It is almost *certain* that the socialists will lose ground in today's election
(5a)   It is *imperative* that the document be returned immediately
(5b)   It is *imperative* that the document should be/is returned immediately[44]

The same is true of the (modal) nouns derived from such adjectives:

(6)    There is a 60% *probability* of rain tomorrow (AE)
(7)    There is a *possibility* that the hostages will be released tomorrow

As far as adjectives/nouns are concerned, the "objective" construction contrasts with an explicitly subjective one (see also § 9.12); compare (4) and (7) with:

(4a)   *I'm* almost *certain* that the socialists will· lose ground in today's election
(7a)   *I think* it is *possible* that the hostages will be released tomorrow

However, modal adverbs are probably often chosen simply because of their positional flexibility:

(8a)   *Perhaps* the treasure is buried here
(8b)   The treasure is *perhaps* buried here
(8c)   The treasure is buried here, *perhaps*

"Objectivity" may also be implied by copula verbs such as *appear, look* and *seem* (and corresponding adverbs):

---

44. In (5a), which is the usual American English version, the desirability meaning results in the use of the subjunctive, whereas the most common British construction has the indicative or uses *should* (5b), see further §§ 7.3.4-7.3.5.

(9)     There *appears* to have been a slight mistake (cp. "...has *ap-parently* been...")
(10)    He *seems* to be such a kind person (cp. "...is *seemingly*...")

## Modal Main Verbs: Explicit Subjectivity (9.12)

9.12    A number of main verbs can express modality when used in the simple present tense and preceded by a 1st person subject. The latter criterion means that the speaker's belief or attitude is presented as explicitly subjective. The verbs involved are **cognitive verbs** (probability: e.g. *think, suppose, wonder*; desirability: e.g. *hope, want, wish*) and **performative verbs** (desirability, e.g. *demand, insist, suggest*; see § 8.4.1):

(1)     I *think* she has already left
(2)     I *wonder* if we could have a look at that?
(3)     I *hope/want/wish* to see him when he gets back
(4)     I *insist* that you write to her again
(5a)    I *suggest* Henry buy the first drink and John the second
(5b)    I *suggest* Henry buys/should buy the first drink and John the second

After a performative verb expressing desirability, as in (4) and (5), the propositional verb is usually in the subjunctive in American English (see *buy* in the 3rd person in (5a), and cp. note on examples (5a) and (5b) in § 9.11).

Nouns derived from modal main verbs can be used in a similar way, e.g.

(6)     *My suggestion is* that this person leave(s)/should leave

## Emphasizing Belief and Attitude (9.13)

9.13    Modal categories may be stressed for contrast. If this happens to expressions of "less than certainty" on the probability scale, they come to indicate "contrast with what is possibly the real state of affairs":

(1)     Joe '*might* do it again (but I doubt it)
(2)     Joe isn't '*likely* to do it again (but I can't guarantee that he won't)
(3)     Joe '*looks* innocent enough (but maybe he isn't)

Otherwise stress simply reinforces the original meaning:

(4)     Accidents '*will* happen
(5)     I '*did* hear what you said
(6)     You (absolutely) '*must* try this chocolate cake

## Modal Redundancy and Complexity (9.14)

9.14    Sometimes the same type of meaning is expressed more than once in the same clause, and this we refer to as **redundancy**. Thus if I say:

(1)     I *fear* that this decision *may* have serious consequences

the element of uncertainty is expressed both in *may* and in *I fear*. The meanings of modal auxiliaries and tense suffixes are usually less explicit than corresponding lexical forms, i.e. they are included in the meanings of the lexical forms but not the other way around: in (1) the meaning of *may* ("it is possible that X") is included in *I fear* ("it is possible that X, and I don't like it"). Different types of modal construction can be used to reinforce the same degree of probability or desirability:

(2)    The paper *may possibly* have been stolen
(3)    *Preferably* the typing *should* be double spaced

Although such forms may be redundant in terms of degree of probability or desirability, they are still significant in terms of situation, see e.g. §§ 9.11-9.12.

Sometimes the coocurrence of different types of modal construction lends modal complexity to the utterance:

(4)    *Perhaps* the paper *should* be copied

But the reinforcement of probability meaning, as in (2), is in fact the most common type. It is important to note that modal categories can be redundant only in a strictly semantic sense. In a pragmatic sense (i.e. in terms of how they are used), the utterance becomes more **tentative** (polite, hesitant, deliberative etc.) for each additional probability signal, whether it is a statement:

(5)    *I don't think* it is *at all inconceivable*, *really*, that she
       *might perhaps* have overheard something, *is it?*

or a request:

(6)    *Might* I *perhaps* ask if you *could possibly* lend me the money
       until tomorrow, *do you think?*

or a question:

(7)    *Is there any possibility at all* that she *might conceivably*
       have overheard something?

**Modality and Communicative Function (9.15.0-9.15.2)**

9.15.0 Modal features are often the linguistic markers of particular **communicative functions of language**. Any utterance represents several types of communicative function, the main categories being

(1)    the **message function**, i.e. the utterance represents a particular kind of message (whether e.g. it conveys information, expresses feelings or induces to action)
(2)    the **interactional function**, i.e. the utterance represents a link in the

interaction between speaker and addressee, in the way e.g. question and answer are linked[45]

(3)     the **textual function**, i.e. the utterance has a place in the wider structure of the text (building on that which has gone before and/or anticipating what is to follow).

The use of modal features is closely related to both (1) and (2). In the following section (§§ 9.15.1-9.15.2) we shall focus especially on aspects of (1), i.e. the typical use of modal features depending on what kind of message the utterance represents.

The **message function** can be divided into a number of different categories, of which the following are the most important ones:

1. **Representatives**: the utterance is concerned with the representation of facts
    a. **Reportives**: the speaker "knows" and states a verifiable fact, with no indication of uncertainty[46]
    b. **Assumptives**: some indication of uncertainty about the facts, or the statement represents the speaker's interpretation of the facts

2. **Expressives**: the utterance is concerned with the speaker's personal feelings, impressions and attitudes
    a. **Evaluatives**: the expression of positive or negative evaluation (value judgments)
    b. **Estimatives**: the expression of feelings and subjective impressions which are not value judgments

3. **Regulatives**: the utterance is concerned with regulating the behavior of (a) speaker or (b) addressee
    a. **Commissives**: the utterance commits the speaker to a certain course of action (as in promises, threats, statements of intent)
    b. **Directives**: the utterance regulates the behavior of the addressee (as in commands, requests, advice)

An utterance may represent more than one message function, though it is usually possible to determine which is the primary one. In the following we shall exemplify those functions which are typically marked by particular modal features.

---

45. In other words, it is primarily this function which determines the choice between the three main types of clause structure, see § 5.0.

46. However, **requests** for information (in the form of questions) are also classified as reportives, because they represent language concerned with fact. In other words, questions and statements may have the same message function, although they represent different interactional functions, see § 5.0.

### Representative language and "probability" (9.15.1)

9.15.1 One of the functions of language is to represent facts. This is called the **representative** function. If representatives are uttered without any indication of uncertainty (the speaker "knows") we call them **reportives**, e.g.

(1)    It is now 10 o'clock

whereas if they reflect the relative probability of the proposition we call them **assumptives**, e.g.

(2)    It must be 10 o'clock now

Reportives can usually be proved true or false, whereas assumptives are not always as easily verifiable as (2), cp. the following text:

(3)    (a)    Mrs. Thatcher announced last night that she has
              decided not to introduce further measures against
              South Africa.
       (b)    At the approaching Commonwealth summit it seems likely
              that she will argue that there is still a chance of
              more movement by Pretoria.
       (c)    She is believed to have underlined her continued op-
              position to sanctions at a private dinner with the
              Queen last night.

(a) is reportive: Mrs. Thatcher's public statement is a matter of record; (b) is assumptive because, although past events may have *indicated* what Mrs. Thatcher will do in the future, the reporter can only guess, hence the expression of "probability," *seems likely*; (c) is also assumptive, the formulation suggesting that this is political gossip which no one is likely to confirm (cp. *is believed to*: passive — who "believes" and on what evidence?). Assumptions about other people's motives, intentions, thoughts and feelings can hardly ever be proved true or false, though we can attempt to justify them as more or less likely on the basis of the evidence at hand.

Modal expressions of relative "probability" are the typical markers of assumptive language, and most kinds of utterances can be given assumptive meaning through the use of such expressions, cp. (3a) with

(3)    (d)    Mrs. Thatcher *may* have announced...
       (e)    Mrs. Thatcher *probably* announced...
       (f)    Mrs. Thatcher *is likely* to have announced...
       (g)    Mrs. Thatcher *seems* to have announced...
       (h)    *It appears* that Mrs. Thatcher announced...
       (i)    *We assume* Mrs. Thatcher announced...
              (etc.)

However, utterances may be assumptive **without** containing probability signals, e.g.

(4)    Our politicians were not ready to face the consequences of
       the oil crisis right away

We can verify the behavior of "our politicians" in terms of what they actually
**did**, but to say that they acted in a certain way because they were "not ready
to face the consequences of the oil crisis" is to make an assumption about their
motives which is hardly verifiable.

On the other hand, the presence of probability signals is no guarantee that
the utterance is in fact assumptive (see also § 9.15.2 (17) and (18)):

(5)    *I believe* it's time for bed now, children!

### Evaluative and directive language, and "desirability" (9.15.2)

9.15.2 Just as "probability" signals tend to characterize the assumptive function of
language, "desirability" signals are among the typical markers of the evaluative
and directive language functions. **Evaluative** utterances are value judgments, i.e.
utterances which show positive or negative speaker attitude:

(6)    He *should* get his hair cut
(7)    Payment *should preferably* be in cash
(8)    *I hope* the two parties will reach an agreement

The evaluative function can also be indicated by other means than desirability
signals:

(9)    Her dress is *beautiful*
(10)   Mr. Morrison is one of the most *excitable firebrands* we
       have had

**Directive** utterances aim at getting the addressee to perform an action:

(11)   *Get* out! (imperative)
(12)   You *must* send the letter immediately
(13)   I *suggest* you talk to her about it

Whether a desirability signal marks the directive or the evaluative function often
depends on the situation. If the speaker can in fact expect the utterance to be
acted upon the function is directive, as when the doctor says:

(14)   You *shouldn't* smoke so much

whereas if it merely expresses a general attitude or "wishful thinking," it should
be classified as evaluative:

(15)   There *shouldn't* be so much violence on television

As in the case of evaluatives, directive utterances are not **necessarily** marked by
desirability signals:

(16)   You will proceed to headquarters at once

In fact, in (16) we find the probability signal *will* instead, which lends special overtones to the directive ("all I have to do is say it, and the future is certain on that point"). Interrogative clauses functioning as directives routinely employ modal-auxiliary past-tense forms to indicate politeness:

```
(17)   Could you tell me the time(, please)?
(18)   Would you mind helping me?
```

## Overview of Modal Auxiliaries: Most Important Forms/Meanings (9.16.1-9.16.5)

### 9.16.1 *Can:*

#### A. The grammatical subject's ability (§§ 9.2.5-9.2.6, 9.5.2 (n.))

```
George can swim
George could swim when he was five (cp. The boat capsized,
but we managed/were able to swim ashore)
Could you help me with this?
```

#### B. Making explicit the stative meaning of the main verb (§ 9.5.2)

```
He could smell the perfume (cp. She smelled the perfume
before buying it)
```

#### C. Theoretical possibility (§ 9.5.2)

```
The door can be locked (cp. The door may be locked)
In those days the door could be locked
```

#### D. Possibility assessed by the speaker (§ 9.5.1)

```
Can she have forgotten about the meeting? (cp. She may have
forgotten about the meeting)
The report could be true (cp. The report might be true)
```

#### E. Logical necessity (only *cannot*; § 9.4.1)

```
The report can't be true (cp. The report must be true)
```

#### F. Permission (§§ 9.10.1-3)

```
You can have the car tonight (cp. You may have the car
tonight)
Can students take books out of the university library?
In those days students could not take books out of the
university library (cp. Yesterday afternoon we were allowed
to go swimming because it was so hot)
Could I borrow it?
```

### 9.16.2 *May:*

#### A. Possibility assessed by the speaker (§ 9.5.1)

```
She may have forgotten about the meeting (cp. Can she have
forgotten about the meeting?)
```

```
The door may be locked (cp. The door can be locked)
He said he might do it
The report might be true (cp. The report could be true)
```

### B. **Permission** (§§ 9.10.1-3)

```
You may take the book home with you, if you like (cp.
Teachers can take books out of the university library)
This book may not be introduced into the U.S.A.
Might I ask what you are paying?
```

### C. **Wish** (§ 9.10.2 n.)

```
May all your dreams come true
```

## 9.16.3 *Must:*

### A. **Logical necessity** (§ 9.4.1)

```
It must have cost a lot
It must not have cost much (AE) (cp. It cannot have cost
much; It does not need/have to cost much if we do it
ourselves; It needn't cost much if we do it ourselves (BE))
```

### B. **Necessity imposed by the speaker** (§ 9.7.1-9.7.2)

```
We must stop him immediately (cp. We have to pay the fine
within 10 days)
You must not tell him (cp. You don't need/have to tell him
if you don't want to; You needn't tell him if you don't want
to (BE))
Bob said I must come and see him
```

## 9.16.4 *Shall:*

### A. **Prediction/confidence** (§§ 8.5.1, 9.3.1)

```
I have no doubt I shall be happy down there (cp. I have no
doubt you will be happy down there)
I had no doubt I should be happy down there
```

### B. **Commitment** (§ 9.8.1)

```
Be patient — you shall have the whole story tomorrow (cp.
You will have...)
No one shall stop me (cp. No one will stop me)
Shall I clear the table now?
Should I clear the table now? (cp. I was to clear the table
while Paul made coffee (§ 8.5.2))
```

### C. **Special meanings of** *should* (no corresponding uses of *shall*):

#### 1) Assumption which may be wrong (§§ 9.3.4, 9.4.3)

```
He should be home by now — unless he has stopped for a drink
(cp. He ought to be home by now)
```

2) Hypothesis, remote idea (§ 9.3.3)

```
If he should arrive early, give him a drink
It is unlikely that she should have been caught up in this
```

3) Obligation, moral evaluation: § 9.9.1)

```
You should see a doctor — if you are so worried about that
bruise (cp. You ought to see a doctor — high blood pressure
can be very dangerous)
She should talk to him right away (cp. She had better talk
to him right away (§ 9.9.3))
```

4) (In the subclause, alternating with the present subjunctive:) Desirability (§ 7.3.5)

```
He demanded that they should release the hostages
It's important that she should be warned immediately (AE
more often: ...that they release.../...that she be...)
```

### 9.16.5 *Will:*

A. **Prediction/confidence** (§§ 8.5.1, 9.3.1-9.3.6)

1) Confidence about the future (§ 9.3.1; past tense: future-in-the-past or non-fact, § 9.3.3)

```
You'll be happy down there — you 'll see
He was sure she would be happy down there
I think she should go — she would be happy down there
```

2) Assumption about the present (§ 9.3.4)

```
The exam will be over by now — it's 12 o'clock (cp. The exam
should be over — so why aren't the students coming out?/The
exam must be over — the students are leaving the building)
Would that be Paul on the phone?
```

3) Confidence based on knowledge of habit (§ 9.3.5)

```
He will talk for hours every time the subject is brought up
Churchill would smoke twenty cigars or more a day (cp. I
used to smoke forty cigarettes a day — now I smoke eighty)
```

4) Confidence based on knowledge of the qualities of the grammatical subject (§ 9.3.6)

```
Lava will float on water
People 'will criticize a new approach
John 'would make a mess of things
```

B. **The grammatical subject's willingness** (§ 9.8.1-9.8.2)

1) Reference to 2nd or 3rd person's willingness

The student just *won't* do his homework
Mr. Smith *will* see you in a moment
Yesterday he just *wouldn't* do his homework
Mr. Smith *would* see him in a moment (she said)
I'm sure Mr. Smith *would* help you if you asked him

## 2) Speaker's commitment

I *will* see that he gets the message
I *will* let you have the money, if you promise not to tell
anyone
I *would* lend you the money if I had any, which I don't

# IV.  THE NOUN PHRASE[1]

## Introduction (10.0)

10.0    The archetypal noun phrase has a noun as head, hence the name. However, not
all the constituents of the noun phrase will necessarily be nouns, in contrast
with the verb phrase, where all the constituents must be verbs. Even the head
of the noun phrase can be a non-noun; in (2) below the heads are adjectives, and
in (3) the head is a pronoun:

```
(1)    (She is moving into)
       some  neglected  old  house  that she bought last month
       PRM   PRM        PRM  H                POM

(2)    The  rich  (are urged to help)  the  poor
       PRM  H                          PRM  H

(3)    The  only  one  there  (was Peter)
       PRM  PRM   H    POM
```

If the head is a non-noun, as in (2) and (3), the most important indicator of
noun-phrase structure is the presence of the definite article (see further § 10.3.2).
        Another difference between noun phrases and verb phrases is that whereas
the verb phrase has a maximum of four premodifiers (usually no more than
three), which can be realized only by particular verbs in a fixed order, it would
be difficult to deal with the structure of the noun-phrase premodifiers without
taking into account at least ten different categories. Several of these can be
realized in any number of ways, as well as being able to recur within the same
NP, and their relative order of occurrence is often not quite stable.
        It will be our task in this section to show that in spite of its greater variety
of form and "looseness" of structure, it is still possible to describe the noun
phrase, with some confidence, as a structural entity.
        Noun phrases may or may not be introduced by a junctive. We have oc-
casionally been using the term "prepositional phrase" about noun phrases that
are introduced by a junctive (in accordance with traditional terminology).
However, as the presence of a junctive has no effect on the structure of the
phrase, such phrases will not be treated as a separate structural category.

---

1. The noun phrase also includes phrase structures with a pronoun as head. However, as the
pronouns are characterized by a number of special morphological, syntactic and semantic
features, the pronominal noun phrase will not be discussed in any detail here, but will be
presented in the next chapter.

## THE STRUCTURE OF THE NOUN PHRASE (10.1.1-10.9.3)

### Head (10.1.1-10.1.4)

#### Nouns as head (10.1.1)

10.1.1  The nouns constitute an open class (see § 7.0) of lexical items characterized by genitive and plural declension. Nouns in the genitive do not often function as head of the noun phrase, but see §§ 10.3.2, 10.6.3 and 14.3.8 below.

As a class, the nouns can be modified by all the pre- and postmodifier types described in § 10. The special features of various subclasses of nouns will be found in §§ 12-14.

#### Adjectives as head (10.1.2-3)

10.1.2  The adjectives, too, make up an open class of lexical items, but their form, unlike the nouns, does not vary according to case or number. Adjectives realize the head of an adjective phrase (see § 21.1.1):

```
(1)     He is very rich
(2)     They are as American as apple pie
(3)     Her identity was completely unknown
```

but the adjective phrase may in turn realize the head of a structure which is unmistakably a noun phrase, the identifying feature being the definite article (see § 10.3.2):[2]

```
(4)     Only the rich patronize this restaurant
(5)     The extremely old need a great deal of attention
(6)     The English and the French were allies
(7)     He was afraid of the unknown
```

Adjectives used in this way have **generic reference** (i.e. they refer to the whole class of whatever they denote), either to **persons in the plural** ((4)-(6)) or to **uncountable abstracts** (7). Thus *the rich* is followed by a plural verb and refers to the whole class of those who are rich, as opposed to e.g. *the rich man*. The English, also plural, refers to the English people, not the individual Englishman/-woman (see also § 10.1.3). Uncountables like *the unknown* refer to a general concept, as opposed to e.g. *He was afraid of the unknown visitor*. Specific reference occurs only when the head is realized by an adjective in the superlative (though see also §§ 10.1.3 and 21.4.1):

---

2. If two adjectives are coordinated, they may function as noun-phrase heads without the presence of a determiner:

```
She was accepted by young and old alike.
```

(8)      She is *the nicest of all the people I know*

and in a few fixed expressions in specific contexts, e.g. *the accused, the Almighty, the deceased*. See also § 20.4.17 n. and § 22.1.5 n.

Noun phrases with an adjective (phrase) as head may in rare cases contain a descriptive (9) or classifying (10) premodifier (epithet or nominator, see §§ 10.5 and 10.6), or a postmodifier (11):

(9)      Only *the filthy rich* patronize this restaurant
(10)     The government has done nothing to help *the London poor*
(11)     The world belongs to *the young in spirit*

### 10.1.3 Adjectives denoting nationality:

(A) Some adjectives denoting nationality can always function as head of the noun phrase, regardless of number and specification, viz. those ending in *-ese*, e.g. *Chinese, Japanese, Portuguese*, besides *Swiss*:

(12)         A *Japanese* / two *Japanese* / the *Japanese* (people)

(B) Some nationality adjectives have a corresponding noun which is used as head except in the generic plural. The noun consists of the adjective + *-man/woman* (or their plural form). In the generic plural, it is the adjective which realizes the head of the noun phrase, preceded by *the*. Thus, for instance, *English, Dutch, French, Irish*:

(13)     An Englishman / two Englishmen / the *English* (people)

(C) Nationality adjectives in *-ish* differ with regard to their ability to occur at the noun phrase head. In most cases, a corresponding noun (with the same root as the adjective) is used for that function, e.g. *Dane/Danish Pole/Polish, Swede/Swedish*. *British* (cp. *Briton*)[3] and *Spanish* (cp. *Spaniard*), however, realize the head when the noun phrase has generic plural reference:

(14)     A Dane / two Danes / (the) Danes
(15)     A Briton / two Britons / the *British*

(D) Nationality adjectives in *-an* and *-i* have the same form as the corresponding noun, which is used and declined as a regular noun, e.g. *American, German, Italian, Norwegian; Israeli, Iraqi, Pakistani*. Only the noun occurs at the head of the noun phrase:

(16)     A German / two Germans / (the) Germans
(17)     A Pakistani / two Pakistanis / (the) Pakistanis

### One *as head (10.1.4)*

10.1.4  *One* is a pro-form (see § 5.9.0 n.) for a countable noun as head, and is declined

---

3. A more recent noun form, *Brit*, is on the increase in informal language.

like a countable noun. It is needed after adjective (18)-(20) and noun (21) premodifiers:

(18)    We should build a new hospital instead of wasting more money
        on *the old one*
(19)    These bags are too small; give me *the large ones*
(20)    He tried to keep up with the horses and grabbed hold of *the*
        *black one's* tail
(21)    She'd prefer a teak table but I want *an oak one*

Note that *old* in (18), without *one*, would be interpreted as having generic, plural
reference. If *one* were missing from (21), the noun *oak* would be mistaken for the
head.

   *One* may be optional after ordinal numbers and adjectives in the comparative
and superlative, i.e. after ordinators (§ 10.4.1-3) other than cardinal numbers.
*One* never occurs (immediately) after genitives, *own*, and cardinal numbers:

(22)    The first and the second volumes were still there, but *the*
        *third (one)*, which was also *the largest (one)*, had
        disappeared
(23)    I thought I had six cups, but I only have *five*. Be sure to
        bring your *own*!

See also § 20.4.15-20.4.18.


**Premodifiers (10.2-10.7.4)**

*Structural overview (10.2)*

10.2   The noun-phrase premodification can be divided into four main "areas" of
       meaning, (1) **specification**, (2) **quantification**, (3) **description**, (4) **classification**,
       each of which is represented by a particular range of premodifiers. In terms of
       defining the boundaries between these areas, they are more like a continuum
       than watertight compartments: specification is signalled farthest from, classifica-
       tion closest to, the head, and the borderline between any two categories is often
       blurred. Corresponding to these semantic categories we have four main groups
       of premodifiers: (1) **Determinative**, (2) **Ordinator**, (3) **Epithet**, (4) **Nominator**:

(1)       D      O                    E                    N
       The  last three beautiful old white Indian saddle blankets
       PRM  PRM  PRM     PRM      PRM  PRM  PRM   PRM       H


Obviously not all of them are always present in the individual noun phrase; (1)
reflects their relative order if two or more are present.

   The categorization of (1) is still not fine enough, because the order within
each category is not random, either. We would not, for instance, say *\*white old*
*beautiful blankets* or *\*saddle Indian blankets*. In the following treatment of each of
the four main categories, therefore, it will be necessary to distinguish several
subcategories.

### Determinative (10.3.1-10.3.2)

10.3.1 The determinative consists of predeterminer (PrD) and determiner (D). Only a few forms can realize the **predeterminer**:

(1)  *All* my life
     PrD  D   H

(2)  *Both* these hats
     PrD    D    H

(3)  *Half* a million[4]
     PrD  D   H

(4)  *Many* a time
     PrD  D  H

(5)  *Quite a gentleman*
     PrD   D     H

(6)  *Such* a fool
     PrD  D   H

(7)  *What* a nuisance
     PrD  D    H

Cp. §§ 20.4.19-20.4.20.

10.3.2 The **determiner** is realized by:
A. The articles, *a, an, the*.
B. The demonstratives, *this, these, that, those*.
C. The *wh*-forms, *which, what, whose*.
D. Genitives, *my, your, John's*, etc.
E. The forms, *any/no/some, a little/a few, each/every, either/neither*.[5]
   Examples:

(8)   *The* girl next door
(9)   *Those* brave men
(10)  *What* brave men? (cp. (7))
(11a) *My* pretty little doll
(11b) *Sandra's* pretty little doll
(11c) *The pretty little girl's* pretty little doll
(12)  *Some/a few* cigarettes

Note that *the* in (11c) does not belong to the whole noun phrase but only to the rankshifted one within the determiner, *the pretty little girl*. Genitives may also classify (i.e. function as nominator), cp. § 10.6.3.

The presence of a definite article or a genitive defines the structure as a noun phrase, even if the head of the noun phrase is not a noun:

(13)  I don't envy *the rich*
(14)  I resent *his/John's taking all the credit*.

As shown by (14), this rule enables us to analyze *-ing* clauses introduced by a genitive as noun phrases with a clause as head (see also §§ 2.7.7, 3.1 n., 3.6). Several quantifiers (most of them complex idioms) cannot be preceded by

---

4. In American English, *half* often modifies the expression of measure directly instead of being a predeterminer: *a half hour, a half dozen eggs*.
5. Cp. §§ 20.4.1-20.4.11, 20.4.20-20.4.21, 20.5.2-20.5.5.

determiners, and so may be regarded as determiners themselves, e.g. *a good deal of, a great many, a lot of, a number of, enough, much*:

(15)    There were *a number of* students present

The plural form of the verb (*were*) shows that *students*, not *number*, is head of the subject noun phrase.

### Ordinator (10.4.0-10.4.3)

10.4.0  The following subcategorization of the ordinator (O1-O3) is based on the most likely order of occurrence of its manifestations.

10.4.1  **(O1) Ordinal numbers** and words of related meaning, e.g. *first, second, other, former, latter, next, last, only, own, same*:

(1)     The *first* three volunteers
(2)     My *only* two decent shirts

10.4.2  **(O2) Cardinal numbers** and words of related meaning, e.g. *two, three, (a) dozen, few, many, numerous, several, various*:

(3)     His next *three* questions
(4)     *Many* older men

O1 and O2 change places if there is no determiner (5):

(5)     *Two last* questions

Note that *hundred, thousand, million and dozen* are treated as regular nouns (adding *-s* in the plural) when, instead of functioning at O2, they realize the head of the noun phrase. If a number precedes them, however, they remain unchanged. Compare:

(6)     There were *four/several thousand* people waiting to see him
        (O2)
(7)     There were many *thousands* of people   (H)
(8)     The police estimated the number of demonstrators at *four thousand*[6]

10.4.3  **(O3) Adjectives in the comparative and superlative**, e.g. *prettier/prettiest, more beautiful/most beautiful*:

(9)     The two *most competent* nurses
(10)    The *longer*, very interesting essay

*More/most, less/least* functioning as quantifiers, besides *fewer/fewest*:

---

6. British English, especially British journalism, sometimes uses the plural with this type: *The Government will cut defence spending by four millions*. This is not possible in American English.

> (11)   We now had *more/less* money to spend
> (12)   *More/fewer/most* people are aware now of the origin of that
>        tradition

A limited set of **restricting adjectives**, e.g. *certain, chief, entire, main, plain, pure, sheer, single, such, whole*:

> (13)   A *certain* innocent charm
> (14)   *Sheer* undiluted malice
> (15)   Two *whole* slices of bread

### Epithet (10.5.0-10.5.4)

10.5.0  The following subcategorization of the epithet (E1-E4) is based on the most likely order of occurrence of its manifestations.

10.5.1  **(E1) Descriptive adjectives.** This is a large, open class of adjectives which are gradable, i.e. they can be turned into the comparative and the superlative, and be modified, for instance, by *very*. They fall into three morphological categories:
      A. **Simple adjectives**, e.g. *high, long, low, odd, sad, short, simple, small, thin.*
      B. **Adjectives derived from verbs**, e.g. *interesting, shocking* (most of them are *-ing* forms), *active, adorable, satisfied, significant.*
      C. **Adjectives derived from nouns**, e.g. *beautiful, childish, dusty, fashionable, lady-like, tight-fisted.*
Their order of occurrence is stylistically determined, though a few rules of thumb may be given:
A. Simple adjectives tend to precede derived ones:

> (1)    His *quiet relaxed* manner
> (2)    Her *hard angry* eyes

and those denoting size tend to precede other simple ones:

> (3)    A *long dark* passage
> (4)    A *large cold* beer

B. Adjectives derived from verbs tend to precede those derived from nouns:

> (5)    A *tiring uneventful* journey
> (6)    An *attractive busty* blonde

C. Short adjectives tend to precede longer ones:

> (7)    Her *soft gentle* hands
> (8)    His *relaxed, good-looking* features

D. Adjectives carrying emotional emphasis tend to precede others:

> (9)    A *beautiful spacious* room
> (10)   A *good long* rest

**10.5.2** **(E2) Participles which retain their verbal meaning**. These are nongradable, but may occasionally be intensified by *much* or other adverbs:

```
(11)    The golden waving corn
(12)    The wet fallen leaves
(13)    A much admired building (cp. *an admired building)
(14)    A carefully described structure (cp. *a described structure)
```

Note that they may themselves have an obligatory premodifier, as in (13) and (14). Adverb premodifiers like *carefully* in (14) are the same as those occurring as adverbials in clauses with the participle as main verb, cp. (17). The verbal content of E2 participles is brought out clearly when they are moved to the predicate of a clause, cp. (15) with (16) and (17):

```
(15)    An exciting story   ==>   The story is (very) exciting
        D   E1      H             S       V            SC
```

```
(16)    A barking dog   ==>   The dog is barking
        D   E2     H          S       V
```

```
(17)    A carefully described structure   ==>
        D        E2               H

        The structure has been described carefully
             S             V                 A
```

**10.5.3** **(E3) The "little" group** has only four members: *little, young, new, old*. These are often preceded by gradable adjectives:

```
(18)    A nice little boy
(19)    An expensive new car
(20)    An elegant young woman
(21)    A crafty old man
```

though they may become gradable themselves and function as E1 when placed before other E3 premodifiers:

```
(22)    Two very old and talkative little ladies
            E1       J      E1       E3
```

Note that (19) acquires a different meaning if *new* is placed before *expensive*: *a new expensive car* (i.e. the old one was expensive, too).

**10.5.4** **(E4) Color adjectives** are primarily descriptive, though they are often used to classify (see § 10.7.3):

```
(23)    A fancy little red electric car
(24)    A quaint old white Gothic country church
```

Color adjectives are frequently submodified by a special set of adjectives, e.g. *bright, dark, pale*:

```
(25)    The leaves on the trees are bright green at this time of
        year
(26)    Her pale/dark blue eyes widened in amazement
```

### Nominator (10.6.0-10.6.3)

10.6.0   The nominator is called thus because nominator premodifiers are those closest
to the head (which is most often a noun), and because some of them are nouns
themselves. Whereas the epithet PRM's describe the head, those of the nominator classify it. They cannot, therefore, be graded or modified by *very*. The
following subcategorization (N1-N3) is based on their most likely order of
occurrence.

10.6.1   **(N1) Adjectives denoting nationality** or geographical origin, derived from
proper nouns: *American, British, European, Gothic, Mediterranean*, etc.:

     (1)     A big green *American* station car
     (2)     Her sparkling blue *Scandinavian* eyes

10.6.2   **(N2) Adjectives denoting type, field or material**, mostly derived from nouns:

     (3)     The European *industrial* revolution
     (4)     A South African *medical* research institution
     (5)     His new *poetic* output
     (6)     A red *wooden* chair

10.6.3   **(N3) Nouns**, either common-case or in the genitive. **Common-case** nouns usually have singular form, even when the noun would be plural as head.
However, in institutionalized labels in British English, the plural form in reference to plural concepts is on the increase, see (12). Note also the plural form
*sales* in expressions like (13):[7]

     (7)     A medical *research* institution
     (8)     An Alpine *walking* stick
     (9)     Illegal *tiger* shooting   (= "...shooting of *tigers*")
     (10)    Chronic *tooth* decay   (= "...decay of *teeth*")
     (11)    A *scissor* sharpener   (as head always plural: *scissors*)
     (12)    The *Courses* Committee   (BE)
     (13)    Our *sales* manager   (BE & AE)

Note that *-ing* forms, besides occurring at E1 and E2 (§§ 10.5.1-10.5.2), can also
function as nouns at N3 (*walking* in (8)).

   Classifying nouns in the **genitive** have to occur immediately before the head,
and are singular or plural depending on the meaning: *a lady's hat* is a hat for
**one** lady, whereas *a ladies' magazine* is a magazine for **many** ladies. If the head
is plural, however, this form is often anticipated by the plural form of the
genitive: *ladies' hats*. Further examples:

     (14)    A deep and soft *bird's* nest
     (15)    A battered *fireman's* helmet

---

7. *Woman* and *man* as nominators follow the number of the head in examples like:
     a.   A *woman* doctor / two *women* doctors
          (cp. *Woman* haters = men who hate *women*)
     b.   A *man* servant / two *men* servants.

```
(16)   A German children's physician
(17)   An examiners' conference
```

Note the ambiguity of phrases like (18) *The fat farmer's wife*, the meaning of which depends on whether the genitive belongs to the determiner (18a) or the nominator (18b):

```
(18a)  The fat farmer's wife   (see also § 10.3.2)
        D   E1    H
              D           H

(8b)   The fat farmer's wife
        D   E1   N3      H
```

Finally, we include **adverbs, rankshifted clauses and phrases** (other than adjectival ones) among the N3's because they tend to classify, and because they occur immediately before, the head. A few of these are idiomatic expressions:

```
(19)   The then king
(20)   Mysterious, far-away places
(21)   His no-nonsense attitude
(22)   (on) a day-to-day basis
```

but for the most part they are unconventional constructions:

```
(23)   Her see-what-I-care shrug
```

### Recategorization of premodifiers (10.7.1-10.7.4)

10.7.1  Epithets 3-4, and (in rare cases) nominators other than the genitive, can be recategorized to become Epithet 1:

```
(1a)   A very inexperienced young teacher
          E1              E3

(1b)   A very young and inexperienced teacher
          E1     J        E1
```

Note that *very* could modify both *young* and *inexperienced* in (1b), because they are coordinated E1 items, whereas in (1a) it only modifies *inexperienced*. A few further examples:

```
(2a)   An old black car
           E4

(2b)   A (very) black, despairing outlook
         E1

(3a)   Two old British army colonels
               N1

(3b)   Two very British old army colonels
           E1

(4a)   A Greek musical instrument
               N2
```

```
(4b)   A very musical family
              E1

(5a)   An English High-Church gentleman
                      N3

(5b)   A very High-Church English gentleman
            E1
```

**10.7.2** Some adjectives that can occur both at E1 and N2 have a different form for each of the two positions:

```
(6)    An economical car   —   Economic legislation
              E                     N2

(7)    A historic occasion  —   A historical novel
            E1                        N2

(8)    A humane act   —   The human race
            E1                     N2

(9)    A poetical story  —   Her poetic writings
            E1                       N2

(10)   An urbane reply  —   An urban district
             E1                      N2
```

**10.7.3** Color adjectives (E4) often change position to N2 when used to classify:

```
(11)   The British black pudding. The American Red Indian
```

**10.7.4** Nationality adjectives (N1) are regularly recategorized to become N3 nouns meaning "language", which in speech is indicated by the head losing its primary stress:

```
(12a)  A 'French 'teacher  (= a teacher from France)
            N1

(12b)  A 'French teacher   (= a teacher of the French language)
            N3
```

**Postmodifiers (10.8.1-10.8.12)**

*Finite clauses (10.8.1)*

**10.8.1** The typical noun-phrase postmodifier is the relative clause. The appositional clause, too, realizes the postmodifier. See §§ 3.7.0-3.7.2.

```
(1)    The lady who forgot her purse                    (relative)
(2)    The first time I saw you                          (relative)
(3)    The idea that she was mad                     (appositional)
```

The other postmodifier categories described below can often be paraphrased by relative clauses:

```
(4)    The girl next door = the girl who lives next door
```

(5)  The person *responsible* = the person *who is responsible*
(6)  The examples *below* = the examples *which can be found below*

For relative pronouns, see § 18.

*Nonfinite clauses (10.8.2)*

10.8.2  The postmodifier clause may be nonfinite (see § 3.7.3):

(7)  (He gave me) another book *to read*                    (cp. relative)
(8)  A book *containing numerous beautiful pictures*        (cp. relative)
(9)  An article *written by Winston Churchill*              (cp. relative)
(10) His desire *to see her*                           (cp. appositional)

Note that not all such expressions are postmodifiers:

(11a) He wants  a  lady <u>to clean</u> <u>his house</u>
                              V          DO
           <u>PRM</u>  <u>H</u>  <u>POM</u>
      <u>S</u>  <u>V</u>  <u>C</u>

      (= ...a lady who will...)

(11b) He wants <u>the lady</u> <u>to clean</u> <u>his house</u>
                   S              V             DO
      <u>S</u>  <u>V</u>  <u>C</u>

*Noun phrases (10.8.3-10.8.6)*

10.8.3  The noun-phrase postmodifier may be realized by another noun phrase, which is usually one **introduced by a junctive** (a prepositional phrase):[8]

(12)  The end *of the story*           (16)  A smile *of recognition*
(13)  The house *in Baker Street*      (17)  The man *for the job*
(14)  A boy *with curly hair*          (18)  His book on *life styles*
(15)  A woman *of influence*           (19)  A whale *of a time*

The head of the postmodifying noun phrase[9] may be in the genitive (see § 14.3.6):

(20)  A friend *of my father's*
(21)  That old car *of hers*

10.8.4  **The junctive can be omitted** in front of the postmodifying noun phrase in the following cases:
(A) In certain expressions of time and place, see also example (4) above:

(22)  His speech *this year* (was better than) the one *last year*
(23)  The only doctor *this side of the river*

---

8. In expressions of clock time, American English often uses the junctives *of, till, after*, besides *to* and *past*, which are the only ones used in British English:
    a.  A quarter *to* two (BE & AE)/a quarter *of (till)* two (AE)
    b.  A quarter *past* two (BE & AE)/a quarter *after* two (AE)
9. If the head of the rankshifted noun phrase is *it*, after the junctives *in, on, round, off*, and if it refers to the same thing as the head of the larger noun phrase, it may be deleted in British English (but not in American English): *Coffee with sugar in (it); a coat with two buttons off (it).*

(B) When the head of the postmodifying noun phrase is one of a particular set of nouns, of which the following are the most frequent: *age, colo(u)r, length, shape, size, weight*:

```
(24)   Women my age
(25)   A hole the size of a penny
```

(C) In connection with the socalled distributive use of the determiner:

```
(26)   Once/twice a week, three times a/each/every month
```

10.8.5  If head and postmodifier refer to the same person or thing etc., we call the postmodifier an **apposition**. The apposition, except for special cases (see below), is without a junctive:

```
(27)   Mike Smart, the Union President[10]
(28)   His friend Larry
(29)   Her birthday present, a book on the Napoleonic Wars
(30)   The novel Wuthering Heights
(31)   The letter A, the noun dog, the word grammar
```

Note that the apposition may be either defining or nondefining.

The apposition may be separated from its head (placed in final position). This always happens after a 3rd person pronoun if the appositional noun phrase is complex, cp. (32) and (33):

```
(32)   He  wasn't  even  sorry,  the little rascal
       H                                 POM
       S-    V      A     SC            -S
```

```
(33)   We the people of the United States...
```

10.8.6  The appositional noun phrase is introduced by a junctive, *of*, in the following cases:

(A) After geographical terms:[11]

```
(34)   The State of New York
(35)   The island of Cyprus
(36)   The City of Canterbury
(37)   The village of Fordenden
```

Note that *river* and *lake* do not take *of*.[12]

(B) In connection with a limited group of terms for seasons and dates:

---

10. In American newspapers, such appositions are often placed before the name, without a definite article: *Union boss Mike Smart*. This practice is gradually making its way into British newspapers as well: *Home Secretary David Waddington*.

11. Note that names of counties are *pre*modifiers in American English (*San Bernardino County*), whereas they are appositions in Britain (*the county of Yorkshire*), in Ireland without article/of (*County Cork*).

12. *Lake* is without the definite article when followed by an appositional name: *Lake Victoria, Lake Ontario*. Names of rivers are **pre**modifiers in American English: *The Mississippi River* (cp. British English, *The river Thames*).

```
(38)   The month of September
(39)   The fateful year of 1939
```

Note that *year* does not take *of* unless premodified by an item other than the determiner:

```
(40)   The year 1939
```

The postmodifier is partitive rather than appositional in the following (i.e. the head denotes a part of something, and the postmodifier indicates what it is a part of):

```
(41)   The summer of 1963
(42)   The spring of 1989
(43)   The fourth of July
```

(C) After particular nouns, notably *firm, game, name, office, science, sense, subject, title* (*of* is sometimes dropped with *title*):

```
(44)   The firm of Johnson and Johnson
(45)   A game of backgammon
(46)   The office of President of the United States
(47)   The science of mathematics
(48)   The title (of) Doctor Honoris Causa
```

### Adjective phrases (10.8.7-10.8.11)

10.8.7 The adjective phrase normally functions as the subject complement or as a noun-phrase premodifier, i.e. its function as a noun-phrase postmodifier is special. Long, weighty adjective phrases frequently realize the noun phrase postmodifier (corresponding to the subject complement of a relative clause):

```
(49)   An adversary too strong to be defeated (= who is too...)
(50)   A project more difficult than he had bargained for
```

though often the modifier is divided, cp. (50) with:

```
(50a) A more difficult project than he had bargained for
         PRM     H                      POM
              M-          H              -M
```

In other words, *project* is modified by the adjective phrase, *more difficult than he had bargained for*, in both examples, but since *project* divides the modifier in (50a), we cannot really call the modifier a **post**modifier there. The same analysis can be applied to superlatives followed by a postmodifier, including *that*-clauses (though it may not always be important to distinguish the latter from relative clauses, cp. § 18.4.1 (8)):

```
(50b) The worst excuse that I've ever heard (cp. the worst that
       I've ever heard)
(50c) The best solution possible (cp.the best possible solution:
       § 10.8.8)
```

Several adjectives in coordination often realize the postmodifier:

```
(51)   A laugh musical but malicious
(52)   The woman, haughty and proud ([,] stood up to defend
       herself)
```

10.8.8  With **simple adjective phrases**, the postmodifier function is linked to particular adjectives, often in noun phrases introduced by a definite determiner and/or an ordinator:

```
(53)   The entire evidence available
(54)   The only documents extant
(55)   The best solution possible
```

Note that where the adjective can come either before or after the noun-phrase head, it gains more weight by being placed in final position, cp. (55) with:

```
(55a)  The best possible solution
```

10.8.9  The adjective phrase often realizes the noun-phrase postmodifier after indefinite pronouns beginning in *any-, no-, some-*; premodifier position is not possible:

```
(56)   Anywhere near. No one special. Something different
```

10.8.10  Certain adjectives and participles mean different things according to whether they realize the post- or the premodifier of the noun phrase:

```
(57)   The members present — the present members
(58)   The hooligans responsible  — a very responsible person
(59)   The mothers concerned (= "involved") — the concerned mothers
       (= "worried")
```

10.8.11  Certain nouns as head tend to be postmodified by particular adjectives, especially in legal expressions of Romance origin:

```
(60)   Court-martial. Heir apparent. Secretary-general.
       The sum total.
```

Some of these expressions are often felt to be compound words, i.e. they may be hyphenated and the second component may take the plural form (*court-martials, secretary-generals*), besides the more formal version (*courts-martial, secretaries general*).

The nouns (in the plural) *matters* and *things*, furthermore, are sometimes followed by a postmodifying adjective, in literary and often humorous style:

```
(61)   His obsession with matters political was exceeded only by
       his passion for all things English.
```

### *Adverbial particles (10.8.12)*

10.8.12 Finally, the noun-phrase postmodifier may be realized by an adverbial particle[13] of time or place:

```
(62)   The examples above (besides the above examples)
(63)   The way out
(64)   The day before
```

### The Structure of the Modification (10.9.1-10.9.3)

### *Coordination (10.9.1)*

10.9.1 Only modifiers of the same type can be coordinated. The indicators of coordination are *and, (n)or, but.* Commas are indicators of coordination where they could be replaced by *and:*

```
(1)    A dark and stormy night
       D  E1    J     E1      H

(2)    Red, white and blue flags
       E4   E4    J    E4    H
```

The ambiguity of (2) illustrates the two kinds of coordination: One corresponds to the coordination of several elliptic noun phrases ("a red, a white and a blue flag" or "red flags, white flags and blue flags"). The other coordinates qualities coexisting in the same object etc. ("flags each of which is red, white and blue").

### *Sequential modification (10.9.2)*

10.9.2 In our classification of premodifiers we noted their relative positions. This method of classification, resulting in analyses like the following:

```
(3)    All these beautiful Indian saddle blankets
       PrD   D      E1      N1     N3      H
```

presupposes the fact that each modifier modifies the whole **sequence** of what follows. Or, to put it differently, each modifier really has a rankshifted noun phrase for its head:

```
(4)    These three beautiful Indian saddle blankets
                                     N3      H
                                     N1       H
                            E1                H
              O2                              H
       D                                H
```

---

13. Adverbial particles are adverbs consisting of one morpheme (§ 1.7), many of which can also function as junctives.

Postmodifiers, too, may represent sequential modification, as in:

```
(5)    The only member of the club with one leg
                   H       POM
                       H              POM
          O1                H
       D                     H
```

### Submodification (10.9.3)

10.9.3 Whereas in sequential modification it is the **head** which is realized by a rankshifted phrase, submodification means that one of its **modifiers** is realized by one:

```
(6)    The Obscene Publications Act
              E1          H
       D              N3        H
```

It is very important in terms of meaning that *obscene* is seen to modify *publications* (submodification) and not *publications act* (sequential modification): the phrase is about a law on *obscene publications*, not an obscene law on publications.

When adjectives in the noun phrase are modified by adverbs, this too is submodification:

```
(7)    A very exciting discovery
         PRM     H
       D   E1            H
```

Postmodifiers, too, are often submodified:

```
(8)    The only teacher in a school with 30 children
                        J D   H        POM
                   H            POM
       D   O1                H
```

i.e. *with 30 children* modifies *school*, not *teacher (in a school)*.

(Frequently, both sub- and sequential modification can be found within the same noun phrase:

```
(9)    The government's unpopular emergency measure power cuts
                                  N3        H      N3    H
          D         H                   N3             H
       D                       E1                H
```

Note that there may be nothing in the **form** of the phrase which indicates whether a sub- or sequential analysis is required. Only the meaning of the words determines the analysis. *An efficient hair remover* and *a superfluous hair remover* look the same, but to occur in the same advertisement they would have to be understood as having different analyses:

```
(10)   An efficient hair remover
                     N3    H
       D    E1             H
```

```
(11)    A superfluous hair remover
   __       E1       H     _____
   D          N3          H
```

Modifiers sometimes modify only **part of the meaning** of the head noun, in a way corresponding to submodification: *A natural scientist* is not a scientist who is natural, but a person who studies *natural science. A heavy smoker* is not a heavy person who smokes, but a person who *smokes heavily. A good baker* is not a baker who is morally good, but a person who is good at baking. Etc. To show this by analysis, however, we would have to go into word structure, which is beyond the scope of this book.

## THE FUNCTIONS OF THE NOUN PHRASE (11.1-11.4)

### NP as Subject, Object, and Subject/Object Complement (11.1)

11.1    The functions as subject, direct object, indirect object, subject complement and object complement are typical of the noun phrase:

```
(1)    John gave  the two girls  a beautiful book
        S    (V)       IO              DO

(2)    The woman in the corner  is   a forensic pathologist
                  S                (V)          SC

(3)    They appointed  Norman  Chief Conductor of the orchestra
         S    (V)        DO                OC
```

The noun phrase, furthermore, can realize the adverbial, and may be rankshifted so as to realize the constituents of another noun phrase, as well as constituents within the adjective/adverb phrase.

### Noun Phrases as Adverbial (11.2.0-11.2.6)

11.2.0  Noun phrases realizing the adverbial are usually signalled by a junctive (i.e. they are prepositional phrases). Particular types of adverbial, however, are quite often realized by a (usually idiomatic) noun phrase without a junctive, some of which will be pointed out in the following.

11.2.1  NP as **conjunct** or **disjunct**:

```
(1)    In the first place, it is a very long way to walk
(2)    With respect, I think we would have managed without you
```

```
(3)    To my regret, she had already left
(4)    She has no doubt been amply rewarded
```

The modal disjunct *no doubt*, as in (4), is not introduced by a junctive.

## 11.2.2 NP as **place adjunct**:[14]

```
(5)    They had breakfast at the hotel
(6)    He ran into the kitchen
(7)    Which way did he go?
(8)    He lives two miles from here
```

Noun phrases with *way* as head (7) never have a junctive. When the noun phrase realizes a place adjunct denoting distance it does not have a junctive (8), except when *for* is used to indicate that the verb has inconclusive meaning (see § 8.1.4), cp.

```
(9a)   She walked another mile up the road
(9b)   She walked on for another mile
```

## 11.2.3 NP as **time/frequency adjunct** is most often introduced by a junctive:

```
(10)   They arrive at two o'clock
(11)   He stayed there for three weeks
(12)   I have met him on several occasions
```

In the following some important exceptions to this will be pointed out:

When the time adjunct is one of **time location** (see § 8.7.1-8.7.2), noun phrases introduced by *every, last, next, some, that, this* occur without a junctive:

```
(13)   They are going to Moscow this year
(14)   She will be famous some day
```

Nor is the junctive needed before the definite article, *that* or a cardinal number if the noun phrase contains further modification:[15]

```
(15)   They left in the morning/They left the morning after the
       funeral
(16)   He came (on) two successive mornings
(17)   It all happened three years ago
(18)   The telephone rang at that moment/The telephone rang that
       very moment
```

---

14. Some junctives have a different form in British and American English ((a) and (b)), or the same idiomatic expression has a different (or no) junctive in one variety as compared with the other ((c) and (d)):

```
       a.   He lives just round the corner (BE)/...just around the corner
            (AE)
       b.   He threw it out of the window (BE)/He threw it out the window
            (AE)
       c.   She lives in Hill Street (BE)/She lives on Hill Street (AE)
       d.   Is Peter at home? (BE)/Is Peter home? (AE)
```

15. In American English, the definite article is usually omitted in the expression *day before yesterday*: "I saw him *day before yesterday*" (BE: "I saw him *the day before yesterday*").

With days of the week, the junctive is either optional, in informal usage (19), or absent (20a and b):

(19)   See you *Saturday*
(20a)  See you *Sunday week/a week on Sunday*   (British English)
(20b)  See you *a week from Sunday*   (American English)

In American English, plural noun phrases, too, may be without a junctive:

(21)   *Evenings* she would write letters
(22)   The store is open *Mondays thru Fridays*

When the time adjunct denotes **duration**, it may be realized by a noun phrase introduced by *all* or *the whole* which does not have a junctive:

(23)   They danced *the whole night long* and slept *all day*

The most common junctive, *for*,[16] can sometimes be omitted in informal usage, particularly after verbs like *last, stay, wait*, but tends to be retained when the adjunct is in initial position:

(24)   Wait *a minute*!
(25)   Can you stay *(for) a while*?
(26)   *For two hours* he waited for something to happen

Noun phrases realizing adjuncts of **frequency** do not have a junctive if they are introduced by *each* or *every*, or if their head is *time(s)*:

(27)   We rehearse *every other week*
(28)   She won the award *three times*

**11.2.4** NP as **degree adjunct** usually has a junctive:

(29)   He doesn't like her *at all*
(30)   She has always *to some extent* worked against him
(31)   She is not *(in) the least* worried about it/worried about it *in the least*

except in a few highly frequent expressions:

(32)   We miss her *a lot*
(33)   He doesn't care *a damn* about her
(34)   It has upset him *a great deal*

**11.2.5** NP as **manner adjunct** normally has a junctive, but the junctive may be left out if the head is *way* (37), and in a few idiomatic expressions like (38):

(35)   He writes *in a way/manner/style* that definitely appeals to me
(36)   Don't talk *like that*!

---

16. A frequent alternative to *for* is *in* in examples like, *He hadn't had a bath in weeks*, i.e. "it was weeks since..."

(37)   Don't you talk *that way* to me!
(38)   I always travel *first class*

**11.2.6** NP as **viewpoint, focus** or **subject adjunct** is always introduced by a junctive:

(39)   His statement is irrelevant *in this respect/from this point of view*   (viewpoint adjunct)
(40)   Not only does she want new clothes, but she wants money *in addition/to boot*   (focus adjunct))
(41)   *With sadness and pride* she accepted the medal on behalf of her son   (subject adjunct)

### The Noun Phrase as a Constituent of Another Noun Phrase (11.3)

**11.3**   A noun phrase can be rankshifted so as to realize the **head** of another noun phrase, see also **sequential modification** (§ 10.9.2):

(1)   American history teachers   (= history teachers in America)
            ―――――   PRM      H
             PRM            H

It may also realize a **premodifier**, which we dealt with under **submodification** (§ 10.9.3):

(2)   American history teachers   (= teachers of American history)
        ――――――   H   ―――――
          PRM      H         H

or a **postmodifier**:

(3)   The house *in Baker Street*      (7)   Women *my age*
(4)   A boy *with curly hair*           (8)   Three times *a week*
(5)   *A friend of my father's*         (9)   Caruso, *the famous singer*
(6)   His speech *last year*           (10)   The letter *A*

As postmodifier the noun phrase is most often introduced by a junctive (i.e. it is a prepositional phrase), as in (3)-(5), though the construction with the genitive (5) is special, see § 14.3.6. The rest of the types exemplified are special by lacking a junctive. In (9) and (10), furthermore, head and postmodifier refer to the same person or thing, in which case we call the postmodifier an **apposition**. See further §§ 10.8.3-10.8.6.

### The Noun Phrase as a Constituent of the Adjective/Adverb phrase (11.4)

**11.4**   The noun phrase may function as **premodifier**, without a junctive, when the AP's head is an adverbial particle (see § 10.8.12), or one of the adjectives *broad, deep, high, long, old, tall, thick* or *wide*:

(1)   (The hospital is) three miles away
                         PRM    H   ―――
                          PRM      H

```
(2)    The accident happened two months ago
(3)    George is six feet tall
(4)    She is only five years old
```

As **postmodifier,** the noun phrase is introduced by a junctive (i.e. it is a prepositional phrase) except after *worth* (9):

```
(5)    (He is) guilty of several serious crimes
                  J     PRM        PRM      H
       _____
          H                    POM
```

```
(6)    Bill is not as tall as the other boy
(7)    She likes you better than Charlie
(8)    I ran too fast for him
(9)    That necklace must be worth a fortune
```

## NUMBER (12.0-12.5.10)

### Introduction (12.0)

12.0   Just as the structure of the verb phrase was seen to reflect the speaker's need to make choices along the dimensions of "time perspective" and "speaker belief and attitude," there are in the noun phrase, too, several such systems of choices. The three **general grammatical systems** of the noun phrase, i.e. those which are represented in just about any noun phrase regardless of its realization, are **number, specification** and **case**. The number system is the subject of the present section.

### The Number System (12.1)

12.1   The number system can be summarized as follows: a noun phrase is either **uncountable** (e.g. *much butter*), or countable. If countable, it is either **singular** (e.g. *a dog*) or **plural** (e.g. *two dogs*). Uncountable noun phrases normally refer to "mass" concepts. Singular noun phrases refer to one member of a class, plural noun phrases to more than one member of a class. However, although these are the typical form/meaning correspondences they may sometimes be broken, as will become apparent in the following.

### Formal Indicators of Number (12.2.1-12.2.3)

*Singular (12.2.1)*

12.2.1 The following formal features are markers of the singular of countable noun phrases.

**Determiners:** *a/an* (the indefinite article), *each, every, (n)either*

```
(1)    A spoon is missing / an idea was hatched
(2)    Each and every room was searched
(3)    Neither solution is satisfactory
```

**Ordinators:** *one* (the first cardinal number), and the ordinal numbers *second, third*, etc.[17]

```
(4)    One minute / the third question
```

**Head:** *one* (as pro-form)

```
(5)    The green dress was awful, and so was the brown one
```

*Plural (12.2.2)*

12.2.2 The following forms are markers of the plural of countable noun phrases.
**Predeterminers:** *both*

```
(6)    Both (the) servants had run off
```

**Determiners:** *these/those* (demonstratives), *a few, a great many, a number of*

```
(7)    These books / a few problems / a number of complaints
```

**Ordinators:** *two, three*, etc. (cardinal numbers except *one*), *few/fewer, many, several, various*

```
(8)    A thousand islands surround the main peninsula
(9)    There were few shoppers in the streets; at least I saw fewer
       shoppers than I did yesterday
(10)   Various suggestions were made
```

**Head:** nouns have the suffix -*s*, though some nouns have individual plural markers; the pro-form *one* has the form *ones*:

```
(11)   These two chairs are yours, and the two red ones are mine
(12)   She brought some of the children but not the little ones
```

---

17. *First*, however, combines equally well with singular and plural:
    *the first question/the first three questions.*

### Uncountable (12.2.3)

12.2.3 The following formal features are markers of the uncountable noun phrase.
**Determiners:** *a little,*[18] *much, a good/great deal of*

```
(13)   A little sugar was needed
(14)   We don't have much sugar
(15)   A good deal of courage was required
```

**Ordinators:** *little, less*

```
(16)   There is little hope that she will survive
(17)   We have less whisky left than I thought
```

**Head:** the pro-form *one* cannot be used; instead, the head may be left out, but this only works with particular (pairs of) adjectives (e.g. *good/bad, old/new*), and colors:

```
(18)   The good news was largely offset by the bad (news)
(19)   If you have no more white wine I'll take some red (wine)
```

### Concord (12.3)

12.3 We have already seen, in the chapter on the verb phrase, how the person and number content of the subject noun phrase is reflected in the form of the first verb from the left (see § 7.3.2). This kind of correspondence we called concord. There may also be concord **between two noun phrases,** when they refer to corresponding numbers:

```
(1a)   She sat in her car   (one person in one car)
(1b)   They sat in their car   (several people in one car)
(1c)   They sat in their cars   (several people in several cars)

(2)    He took off his coat — they took off their coats
(3)    He became a member in 1985 — they became members in 1985
```

Most idiomatic expressions do not show concord:

```
(4)    The parents finally made up their mind(s)
(5)    Many diplomats were taken hostage
(6)    Women have a better ear for music than men
```

As shown by (1b)-(1c), it is the meaning of the noun phrases which determines the question of noun-phrase concord. This is also why there is no concord in the following:

---

18. Note the ambiguity of *a little cake*:

$$\underset{D}{\text{a little}} \text{ (sweet) } \underset{H}{\text{cake}} \text{ (uncountable)}$$

$$\underset{D}{\text{a}} \text{ (sweet) } \underset{E3}{\text{little}} \underset{H}{\text{cake}} \text{ (singular)}$$

(7)    His abilities were *a disappointment*   (i.e. *the fact* that his
       abilities were *poor*)
(8)    The children are *a rough bunch*

### The Uncountable/Countable Distinction (12.4.1-12.4.5)

#### Nouns and countability (12.4.1)

12.4.1 Most nouns can occur as either countable or uncountable depending on the
context, but each tends to be primarily one or the other.
    Those which are **primarily countable**, i.e. those which nearly always function
as the head of noun phrases such as those described in §§ 12.2.1-12.2.2, include
for example *boy, dog, duck, fish, sheep; aircraft, beach, chair, cloud, field, river, tool;
advantage, feeling, idea, situation, spectacle.*
    Those which are **primarily uncountable**, i.e. those which nearly always func-
tion as the head of noun phrases such as those described in § 12.2.3, include for
example *butter, hay, ink, money, sugar, water; lightning, thunder, music; advice,
information, knowledge, progress; luck, patience, wisdom.*
    Those which are equally common in **countable and uncountable** noun
phrases, sometimes with a change of meaning involving more than just count-
ability, include for example *drink, fire, glass, hair, ice, light, noise, paper, stone,
wood; business, conversation, desire, detail, life, pleasure, size, speech, thought; beauty,
genius, youth.*

#### Uncountable nouns of plural form (12.4.2)

12.4.2 Some nouns can add the plural suffix without becoming modifiable by cardinal
numbers, which is why we regard the resulting noun phrase as uncountable.
A. With some of these nouns, the plural form is not the more frequent one, but
when it occurs it is accompanied by plural verbal concord:

(1)    *The waters* of this mighty river *lie* before us
(2)    Their *doubts were* allayed
(3)    I was being dragged through *the woods*

B. Some nouns always, or nearly always, have plural form and plural concord
(e.g. *alms, arms* ("weapons"), *clothes, goods, oats, proceeds, tights, riches, thanks, tid-
ings, wages, wares*):

(4)    Your *tights are* in the top drawer
(5)    *My wages are* not enough to support a family
       (but: I earn *an honest wage*)
(6)    The house was burned to *ashes*
       (but: *the ash from his cigar* fell on her dress)

C. Some original plurals have become uncountables proper, i.e. they end in *-s*
but behave like genuine uncountable nouns in every other respect (e.g. *measles,*

*news, phonetics, politics; billiards, checkers* (American English), *draughts* (British English), *darts*:

```
(7)    The news was devastating
(8)    Politics is a way of life with her
(9)    Acoustics is the scientific study of sound
```

However, nouns in *-ics* may take a plural verb if the meaning is more concrete:

```
(10)   His politics are somewhat wishy-washy  ("political views")
(11)   The acoustics of this hall are appalling
```

### *Making uncountable noun phrases countable (12.4.3-12.4.4)*

12.4.3 Uncountable noun phrases can always be made countable by means of a partitive *of*-construction (see 10.8.6 n.) with a countable "prop" word as head. The prop word which can be applied most generally is *piece*:

```
(12)   A piece of cake / paper / advice / furniture etc.
       (two etc. pieces...)
```

*Item* denotes a single article in an inventory or agenda:

```
(13)   An item of news / furniture (e.g. in an auctioneer's pro-
       gram) / information
```

The use of *bit* can sometimes make the noun phrase countable, but more often the noun phrase remains uncountable:

```
(14)   Several bits of paper (but a bit of sugar is a little sugar,
       not a piece of sugar)
```

Certain uncountable nouns tend to go together with particular prop words, depending on the kind of substance or condition (etc.) they refer to, e.g.

```
(15)   A lump of coal / meat / sugar (etc.)
(16)   A glass of milk (etc.)
(17)   A pound of butter (etc.)
(18)   An attack of fever / malaria (etc)
```

A few prop words can only be used with particular nouns, e.g.

```
(19)   A loaf of bread, a bar of chocolate / soap, a sheet of
       paper / metal
(20)   A pang of remorse, a peal of thunder / laughter (cp. a
       laugh), a stroke of luck / genius
```

12.4.4 The possibility of turning uncountable noun phrases into countable (or at least singular) ones without using the partitive *of*-construction is more limited. This usage, too, may indicate a quantity or portion of something (21), but also a particular kind ((22), (23)), manifestation (24) or result (25):

```
(21)   Two beers, please
(22)   We need someone with a knowledge of linguistics
(23)   These are both American wines / tobaccos
```

```
(24)   He could never forget their many kindnesses
(25)   Her survival is a comfort to me
```

### Making countable noun phrases uncountable (12.4.5)

12.4.5 Countable nouns may become uncountable to denote the substance or concept of what they refer to. Such noun phrases usually have generic reference (see § 13.3).

**Substance**, e.g.

```
(26)   What kinds of apple do you grow in your garden?
       (also ..kinds of apples..)
(27)   Mary was hungry, so she had a little lamb (salmon,
       duck, etc.)¹⁹
(28)   Any man might succumb to a few inches of bare leg
(29)   Beech makes better firewood than birch
```

**Concepts**, e.g.

```
(30)   He hates school
(31)   With this model you get a lot of car at a reasonable price
(32)   They went over the plan once more in detail
(33)   Talk shop, send word (and other idioms)
```

## The Singular/Plural Distinction (12.5.0-12.5.10)

### Nouns and the singular/plural distinction (12.5.0)

12.5.0 Nouns realizing the head of the noun phrase normally have plural form if their content includes the meaning of "more than one." This general rule also covers cases where several coordinated modifiers, each referring to one unit, together add up to more than one, thus requiring the head to be in the plural:

```
(1)    One and a half hours   (cp. an hour and a half)
(2)    The first, second and third prizes
(3)    Chapters one and two
(4)    The film was for children between the ages of 12 and 16
```

However, as in the case of the uncountable/countable distinction, there may sometimes be discrepancies between form and content.

### Same form in singular and plural (12.5.1-12.5.7)

12.5.1 A number of nouns are unchanged in the plural and so have the same form in plural as in singular noun phrases (§§ 12.5.1-12.5.6). Likewise, a number of originally plural forms do not have a singular, the plural form being used also in singular noun phrases (§ 12.5.7). The other plural/singular characteristics of the phrase are normal.

---

19. The difference between the individual animal and the animal thought of as meat is often lexicalized: *calf/veal, deer/venison, ox/ beef, pig/pork, sheep/mutton.*

12.5.2 Certain **animal names** do not have a plural form, e.g. *cod, deer, grouse, mackerel, salmon,*[20] *sheep, trout*:

```
(1)    About a hundred deer had been shot
(2)    All the sheep had been brought in by nightfall
```

Some animal names have the same form in the plural only when referring to the animals in the mass, as game, whereas the regular plural is used about individual animals, e.g. *buffalo, duck, fish, fowl*:

```
(3a)   The Indians were following a herd of buffalo
(3b)   Three buffaloes were grazing peacefully
(4a)   How many fish have you caught?
(4b)   He could see three little fishes near the bottom[21]
```

12.5.3 **Nationality names** in *-ese* (e.g. *Chinese, Japanese, Portuguese*), and *Swiss*, do not have a plural form:

```
(5)    A Portuguese was talking to two Chinese
```

12.5.4 Some **units of measure** can be unchanged in the plural, e.g. *foot* and *pound*, especially before a numeral, cp.

```
(6a)   She is only five foot ten
(6b)   She is five feet (tall)
(7a)   The book costs four pound(s) twenty      (British English)
(7b)   The book costs four pounds               (British English)
```

Some do not have a plural form at all, e.g. *horsepower, (kilo)hertz*, informal money terms such as *grand* "a thousand dollars/pounds," British English *p* /pi:/ "penny", *quid* "pound":

```
(8)    The engine has fifty horsepower
(9)    Two kilohertz equals 2000 hertz
(10)   They charge you 50p
(11)   It cost me ten quid (the corresponding American expression
       has the regular plural: ten bucks)
```

and certain nouns used in partitive constructions, e.g. *head*:

```
(12)   I sold him thirty head of cattle
```

12.5.5 *Kind* and *sort* often have the singular form in the following plural idiomatic constructions (colloquial language):

```
(13)   Those kind/sort of apples (besides those kinds/sorts of
       apple(s))
```

---

20. Also plural *salmons* in American English.
21. *Fishes* is often used in speech with children; it tends to refer to small fish.

whereas they always take -s when more than one type is being referred to (see § 12.4.5):

(14)    Three different *sorts* of apple(s)

12.5.6  Some **individual nouns** such as *aircraft, counsel* (lawyer), *series, species* do not change their form in the plural:

(15)    *Three aircraft* were shot down
(16)    *The two counsel* were talking to the judge
(17)    *One series* is interesting, *the other two series* are boring

12.5.7  A number of originally plural forms do not have a singular, the plural form being used also in singular noun phrases, e.g. *gallows, headquarters, innings, means, works* (= *factory*):

(18)    *Our present headquarters* is five miles from here
(19a)   *The quickest means of getting there* is by boat
(19b)   *All possible means* have been tried
(20)    *The public gasworks* pollutes more than any other factory

### Plural nouns denoting two-component items (12.5.8)

12.5.8  A number of nouns refer to articles that are conceived of as consisting of two components. Such nouns have plural form and concord, but can be used in the singular or after cardinal numbers only as part of a partitive construction with *a pair of*. They include terms for various instruments (e.g. *binoculars, compasses, glasses, pincers, scales, scissors, tongs*) and items of clothing (e.g. *pants,*[22] *shorts, tights, trousers*, British English *braces, knickers, pyjamas*, American English *suspenders, pajamas*):

(21)    *My scissors* are gone
(22)    I need *(some/a pair of) scissors* for this job
(23)    He needs *two pairs of shorts*

### Collective nouns (12.5.9)

12.5.9  Nouns referring to a group of individuals are constructed regularly as either singular or plural. In British English, however, such collective nouns may in the singular take plural concord if they are thought of as a collection of individuals rather than a single undivided body. In American English, the singular form of such nouns is nearly always followed by a singular verb, though subsequent pronouns referring to the group may, as in British English, be in the plural. Compare:

(24a)   *Our staff is* growing
(24b)   *The staff have all* gone home

---

22. There are many characteristic differences between American and British English in the use of these terms, e.g. *pants* (AE "trousers," BE "underpants"), *shorts* (AE "underpants" besides "trousers ending above the knees").

```
(25a)  The orchestra are playing better now, aren't they?  (BE)
(25b)  The orchestra is playing better now, isn't it?  (AE & BE)
(25c)  The orchestra is playing better now, aren't they?  (AE)
(26)   The orchestra is touring Russia at the moment, isn't it?
(27)   Both orchestras are touring Russia at the moment, aren't
       they?
```

Other examples of collective nouns: *audience, class, committee, crew, crowd, family, government, team; the aristocracy, the public; (the) Congress, Parliament.*

The relative pronouns *who* and *which* are used differently when the antecedent is a collective noun: *which* is used when the noun refers to an undivided body, whereas *who* is used when the noun refers to a collection of individuals, e.g.

```
(28)   Our staff, which is growing...
(29)   The staff, who have all gone home...
```

### Plural nouns without plural form (12.5.10)

12.5.10 A few nouns, notably *cattle, clergy, gentry, police,* are always constructed as plural:

```
(30)   The rancher had a thousand cattle up for sale
(31)   Most police wear uniforms
```

## SPECIFICATION (13.1-13.6.3)

### The System of Specification (13.1)

13.1 The system of specification is a three-term one: A noun phrase has either **generic** or **specific reference**. If it is specific, it is **indefinite specific** or **definite specific**.

(A) **Generic reference** (cp. *genus*) means reference to the category or general concept of what the noun phrase denotes, as opposed to a particular member or manifestation of the category. Thus if I say,

```
(1)    Next year I'll buy a car
```

I am not thinking of a **particular** car, but "any member of the category of cars." Likewise,

```
(2)    I like cats and dogs
(3)    There is more caffeine in tea than in coffee
(4)    The situation calls for kindness and consideration
```

(B) **Indefinite specific reference**. "Specific reference" as such means reference to a specific member or manifestation of a category. It is "indefinite" when the speaker assumes that this member or manifestation has not previously been introduced to, and cannot be immediately identified by, the addressee:

```
(5)    He was invited out by a beautiful woman yesterday
(6)    There is an alligator in the bathtub
(7)    There is some chocolate in the cupboard
(8)    I have some information for you
```

(C) **Definite specific reference** means reference to a specific member or manifestation of a category when the speaker is assuming that this member or manifestation has already been introduced to or identified by the addressee:

```
(9)    The woman is a professor of history
(10)   The chocolate was eaten by the alligator
(11)   I wish I had had the information yesterday
```

In other words, utterances like (9)-(11) presuppose utterances like (5)-(8).

Nouns fall into two basic classes with regard to their use with specific reference: **common nouns** are nouns of lexical content which can become definite specific by means of determiners, as in (9)-(11); **proper nouns** are arbitrary designations which uniquely identify a particular member or manifestation of an understood category, i.e. they do not need a determiner:

```
(12)   I like Bob better than Joe
(13)   She has a cousin in Edinburgh
(14)   He wants you back by Saturday/Christmas
```

### Formal Indicators of Specification (13.2)

13.2    The most important constituent of the noun phrase with regard to specification is the determiner. The following pattern of form/reference correspondences is typical of common nouns (though not exhaustive):

|            | Generic     | Indefinite specific | Definite specific |
|------------|-------------|---------------------|-------------------|
| **Sing.**  | *any/a/an*  | *a/an*              | *the*             |
| **Plur.**  | *any/zero*  | *some/a few*        | *the*             |
| **Uncount.** | *any/zero* | *some/a little*     | *the*             |

Proper nouns, capitalized in writing, usually realize the head of a simple noun phrase and have singular form, see (12)-(14) above.

Elaboration, examples and exceptions will be given in the following. For specification in connection with pronouns, see § 13.6.

### Generic Reference (13.3.0-13.3.7)

13.3.0 Noun phrases referring to a semantic category (e.g. a species, class, substance, concept) are called generic:

```
(1)    Do you have a pencil?    (any member of the category of
       pencils, not a particular pencil)
(2)    She is allergic to flowers
(3)    Oil and vinegar do not mix
(4)    Let's leave it to chance
```

Both descriptive and classifying noun-phrase constituents may contribute to the definition of a category:

```
(5)    I like big dogs
(6)    He collects gaudy Indian saddle blankets
```

The size of the category is irrelevant:

```
(7)    Beautiful little girls with blue eyes and golden hair
       answering to the name of Lisa ought to be in bed by now!
```

The reference may be generic within the context of a given situation:

```
(8)    A newly qualified teacher is paid between eight and ten
       thousand a year  (understood: in this country)
(9)    Secretaries are having a hard time at the university
(10)   Conditions were appalling
(11)   Things didn't change
(12)   Visibility was nil
```

Referring generically to "secretaries" in (9) is a way of avoiding the claim that "(all) the secretaries are having a hard time at the university." Generic reference and indefinite specific reference come very close in this example, and in examples like *"Members of the Communist Party* led the demonstration," which can be seen in the fact that subsequent personal pronouns tend to have definite specific reference: *"They* were singing The Red Flag."

To explain the generic use of the indefinite article in (1) above, we paraphrased it by means of the determiner *any.* Noun phrases introduced by *any* are in fact often used to make it explicit that generic reference is meant, and that the speaker is not thinking of particular individuals or manifestations:

```
(13)   She wants to marry a man from Denmark — any man from Denmark
```

*A man from Denmark* is ambiguous (it might refer to a particular man), but the addition of *any man...* makes it unambiguously generic.

Whereas the use of generic noun phrases is not limited to particular types of clause, there are two cases in which reference is always generic:
(A) when the clause denies the existence of whatever the noun phrase refers to:

```
(14)   What policeman? — I did not see any policeman
(15)   There weren't any people in the room
(16)   We have no whisky left
```

(B) when the noun phrase realizes the subject complement of a clause expressing classification, or has related functions:

```
(17)   This is not coffee, this is mud
(18)   My father is a teacher
(19)   As/being a priest I can only denounce such actions
(20)   Ms. Smith, (who is) a former call girl, headed the
       demonstration
```

If there is only one member of the class at a time, the article may be dropped:

```
(21)   She wants to become prime minister
```

as it may if only the qualities of the class are referred to:

```
(22)   The author is more poet than novelist
(23)   He is not linguist enough to understand this kind of
       analysis
```

13.3.1 **Singular noun phrases** often take the indefinite article when generic, as in definitions referring to any representative member of the class. In formal language, the definite article, too, may be used, conjuring up the typical specimen:

```
(24)   A dog is a four-legged flesh-eating domestic animal
(25)   The dog is man's best friend²³
(26)   The computer has revolutionized our lives
```

In certain idioms containing a generic noun phrase, only the definite article is possible:

```
(27)   Where did you learn to play the piano (the violin, etc.) ?
(28)   She is down with (the) flu
(29)   Stop playing the fool!
```

The determiners *any* (stressed), *no, every* and *what* are also found:

```
(30)   Any woman would tell you that/No woman would admit that
(31)   Every child knows that!
(32)   What fool would make the same mistake twice?
```

13.3.2 **Plural and uncountable noun phrases** are without a determiner when used generically, or take the determiners *any* (unstressed), *no*:

```
(33)   Cats hate dogs
(34)   American poets have always been influenced by the concept
       of the frontier
(35)   Blood is thicker than water
(36)   She has written a book on life in ancient Greece
(37)   They couldn't get any help/They could get no help
```

---

23. Note that generic *man* and *woman* occur without any article in the sense of "-kind" (*man'kind, 'mankind* vs. *womankind*)
```
       a.      Man is mortal
       b.      Woman's life span is longer than man's
```

A notable exception is noun phrases with an adjective as head (see also § 10.1.2):

(38)   Funerals are for *the living*, not for *the dead*
(39)   These artists are interested mainly in *the obscene* and *the grotesque*

### Generic reference and countability (13.3.3-13.3.7)

13.3.3   When a countable noun of singular form is used in an uncountable noun phrase, i.e. without a determiner, it often becomes explicitly generic (but see also §§ 13.5.6-13.5.7):

(40)   He saw nothing but bare black branches on a background of grey *cloud*
(41)   The third little pig built his house of *brick*
(42)   The Communists are discovering the advantages of *capitalist society*
(43)   Sorry, but Mr. Johnson is in *conference* at the moment

The following are some special cases of this.

13.3.4   Countable nouns become uncountable, i.e. drop the determiner, when they are juxtaposed, whether listed or contrasted:

(44)   This 20-year-old volunteer in the SAS killed his enemies with *knife*, *gun* and *grenade*.
(45)   To fight for *king* and *country* is what a soldier must do
(46)   From *farm boy* to *prime minister*, *head* to *toe*, *top* to *bottom*, etc. (note also: from *east* to *west*, *left* to *right*)

and when the noun phrase, as subject complement of a causal, concessive or conditional clause, is fronted (cp. 13.3.0 (B) above):

(47)   *Idiot* that I was, I forgot to give her the key
(48)   *Pauper* though he is, he can always find the wherewithal to help those worse off than himself

13.3.5   Countable nouns denoting cultural or universal "institutions" (i.e. in a wider as well as in a narrow sense of the word) become uncountable/generic when referred to in terms of their social significance rather than as physical phenomena. The fact that they are generic frequently means that the article is dropped. Such noun phrases, often introduced by a junctive (i.e. prepositional phrases), tend to be idiomatic:
(A) Institutions proper —

(49)   Go to *church/college/prison/school* etc.[24]
(50)   They took their dispute to *court*

---

24. In British English, *hospital* and *university* are treated in the same way, but not in American English:
  a.   He is in *the hospital*
  b.   She wants to go to *a/the university*.

Thus we do not say, *Their children are at schools*, even if they go to different schools.

(B) Household "institutions," including meals —

```
(51)    How early do you serve breakfast?
(52)    She liked to discuss her problems over lunch
(53)    John is in bed, so we won't have the pleasure of his company
        at table
```

(C) Means of transportation (signalled by *by* or *on*) —

```
(54)    I always travel by boat/bus/car/plane/train (etc.)
(55)    We can get to the island by air or by sea
(56)    If we go by land, we can either go on foot or on horseback
```

(D) Times of the day and seasons of the year —

```
(57)    They would get up at dawn
(58)    He came at dusk and stayed till morning
(59)    I love New York by night
(60)    Spring came early that year, but she couldn't wait for
        summer
```

The determiner is necessary, on the other hand, if the uncountable noun phrase refers to the whole of the time period:

```
(61)    The summer is hot and dry in that part of the world
```

After the junctive *in*, times of the day need the determiner, whereas seasons of the year behave less consistently, the determiner being required in American English but not in British English:

```
(62)    She always came home late in the evening
(63)    They would go skiing in (the) winter   (BE)
(64)    I love Paris in the springtime/...in the fall   (AE)
```

13.3.6 The determiner is missing in a number of idiomatic expressions, where a countable noun functions as uncountable and generic. Such expressions consist of verb + object ("object verbs," see § 7.9.3), e.g. *cast anchor, keep house, lose heart, lose sight (of), take offence, take shape, take shelter, tend shop/bar* (American English), *turn tail*:

```
(65)    She had kept house for him for twenty years
(66)    He had turned tail as soon as it became apparent they
        weren't going to win
```

or are simple noun phrases introduced by a junctive (prepositional phrases), e.g. *at bottom, at hand, at present* (see also § 13.4.4 n.), *at/on sight, by heart, on display, on top, uphill*:

```
(67)    He is to be shot on sight
(68)    I don't read music, I just play by ear
```

In other idiomatic expressions, the determiner is realized by the definite article, e.g.

```
(69)    Jim likes to play the fool
(70)    Gladiators were expected to fight to the death    (but: The
        Emperor had the gladiators put to death)
(71)    They bought books by the dozen/hundred/thousand/million
```

or, more frequently, by the indefinite article, e.g.

```
(72)    She loves men who smoke a pipe
(73)    We naturally take an interest in the matter
(74)    They asked him to take a seat
(75)    I don't as a rule accept bribes
```

13.3.7  Terms for diseases are normally uncountable and generic, and so are constructed without a determiner:

```
(76)    He has appendicitis/bronchitis/laryngitis/tuberculosis
```

but *flu, gout, plague* and plural forms like *measles* often take the definite article, *cold* and *fever* normally using the indefinite article:

```
(77)    She is down with (the) flu/(the) measles
(78)    He has a touch of (the) gout
(79)    Don't catch (a) cold now!
(80a)   I think she's got a fever (= a (high) temperature)
(80b)   I think she's got fever (e.g. malaria)
```

**Specific Reference (13.4.0-13.4.5)**

13.4.0  Specific reference is used when the speaker refers to a specific member or manifestation of a category. **Definite specific** reference, as opposed to **indefinite specific** reference, assumes that this member or manifestation can be immediately identified by the addressee. The justification for such an assumption is the fulfillment of either of two contextual conditions: whatever the speaker is referring to (1) has been mentioned or implied in the preceding part of the text — **textual specificity**; or (2) belongs to the speaker and addressee's shared knowledge of the situation/culture/world — **situational specificity**.

*Textual specificity (13.4.1-13.4.4)*

13.4.1  Typically, when something is mentioned for the first time it is given **indefinite specific** reference, the determiner being realized by the indefinite article (in the singular), by *some/a few/a number of* (in the plural) or by *some/a little* (in uncountable phrases). Subsequent mention has **definite specific** reference, most often signalled by the definite article as determiner, or by a personal pronoun (see also § 6.3):

(1)    *A man* and *a woman* were leaving the hotel; *the woman/she* was
       obviously much older than *the man/him*
(2)    *A few people* had already left for the day, *the women* to go
       shopping, *the men* to have a drink or two at the local bar
(3)    I bought *some plain flour* yesterday, but *it* is full of
       maggots

A number of other forms realizing the determiner signal definite specific reference, e.g. the demonstratives and the forms *each* and *which*:

(4)    She has submitted two possible solutions. *Which solution* do
       you prefer?
(5)    There were several refugees waiting outside. *These people*
       had spent the night in the street, having nowhere to go
(6)    Two little boys came up to me and said they were hungry; I
       gave *each boy* an apple

Genitive determiners are most often definite specific, making the whole noun phrase definite specific (generic genitives tend to become nominators, see § 10.6.3):

(7)    *The boys' father/their father* thanked me profusely

*Every*, apart from having generic reference (see § 13.3.1 (31)), can also be definite specific:

(8)    Several students had answered the question, but *every
       (single) one of them* had done it wrong

13.4.2  The natural direction of the reference is that exemplified by (1)-(8): the definite specific noun phrases refer to something mentioned previously. In terms of its direction, in other words, definite reference is most often **anaphoric**. Reference to something that follows is called **cataphoric**. Compare:

(9a)   I'm sure *Emily* could do the job, if you'd be willing to give
       *the girl* a chance   (anaphoric reference)
(9b)   If you'd be willing to give *the girl* a chance, I'm sure
       *Emily* could do the job   (cataphoric reference)

13.4.3  Definite specific reference may be justified even if whatever is being referred to has been mentioned only by implication. This is known as **implicit textual specificity**:

(10)   She has just had *a baby* but refuses to say who *the father*
       is
(11)   *A loud bark* from the other side of the gate made her jump,
       but *the dog* didn't come out
(12)   TV has become the young and impressionable viewer's
       instruction manual in crime and violence, and yet nobody
       takes *the problem* seriously

Thus in (10), although no father has been mentioned before the occurrence of *the father*, definite specific reference is still justified because a baby has been referred to: for every baby there must be a father. Similarly, in (11), a loud bark implies the presence of a dog, which can subsequently be referred to as *the dog*. In (12), the description of what TV does to "the young and impressionable viewer" is strongly negative, implying that the effect of TV is a problem; subsequent reference to this problem, therefore, will be definite specific.

13.4.4 Finally, the presence of defining modifiers within the noun phrase itself may bring about definite specific reference. In the premodification, certain **ordinators** that are defining usually imply definite specific reference, e.g. (O1) ordinal numbers, *former, latter, next, last, only, same*, and (O3) superlatives:

(13) The first volunteer, the 19th century (but: *to want a second opinion; to see a third possibility*), the former alternative, the next station, the only solution, the best brands

Other types of premodifier, but especially **postmodifiers**, may be used as defining. The noun phrase will have definite specific reference if the definition is felt to be precise and unambiguous, as in (14)-(20):

(14) I need *the small blue pronouncing dictionary* (cp. I need *a pronouncing dictionary*)
(15) I'm going to wear *my new suit* tonight
(16) She heard *the sound of a gun* (cp. She heard *a sound from outside*)
(17) He was under *the influence of alcohol* when it happened
(18) *The word "hippopotamus"* is a difficult one to spell
(19) Why not invite *the girl that you met last night* (see also § 3.7.1)
(20) *The fact that he did it* is less interesting than *the question of why he did it*

### Situational specificity (13.4.5)

13.4.5 Definite specific reference may be based on the speaker and addressee's shared experience or knowledge of the situation, the social environment, the subject, the culture, or the world in general. We call this situational specificity:

(21) Open *the door*, please! (the situation makes it clear which door)
(22) He sat down and turned on *the TV* (i.e. that particular medium, though there may be several TV sets in the house)
(23) *The police* have arrested several demonstrators (there is only one police force)
(24) How do you say this *in the singular, the plural, the passive* etc.
(25) There is no need to discuss *the past*, or even *the present*, when we should be planning *the future*[25]

---

25. In British English, *future* lacks a determiner after the junctive *in* if the meaning is "from now on": *I want you to be more careful in future* (but: *Nobody knows what will happen in the future*; American English has *...in the future* in either case). *Present* has no determiner after *at* in either variety: *We can't help you at present.*

```
(26)   We spent all (the) afternoon trying to work it out²⁶
(27)   (To) the left/right/north (etc.)
(28)   The air / the ground / the sea / the sky
(29)   The moon / the sun / the equator / etc.
(30)   Bob returned home from America only last Christmas
```

Situational specificity and implicit textual specificity frequently go hand in hand, as in:

```
(31)   It was a nice house, but the living room was too small and
       the kitchen not very well equipped
```

i.e. speaker and addressee know that the existence of a living room and a kitchen has been implied by the word *house*, because such knowledge is part of their shared cultural background.

## Proper Nouns and Common Nouns (13.5.0-13.5.8)

### *Proper nouns and common nouns contrasted (13.5.0)*

13.5.0  So far we have been dealing mainly with common nouns, i.e. nouns of lexical content denoting a class or general concept, which can have definite specific reference only if preceded by a definite determiner. Let us now look at the category of proper nouns. Proper nouns are usually arbitrary designations (e.g. *James, Bond, 007, London, America, Unesco*), empty of lexical content, which are used to uniquely identify one particular member or manifestation of an understood lexical category. Thus they do not need a determiner, their definiteness being based on situational specificity, see § 13.4.5. They most often realize the head of a simple noun phrase, though modifiers are by no means uncommon (e.g. *Little John, Greater London*).

Although proper nouns do not need a determiner for the sake of their specificity, proper nouns of plural form always take the definite article (e.g. *the Netherlands, the Johnsons*).

Proper nouns are usually capitalized in writing.

Linguistic forms hardly ever have just one function, and this also applies to proper and common nouns: forms normally used as proper nouns are sometimes treated as common nouns, and vice versa. Such recategorization will be dealt with in the following. Typical proper nouns include names of **persons** and personified objects/animals (*Lisa, Mr. Williamson, Dr. Jenkins, Fido*), **institutions** (*Parliament, Nato, Heaven, Hell*), **places** (*Asia, Britain, San Francisco, Loch Ness*), **holidays** (*Christmas, Easter*), **days of the week/months of the year** (*Monday, Tuesday*, etc.; *January, February*, etc.).

---

26. Time periods often do not have a determiner after *all* (in American English the determiner is practically always missing after *all*), and never when *all* occurs in a negative clause: *I haven't seen her all summer.*

### Proper nouns used as common nouns (13.5.1-13.5.5)

13.5.1 Proper nouns are sometimes treated more or less like common nouns by means of a determiner, for instance when a name in itself is not enough for identification:

(1)    There is *a Mr. Smith* to see you
(2)    *A Dr. Johnson* was there to see him — it was, in fact, *the Dr. Johnson*
(3)    Let's welcome *the new Mrs. Smith* to the family

or when a family name is used in the plural with reference to the members of the family:

(4)    Have you invited *the Johnsons*?

13.5.2 As indicated by example (3), the determiner is often used in connection with a defining (pre- or post-) modifier. This is also the case when only a particular aspect of what the proper noun refers to is focused on:

(5)    The mature Mozart   (i.e. the works of Mozart in his mature years)
(6)    The Chicago of Al Capone
(7)    He is *a different Tom* — not *the Tom that I used to know years ago in Paris*

There is no determiner, however, if the defining modifier enters into a fixed combination with the proper noun so that a new, compound, proper noun is formed:

(8)    Ancient Rome, Greater London, North America

13.5.3 A nondefining modifier, too, may take a determiner:

(9)    As *the late Mrs. Crippen* used to say...
(10)   "Here is a little something for you," said *the kind-hearted Mrs. Hopkins*

but there is no determiner if a more personal note is sounded:

(11)   Good old Charlie Brown
(12)   Young Smith

Note also examples like the following, frequently found in journalism:

(13)   Charming 96-year-old Jennifer Hayden

13.5.4 Clear instances of recategorization, i.e. of proper nouns becoming common nouns, are when the proper noun is used about other people or places to indicate that they have the qualities normally associated with the proper noun:

```
(14)   He is a regular little Hitler
(15)   This century hasn't seen many Napoleons
(16)   Copenhagen is sometimes called the Paris of the North
```

or when a name denotes a work of art by a particular artist:

```
(17)   The museum owns a Picasso and a Goya; the Goya is said to
       be one of his finest pieces
```

13.5.5  Terms for times of the day, days of the week, and months, include both proper nouns and common nouns. They occur without a determiner when they refer to the nearest such time, as viewed from the speaker's present, cp. the use of *next* and *last* in some of these expressions, and before the noun *year*:

```
(18)   Charles is coming on Saturday
(19)   Next Thursday is Valentine's Day
(20)   I saw him last night
(21)   I'll see you in September
(22)   She is going to visit China next year
```

But if they are unrelated to the speaker's present, they behave like common nouns in requiring a determiner:

```
(23)   Charles   came   on   the   Saturday   and   left   the   following
       Wednesday
(24)   They gave a party the last night we were there[27]
(25)   They left the island in (the) January (of) 1981
```

### *Common nouns used as proper nouns (13.5.6-13.5.7)*

13.5.6  Original common nouns may become proper nouns while retaining the deter miner (realized by the definite article). For instance, phenomena that are always given definite specific reference because they are unique and universal tend to be conceived of as proper nouns:

```
(26)   The moon, the sun, (the) earth, the aurora borealis/northern
       lights
```

The same happens to culturally unique institutions, concepts, etc.:

```
(27)   The State, the President, the Queen, the Church, the Navy,
       the Tower, the Channel, the Conquest, the Bible, the Devil
```

The determiner may not be the only modifier:

```
(28)   The   White   House,   (the   Houses   of)   Parliament,   the
       International Court of Justice, the Church of England, the
       Tower of London, the Yellow Sea, the Lake District, the Old
       Testament, the (Holy) Bible
```

---

27. In British English, the determiner is optional before *next day*; this is not the case in American English:

```
       a.   Next day they received a report on his findings (BE)
       b.   The next day they received a report on his findings (AE & BE)
```

The determiner is part of the noun phrase, not part of the name: it is usually not capitalized (or in italics) like the rest of the name, and it can be replaced by another determiner, e.g.

(29)   Can I borrow your *Bible*?
(30)   Was it in the *Daily Telegraph*? — In yesterday's *Daily Telegraph*, yes

The determiner is usually also retained when only initials are used, except where the initials are pronounced and written as a new word (acronym), cp.

(31)   The UN, the US, the YMCA   (but CBS, IBM, ITV, where there is no determiner in the original name)
(32)   Nato, Opec, Unesco

The common noun, sometimes implicit, may be premodified by a proper noun (or an adjective derived from one):

(33)   The Argentine (Republic) (= *Argentina*), the London Library, the Atlantic (Ocean), the Straits of Messina

The determiner is sometimes dropped, so that the noun phrase attains full (idiomatic) proper-noun status:

(34)   Parliament, (the) Congress, Central Park, Buckingham Palace, Carnegie Hall, Tower Bridge, Fisherman's Wharf, Hudson Bay

13.5.7  In other cases the question of dropping the determiner is linked to the type of institution, geographical location, etc.:

(A) **Family relationship terms** are used as proper nouns by the family, without a determiner:

(35)   Father, Dad/Daddy, Mother, Mum/Mummy (BE), Mom (AE), Uncle, Grandpa, Grandma, etc.

(B) Certain **religious "institutions"** never have a determiner:

(36)   Is he in *heaven* or is he in *hell*, that damned elusive Pimpernel? (also *paradise* and *purgatory*)

(C) **Street names** are usually without a determiner:

(37)   Fleet Street, Fifth Avenue   (but *the Mall*, *the Strand*)

(D) **Names of newspapers** generally have a determiner (38). **Magazines and journals** generally do not, but this tendency is less consistent (39):

(38)   *The Times, the Sun, the Daily Telegraph, the New York Herald Tribune, the Albuquerque Journal, the Washington Post*
(39)   *New Scientist, Time, Outdoor Life, Trout and Salmon, She, Studies in Higher Education, Ageing and Society, Journal of Linguistics, the Journal of Parasitology*

See also 13.5.6 (30).

*Proper nouns which always take the definite article (13.5.8)*

13.5.8  Some proper nouns take the definite article although this cannot be explained as reflecting a development from common-noun to proper-noun status:
(A)  Proper nouns in the **plural** always take *the*:

(40)   The Alps, the Hebrides, the Midlands, the Netherlands

(B)  **River names** take *the*:

(41)   The (River) Avon, the (River) Thames  (BE)
(42)   The Hudson (River), the Mississippi (River)  (AE)

except when they postmodify names of towns, in the type: *Stratford-on-Avon, Newcastle-on-Tyne*.

(C)  **Seas** and **oceans** take *the*:

(43)   The Atlantic/Pacific/etc. (Ocean)
(44)   The Mediterranean (Sea)

(D)  **Names of ships** take *the* if they are not in apposition:

(45)   The Queen Elizabeth, the Seven Seas, the Titanic
(46)   The steamship Titanic

(E)  The use of *the* is idiomatic with a number of **individual place names**:

(47)   The Crimea, the Hague, the Kremlin, the Orient, the Ukraine
       etc.

## Specification in Pronominal Noun Phrases (13.6.1-13.6.3)

13.6.1  The **personal pronouns** (including the *-self* forms, see § 16) usually have situational specificity in the 1st and 2nd person: *I/we, you*. In the 3rd person, their specificity is normally textual, whether anaphoric (1) or cataphoric (2), though it may occasionally be situational (3):

(1)    I invited Mrs. Robinson, but *she* hasn't come
(2)    Although *she* was invited weeks ago, Mrs. Robinson hasn't
       come
(3)    Look, *he* is running away with my bag!

The personal pronouns have either definite specific, or generic, reference. If something is referred to the first time as specific, whether indefinite or definite, it will be given definite specific reference (through the pronoun) the second time:

(4)    *Two women* were being shouted at by *a little boy*, but *they*
       ignored *him*
(5)    *The little boy* was shouting at *the two women*, but *they*
       ignored *him*

If the concept is given generic reference the first time it is mentioned, it will be generic the second time, too, when referred to by the pronoun:

(6)    *A cat* will attack if *it* is cornered
(7)    *Religious fanatics* are as dangerous to *themselves* as *they* are to others

13.6.2    Generic reference which does not depend on the concept having been mentioned earlier in the text is found with *we, you, one* and *they*:

(8)    *They* say that falling in love is wonderful
(9)    *We* wouldn't do it like that in Britain
(10)   *We* never think of death until *we* are facing it
(11)   *One* should always be on *one's* guard    (BE and formal written AE)
(12)   One should always be on *his/her* guard    (informal AE)[28]
(13)   *You* should never be afraid of doing what is right

All four forms refer to people in general, but *they* is used when the 1st and 2nd person are being excluded. In contrast, *we* includes the 1st ((9), (10)) and sometimes the 2nd person (10), see also § 15.3.2. *One* includes especially the first person, and *you*, the 2nd person.

13.6.3    If we need a pronoun with indefinite specific reference, or one where generic reference is marked formally, we have to turn to a special set of **indefinite pronouns** (see § 20):

|  | Indefinite specific | Generic |
|---|---|---|
| Singular | *one* | *one* |
|  |  | *none* |
| Plural & uncountable | *some* | *any* |
|  |  | *none* |

Like the personal pronouns, these indefinite pronouns usually refer to something mentioned earlier in the text (anaphoric reference), but unlike the personal pronouns their specification does not depend on the specification of the noun phrase to which they refer:

(14)   A group of *children* were playing football on the lawn. *One* of them recognized her and waved his hand in greeting (generic + indefinite specific)
(15)   She loved *those roses* so I gave her *some*    (definite specific + indefinite specific)

---

28. Informal American English has a form of *he* (or *she*, see § 15.3.7) after *one* has been used the first time.

(16)   I have a bottle of *wine*, if you would care for *some*?
       (generic + indefinite specific)
(17)   Why shouldn't I buy myself *a car*? Everybody else has *one*
       (generic + generic)
(18)   You can take *the beers in the fridge*, if there're *any* left
       (definite specific + generic)
(19)   He went for *some wine*, but there was *none* in the cellar
       (indefinite specific + generic)

Cataphoric reference to an *of*-postmodifier is also common, in fact with *none* this
is probably the most common construction:

(20)   *Some* of *these paintings* are for sale
(21)   *None* of *my friends* know I'm here

The specification of other pronouns tends to coincide with that of the same
forms when they function as determiner, see §§ 13.3-13.4 and Ch. V.


## CASE (14.1-14.4.5)


### The Case System (14.1)

14.1   English has three cases: the **subjective**, the **objective** and the **genitive** case.
These are formal distinctions[29] whose "purpose" is to suggest how the noun
phrase functions grammatically, and since two of them often mark noun phrases
functioning as subject and object, respectively, they have been named accordingly. The pronouns have all three distinctions, whereas in the nouns the functions
of the subjective and the objective case are concentrated in one **common case**
which contrasts with the genitive.

---

29. The case roles discussed in § 6.4 are primarily of a semantic nature, and cannot be directly
related to the formal case system.

**The Case Forms (14.2.1-14.2.4)**

*Nouns (14.2.1)*

14.2.1 The nouns exhibit the following case forms:

|               | Singular | Plural  |
|---------------|----------|---------|
| Common case   | *girl*   | *girls* |
|               | *lady*   | *ladies* |
|               | *woman*  | *women* |
| Genitive      | *girl's* | *girls'* |
|               | *lady's* | *ladies'* |
|               | *woman's* | *women's* |

Note that the formal contrasts are fewer in the spoken language: the pronunciation of the vast majority of nouns ending in -*s* in the plural does not distinguish between common case plural, genitive singular, and genitive plural. This is why a construction with an *of*-postmodifier is often preferred to one with a genitive plural (*the sister of the boys* rather than *the boys' sister*).

If the noun ends in a "voiced s" (i.e. the sound rendered as /z/ in phonemic transcription) in the common case singular, the written language most often constructs the genitive by adding an apostrophe, but no *s*, whereas the spoken language usually adds /ɪz/:

```
(1)    Written language:    Simms' (besides Simms's) wife
                            Dickens' (besides Dickens's) house
       Spoken language:    /'sɪmzɪz (besides 'sɪmz) 'waɪf/
                            /'dɪkɪnzɪz (besides 'dɪkɪnz) 'haus/
```

If in the common case singular the pronunciation of the noun ends in /iːz/, however, the spoken language usually does not add /ɪz/:

```
(2)    Euripides' plays, Socrates' wife   (Greek names)
```

Certain institutional names, and abstracts used in the fixed expression *for...sake*, ending in /s/ or /z/ never take a genitive suffix other than, in writing, the apostrophe:

```
(3)    Guy Fawkes' Day, St. Giles' Hospital
(4)    For goodness' sake, for conscience' sake
```

*Pronouns (14.2.2-14.2.4)*

14.2.2 The most extensive manifestation of the case system is to be found in the **personal pronouns**:

|              | Singular |        | Sg/Pl   | Plural  |         |
| ------------ | -------- | ------ | ------- | ------- | ------- |
|              | 1st psn  | 3rd psn | 2nd psn | 1st psn | 3rd psn |
| Subjective   |          | *he*    |         |         |         |
| case         | *I*      | *she*   |         | *we*    | *they*  |
|              |          | *it*    |         |         |         |
|              |          |         | *you*   |         |         |
| Objective    |          | *him*   |         |         |         |
| case         | *me*     | *her*   |         | *us*    | *them*  |
|              |          | *it*    |         |         |         |
| Geni- 1      |          | *his*   |         |         |         |
| tive         | *my*     | *her*   | *your*  | *our*   | *their* |
| case         |          | *its*   |         |         |         |
| 2            |          | *his*   |         |         |         |
|              | *mine*   | *hers*  | *yours* | *ours*  | *theirs* |
|              |          | *(its)* |         |         |         |

*Its* hardly ever occurs in the genitive 2 function.

As what we have called Genitive 1 and Genitive 2 differ not only formally but also functionally (see § 14.3.6-14.3.8), it would not have been unreasonable to regard the pronominal case system as having four terms instead of three. However, in deference to traditional terminology we will use the term "genitive" for both of them.

14.2.3 The **relative pronouns** and the **interrogative pronouns** share one item which varies according to case, viz. (subjective case) *who*, (objective case) *whom*, (genitive) *whose*:

```
(5)    Who do you think you're talking to?
(6)    I don't know who(m) to ask
(7)    The girl, who(m) I had never met before, was younger than
       I had expected
(8)    Is that the lady whose car was stolen?
```

As indicated, the subjective case is used to a large extent as a common case at the expense of the objective case, especially in informal language. The objective case is obligatory after a junctive (preposition), but this construction is not very common in the spoken language. Compare:

(9)   He is one of those people *of whom* posterity will say that
      he did his best
(10)  I don't know *who* you're talking *about*

14.2.4  The **indefinite pronouns**, *some-, any-, no-, everybody/one*, are like the nouns in adding *-s* in the genitive and not distinguishing between a subjective and an objective case:

(11)  It isn't *anybody's* fault, really

**The Functions of the Case Forms (14.3.1-14.3.8)**

*Overview (14.3.1)*

14.3.1  Whereas options both within the number system and the specification system were seen to depend on the reference of the noun phrase, i.e. on aspects of noun phrase meaning, the choice of case form is primarily based on the syntactic function of the noun phrase (the functions of the noun phrase have been dealt with in § 11).

Some typical case-form/NP-function correspondences have been outlined in the following table. See also § 14.3.2 ff.

| **FORMAL CASE SYSTEM:** | | **NP FUNCTIONS as:** |
|---|---|---|
| **H in NP:**<br>**1) Noun**<br>**2) Indef.pron.** | **H in NP:**<br>**1) Pers.pron.**<br>**2)** *who* | |
| Common case | Subjective case | Subject<br>Subject Complement |
| | Objective case | Direct object<br>Indirect object<br>Object complement<br>Adverbial<br>Any constituent introduced by Junctive |
| Genitive | Genitive 1 | Determiner<br>Nominator |
| | Genitive 2 | Head |

It is important to realize that just as the same form may have several syntactic functions, as indicated by the table in § 14.3.1, the same function can be realized by two different forms. The latter fact does not emerge from the table but has been taken into account in the following comments on the case-form realization of particular functions.

### *The subjective and the objective case (14.3.2-14.3.5)*

14.3.2  The subjective/objective case **as subject:** The subjective case is used in finite clauses,[30] whereas nonfinite clauses use the objective case –

(1)    *She* wants *me* to leave
(2)    *Me* apologize to him – never!

14.3.3  The subjective/objective case **as subject complement:** The subjective case is used in very formal language, whereas the stylistically neutral, hence most common, realization is the objective case —

(3)    It is *I*; this is *she*
(4)    It was *him*; next time it might be you or *me*

There is a tendency to use the subjective case in the subject complement of cleft clauses, especially before a relative clause with *who* as subject:

(5)    It was *he* who fired the fatal shot

14.3.4  The subjective/objective case **as direct/indirect object, object complement, adverbial**: Only the objective (and common) case occurs. The object complement, and adverbials without a junctive, are never realized by a pronoun. For examples, see §§ 11.1-11.2).

14.3.5  The subjective/objective case **as any constituent introduced by a junctive:** only the objective (and common) case occurs, regardless of the function of J + NP:

(6)    She was smiling *at him*
(7)    He gave it *to her*

With some junctives which can introduce clauses as well as noun phrases (e.g. *as* and *than*), the objective case alternates with the subjective case. Although the

---

30. Finite clauses with an objective form as subject are considered "incorrect":
        a.     Me and Tom tried to help them/We tried...them, Tom and me.
Speakers of standard English have a general awareness of this, but in their effort to avoid the objective case they often replace it by the subjective case even where the former would be the more "correct" form; such linguistic behavior is called "hypercorrection":
        b.     They arrived after my wife and I.
The expression, *between you and I*, is now probably more frequent than *between you and me*. A *-self* form is often used to avoid the problem of choosing between the subjective and the objective case (see § 16.3.7):
        c.     She sent a letter to my brother and *myself*.

objective case is by far the more common form, some speakers would use the subjective case if the noun phrase is felt to represent the subject:

```
(8)     Nobody knows that better than me    ...better than I (do)
                                   J    H                 J    S   (V)
                              ————————  —————        ————————  ———————
                                 H      POM             H      POM
        ——————  ———  ————  —————————————————     —————————————————————
          S      V   DO            A                        A
```

```
(9)     You are as bad as him      ...as bad as he (is)
                        J    H                J    S   (V)
               —————  ———————————       —————  ———————————
                J  H     POM              J  H     POM
        —————  ———  ——————————————     ——————————————————
          S     V       SC                     SC
```

With *as* and *than*, however, there is sometimes a difference of meaning involved in the subjective/objective-case distinction:

```
(10)    She hates Chris as much as I (do)
(11)    She hates Chris as much as (she hates) me
```

### The genitive (14.3.6-14.3.8)

14.3.6 The genitive **as determiner:** The most common function of the genitive noun phrase is as determiner,

```
(12a) The girl's dress      12b)   Her dress
         D     H                   ——————  —————
      ——————  —————                  D       H
        D       H
```

In this function the genitive most frequently has definite specific reference, lending definite specific reference to the rest of the noun phrase as well (as in *Peter's hat*). If the determiner is needed for other meanings besides those conveyed by the genitive, the genitive is moved to the postmodifier and, as far as the personal pronouns are concerned, given the form of genitive 2.[31] For instance, when we want the noun phrase as a whole to have indefinite or generic reference:

```
(13)    A friend of my mother's had come to see us      (not "my
        mother's friend" unless she only has one friend)
(14)    I borrowed two books of hers
(15)    That is no concern of mine
```

or when the determiner is occupied by a demonstrative pronoun:

```
(16)    That funny nose of yours
```

It is important to realize that the genitive form is a feature of the whole of the rankshifted noun phrase and not just of the head. In other words, the genitive

---

31. Genitive 1 occurs when *own* is head of the genitive: *They have a small house of their own*

suffix is attached to the last constituent of the rankshifted noun phrase, which is not always the (only) head:

(17)   *John and Mary's* car (the rankshifted NP has two coordinated H's)
(18)   In *a day or two's* time
(19)   *My father-in-law's* briefcase   (the rankshifted NP has a POM realized by J + NP)
(20)   *The Queen of England's* heir

This type of construction has traditionally been referred to as the **group genitive**. In colloquial language, the group genitive sometimes occurs also when the postmodifier of the rankshifted noun phrase is not part of a fixed expression like those of (19) and (20):

(21)   *One of the girls in my class's* grandmother

but otherwise the construction is avoided by turning the genitive noun phrase into an *of*-postmodifier:

(22)   The grandmother *of one of the girls in my class*

14.3.7   The genitive **as nominator (N3):** The choice between the genitive and the common case here is idiomatically determined —

(23)   A bird's nest —   A horse shoe
       $\dfrac{\quad\overline{\text{N}\quad\text{H}}\quad}{\overline{\text{D}}\quad\text{H}}$   $\dfrac{\quad\overline{\text{N}\quad\text{H}}\quad}{\overline{\text{D}}\quad\text{H}}$

(24)   A *driver's* license (AE)   — A *driving/driver's* licence (BE)

As a nominator the genitive has generic reference, i.e. it classifies the head (see § 10.6.3), whereas specification (any type), of the noun phrase as a whole, is taken care of by the determiner. This is why personal pronouns are extremely rare in the function of nominator (*a his-and-her shop*).

Note that noun phrases may be ambiguous as to whether the genitive functions as determiner or nominator (though when it functions as nominator the ensuing head usually loses its main stress):

(25)   The prize was awarded to *some outstanding children's physicians*

compare:

(25a)  some outstanding 'children's phy'sicians
       $\dfrac{\overline{\text{D}\qquad\text{E}\qquad\qquad\text{H}}}{\text{D}}\qquad\dfrac{\quad}{\text{H}}$

(25b)  some outstanding 'children's physicians
       $\dfrac{\overline{\text{D}\qquad\text{E}}}{}\quad\dfrac{\overline{\text{N}\qquad\qquad\text{H}}}{\text{H}}$

14.3.8 The genitive **as head:** Besides functioning as determiner or nominator in a noun phrase (see §§ 14.3.6-14.3.7), the genitive may also occur independently, in which case pronouns have the genitive 2 form. Compare:

(26)  Here is your book — That's my pen — Have you seen Tim's hat?
         D   H                  D  H                       D      H
              S                    SC                           DO

(27)  Here is yours — That's mine — Have you seen Tim's?
         (H)              (H)                      (H)
          S                SC                       DO

Note that it would also be possible, in (27), to regard *Tim's* as the determiner of an elliptic noun phrase.

In § 14.3.6 we saw examples of noun phrases with a genitive as head realizing the postmodifier, of the type,

(28)  A friend of my mother's            A friend of ours
                 J  D     H                        J   H
         D   H      POM                   D   H    POM

Such noun phrases also function as adverbials of place, in reference to certain businesses, institutions or somebody's home (pronouns do not occur in this function):

(29)  He is off *to the dentist's* (clinic)/*the grocer's* (shop)
(30)  You really must visit *St. Paul's* (Cathedral)
(31)  I spent the weekend *at my brother's* (home)

**Use of the Genitive: Semantic Considerations (14.4.0-14.4.5)**

*Genitive vs.* **of**-*postmodifier (14.4.0-14.4.3)*

14.4.0 The genitive alternates with the *of*-postmodifier. The following **tendencies** in the use of the two constructions apply only to nouns, as there are no corresponding restrictions on the use of pronominal genitives, see § 14.4.3.

14.4.1 The **GENITIVE** is used with reference to —
(A) **persons, animals** or **personified objects/concepts**:

(1)   *Joe's* problems, *the dog's* tail, *the doll's* pretty dress

including organizational bodies and institutions:

(2)   *The government's* plan, *the firm's* personnel

In literary language, it is possible to use the genitive with things or concepts that can be thought of as having a kind of organic existence of their own; this is sometimes done in accordance with the principle that new/important items of information tend to occur after given/less important items (see §§ 4.2.0 and 6.3). Compare (3) with (4):

(3)    *The mind's* development, *the play's* true importance, *the
       scheme's* implementation
(4)    The development *of the mind*, the importance *of the play*,
       etc.

This is also true for geographical locations, when they are personified or
thought of in terms of the people inhabiting them, cp.

(5)    *America's* intervention, *Britain's* economy, *the earth's*
       resources, *the sun's* rays
(6)    The economy *of Britain*, the resources *of the earth*

(B) **units of time and distance**:

(7)    *Yesterday's* news, *six months'* leave, (at) *a yard's* distance,
       *a cable's* length, *a stone's* throw

The genitive can be used, furthermore,
(C) when the **head** is realized by the nouns *edge, end, sake, surface, worth* (the
genitive is obligatory with *worth*):

(8)    At *the river's* edge/*journey's* end (or *at the edge/end
       of...*), on *the lake's* surface (or *on the surface of...*)
(9)    For *efficiency's* sake
(10)   *Their money's* worth

(D) when it would be **difficult to fit in an *of*-postmodifier** without risking
clumsiness or ambiguity, because there are other postmodifiers:

(11)   *The book's* solution *to these problems*
       (cp. The solution *of the book to these problems*)
(12)   *His journey's* development *into a nightmare*
       (cp. The development *of his journey into a nightmare*)

14.4.2   The *OF*-POSTMODIFIER is the construction generally used
         (A) with **things** and **abstracts** (though see also § 14.4.5):

(13)   The fields *of the farm*, the top *of the table*, the importance
       *of the play*, the fall *of the Roman Empire*, the destruction
       *of the forest*

(B) **to prevent a relative clause from getting separated** from its antecedent (see
also §§ 14.2.1, 14.3.6 (21)-(22)):

(14)   The brother *of the girl who had bought the pretty dress*
       (cp. The girl's brother who had bought the pretty dress)

(C) when the **head** of the noun phrase which might have been in the genitive
is an **adjective**:

(15)   The inability *of the weak* to defend themselves

14.4.3 The above restrictions on the use of the genitive do not apply to **PRO-NOMINAL GENITIVES**, cp.:

```
(16)   The fields of the farm — the farm whose fields...
(17)   The fall of the Roman Empire — its fall
(18)   The destruction of the forest — its destruction
```

*Possessive, subjective, objective genitive (14.4.4-14.4.5)*

14.4.4 The main syntactic function of the genitive, as we have seen, is to connect a noun phrase in a premodifier to its head. The typical semantic content of this relationship is that the head "belongs to" whatever the premodifier noun phrase refers to. This use of the genitive is known by tradition as the **possessive genitive**, although "ownership," as in (19), is only a subcategory of its meaning, e.g.

```
(19)   Celia's money    (cp. Celia has some money)
(20)   The cat's paws   (cp. The cat has paws)
(21)   South Africa's dilemma  (cp. South Africa has a dilemma)
```

Furthermore, genitive and head may correspond to subject and verbal, when the head is realized by a noun derived from a verb, in which case we refer to the genitive as the **subjective genitive**:

```
(22)   The President's arrival  (cp. The President arrived)
(23)   The court's decision  (cp. The court decided)
(24)   Her hatred of her stepmother  (cp. She hated...)
```

Finally, the genitive may correspond to the object of the verbal content of the head noun, in which case we call it the **objective genitive**:

```
(25)   The President's assassination  (cp. Somebody assassinated
       the President)
(26)   Their release  (cp. Somebody released them)
(27)   Germany's defeat  (cp. Somebody defeated Germany)
```

Note that sentences like:

```
(28)   She took my picture
(29)   He arranged Jonathan's donation
```

are ambiguous with regard to whether the genitive is possessive or objective (28), or subjective or objective (29). To ensure the interpretation of the genitive as objective, a *by*-postmodifier corresponding to the subject is often added:

```
(30)   Denmark's liberation by Britain
```

whereas an *of*-postmodifier corresponding to the object may be added if the genitive is to be unequivocally subjective:

```
(31)   Britain's liberation of Denmark
```

14.4.5  Both the subjective and the objective genitive may be replaced by the *of-*
postmodifier, though the genitive is the predominant form with personal names,
cp.:

(32)    The arrival *of the President*
(33)    The assassination *of the President*
(34)    *Bill's* resignation   (cp. *Bill resigned*)
(35)    *Bill's* promotion   (cp. Somebody *promoted Bill*)

# V.  PRONOUNS AND PRONOMINAL NOUN PHRASES

**Introduction (15.0.0-15.0.4)**

15.0.0  A noun phrase with a pronoun as head is called a pronominal noun phrase. So far, in our discussion of the noun phrase, we have focused especially on noun phrases that have a noun as head, although pronominal noun phrases were seen to participate in the three general systems of the noun phrase (number, specification and case, see §§ 12-14 *passim*). Much of what was said about the syntactic functions (§ 11) of the noun phrase in general applies to pronominal noun phrases as well, especially as regards its functions in the clause. However, the pronouns do have a number of special morphological and syntactic characteristics, often semantically determined, which have an influence on the structure and semantics of the noun phrase in which they occur.

15.0.1  The pronouns can be grouped as follows:

| | |
|---|---|
| **Personal** pronouns: | *I/me/my/mine, you/your/yours, he/him/his, we/us/our/ours*, etc. |
| *-self* **forms:** | *myself, yourself, himself, ourselves*, etc. |
| **Demonstrative** pronouns: | *this/these, that/those*, etc. |
| **Relative** pronouns: | *who/whom/whose, which, that*, etc. |
| **Interrogative** pronouns: | *who/whom/whose, which, what*, etc. |
| **Indefinite** pronouns: | *some(-body/one/thing), any(-body/one/thing), none/no(-body/one/thing), one, each, every(-body/one/thing)*, etc. |

15.0.2  The traditional name, "pronoun," is misleading if by this we understand a pro-form that replaces only the (head) noun. Only the form *one* is regularly used in this function, see (2) and (4) below. The typical function of a pronoun is in fact to replace a whole noun phrase, including all pre- and postmodifiers, which is why pronominal noun phrases are usually simple. Compare:

```
(1)    I want to buy the beautiful red dress that I saw in the
       window yesterday — I hope you haven't sold it.
(2)    I don't particularly care for that green dress — I liked the
       beautiful red one that I saw in the window yesterday better.
(3)    The young man's hat was lying on his suitcase
(4)    The black horse's saddle was heavier than the white one's
```

Sometimes the pronominal noun phrase has a postmodifier (5)-(7), whereas premodifiers do not occur except in a few fixed expressions (8)-(9) and in the case of *all* + demonstrative pronoun (10):

(5)     Tell me *something I don't know*
(6)     *Those in the middle* were being squashed
(7)     *What else* can I say?
(8)     Think of what would happen to *poor little me*!
(9)     I think we should give her *a little something* in token of our appreciation
(10)    *All this* is giving me a headache

15.0.3  Apart from realizing the **head** of a simple noun phrase, or being the head of a noun phrase with a postmodifier as in (5)-(7), the pronouns also frequently function as **determiners** (see § 10.3.2) in a noun phrase with a noun as head; such noun phrases, of course, are not called "pronominal":

(11)    *This puzzling answer* was ignored
(12)    *What business* is it of yours?
(13)    *Her daughter* lives in Japan

For other functions of the pronouns, see e.g. §§ 20.4. See also §§ 5.8-5.9.

15.0.4  The **functions of the pronominal noun phrase** are almost the same as those of the noun phrase in general, i.e. pronominal noun phrases occur at S, DO, IO, SC and in functions where the noun phrase is introduced by a junctive (i.e. where it is a prepositional phrase):

(14)    *Who* brought *them to you*   (S, DO, A)
(15)    Sheila gave *him* a present   (IO)
(16)    The burglar was *me*   (SC)
(17)    We have a picture *like this* at home   (POM in NP)
(18)    He was aware *of something*   (POM in AP)

though there are some functions, especially some adverbial functions, in which the pronominal noun phrase would be unacceptable in most contexts. Thus, whereas (19a) is immediately acceptable as the pronominalized version of (19), (19b) is not:

(19)    Denis met Amy in the park
        a.      *He* often met *her* in the park
        b.      *He often met her *in it*

Even in such adverbial functions, however, the pronominal noun phrase is often represented by certain specialized forms, e.g. *here, there, now, then, where, when*:

(20)    He often met her *there/Where* did he meet her?

In the present book these forms are regarded as marginal pronouns realizing the head of a simple pronominal noun phrase. Traditionally they have been regarded as adverbs, but their precise label in terms of word class is less important than the fact that they are pro-forms which, at clause level, function as adverbials. This is why they are sometimes referred to as "proadverbials," see §§ 17.5.1, 18.5.2, 19.5.1, 20.5.1.

## PERSONAL PRONOUNS (15.1-15.5.3)

### Definition (15.1)

15.1 The personal pronouns have been thus named because they make up a system of formal distinctions between the 1st, 2nd and 3rd person (*I*, *you*, *he/she/it*, in the singular). The system is shared by the *-self* forms (*myself*, *yourself*, *him-/her-/itself*), but as the functions of the latter are quite unique, we will treat the *-self* forms separately (§ 16).

The table in § 14.2.2 represents the systems of the personal pronouns, showing formal contrasts in terms of number, case, person and gender.

### Modification (15.2)

15.2 Personal pronouns most often realize simple noun phrases, i.e. they usually do not have any modifiers. They do occasionally, however, have a postmodifier realized by a nondefining[32] relative clause, or one of the forms *all*, *both*, *each* and (after a genitive) *own*:

(1) She remained unrewarded, whereas *he, who had accomplished far less than she*, was paid handsomely
(2) *We all/both/each* shook hands with her and thanked her
(3) She changed the song and made it *her own*

Appositions (see § 10.8.5), too, are sometimes possible:

(3) *We bachelors* have to be on our guard, you know
(4) Are you sure *you people* know what you're doing?
(5) *You three* work in the next room, and *you four* stay here

With cardinal numbers, as in (5), an alternative construction is one where the number becomes the head, the pronoun becoming the postmodifier: *the three of you*, etc.

---

32. Personal pronouns do not have defining postmodifiers in present-day English, though this construction is quite common in proverbs and in the language of the Bible:

a.  *He* who laughs last laughs longest.
b.  Children, how hard it is for *them* that trust in riches to enter into the kingdom of God (Mark 10.24).

**Grammatical Systems (15.3.0-15.3.7)**

15.3.0  The grammatical systems of the personal pronouns are **number, case, person**
and **gender**. Although the personal pronouns play an important part in the
specification system by always being either definite specific or generic, they do
not show formal variation in terms of specification, i.e. their two specification
values, definite specific and generic, cannot be distinguished by the form of the
pronoun. See § 13.6 on specification in the pronominal noun phrase.

*Number (15.3.1-2)*

15.3.1  The personal pronouns participate in the general number system of the noun
phrase (§ 12), by taking number-specific form in accordance with the noun
phrase they replace, or according to situational context, though their formal
number distinctions are irregular as compared with the +/- *s*-suffix of the
nouns:

| | |
|---|---|
| Singular: | *I, you, he/she/it* (*me* etc., *my* etc.) |
| Plural: | *we, you, they* (*us* etc., *our* etc.) |
| Uncountable (of neuter gender only): | *it, its* |

See also §§ 20.4.20-22 on forms with duality meaning.

15.3.2  **Use of *we*:** *We* refers to "me and somebody else." If "somebody else" includes
the 2nd person, *we* is called **inclusive**. If the 2nd person is not included, *we* is
called **exclusive**. Compare:

(1)     *We* never see each other any more (you and I and perhaps some
        other people)
(2)     *We* never see each other any more (Carol and I)

*We*, furthermore, is used as the socalled "editorial *we*" when there is only one
editor/author (3), and as "patronizing *we*" (4); whereas as "majestic *we*," used
by the monarch about him- or herself, it is now archaic (5):[33]

(3)     *We* will now proceed to a different problem, which is related
        to the one *we* discussed in chapter four
(4)     (Nurse to patient) How are *we* feeling today?
(5)     *We* are not amused   (attributed to Queen Victoria)

See also § 13.6.2.

---

33. Margaret Thatcher was sometimes criticized for using *we* in a way that was indistin-
guishable from the "majestic *we*," in reference to (herself as leader of) the British government.

*Case (15.3.3)*

15.3.3  The personal pronouns contribute to the case system of the noun phrase, in fact, they have retained a more elaborate case system than the common-case/genitive distinction of the nouns:

| | |
|---|---|
| Subjective case: | *I, he/she/it, you, we, they* |
| Objective case: | *me, him/her/it, you, us, them* |
| Genitive 1: | *my, his/her/its, your, our, their* |
| Genitive 2: | *mine, his/hers, yours, ours, theirs* |

For details of the system, see § 14.2.2 ff.

*Person (15.3.4)*

15.3.4  This system, peculiar to the personal pronouns (see § 15.1), covers the following form/reference correspondences:

1st person ==> the speaker
2nd person ==> the addressee
3rd person ==> other people, things or concepts

Note that *we, you* and *they* can also be used generically, in which case the differences between them in terms of person become somewhat blurred. See § 13.6.2.

*Gender (15.3.5-15.3.7)*

15.3.5  Formal gender distinctions are found only in the pronouns, and only in the 3rd person singular. The personal pronouns distinguish between *he, she* and *it*. The gender distinctions refer to **natural gender**, i.e. male persons are referred to by *he* (masculine), female persons by *she* (feminine), and animals, objects and concepts by *it* (neuter). Exceptions to this rule are for the most part due to the fact that certain animals (regardless of sex), objects and concepts may be subjectively associated with either masculine or feminine qualities.

15.3.6  **Animals**, in other words, are referred to by *it* unless there are special reasons to do otherwise. Thus, if the sex of the animal is focused on (through the use of nouns like *bitch, mare, tomcat,* etc.), *he/she* is used. *He/she* is also used when the speaker is showing interest in the animal (the particular animal or the breed or species); in such cases, if the sex of the animal is irrelevant or unknown, *he* is used more frequently than *she*, though one very common pet, the cat, tends to be referred to by *she*. Note that pets are often personified to the point of taking *who* (7) as relative pronoun (see § 18.3.2), other animals requiring *which*:

```
(6)    A dog had run out in front of our car, and we had crashed
       trying to avoid it
(7)    The bitch was feeding her puppies, except one who was busy
       chasing his tail
(8)    If a cat loses her appetite, it may not be because there is
       something wrong with her
```

**Terms for little children** (e.g. *baby, child, infant*) are referred to by *he/she*, unless the child's sex is unknown or irrelevant, in which case *it* is used (though not by the child's own family):

```
(9)    The baby had dropped its rattle, and it was crying for its
       mother
```

**Means of transport**, though normally referred to by *it* like most "things," frequently take *she* (especially ships):

```
(10)   The psychological effect of the sinking of the Bismarck
       should not to be underestimated, because she was the pride
       of the German navy
(11)   I finally decided to get rid of my old car, after she had
       served me well for nearly fifteen years
```

**Countries** are referred to by *it* when thought of in terms of geography, and by *she* when conceived of as nations:

```
(12)   Canada is a huge country in terms of square miles, though
       in terms of population it is quite small
(13)   Canada's attitude toward her big ally to the south has
       always been ambivalent
```

**Literary personification**: There is in principle no limit to the type of phenomenon which may be personified in literary language. By convention, however, certain natural phenomena such as the sun (*he*), the moon (*she*), rivers (*he*), etc., as well as philosophical concepts like "freedom" (*she*) "justice" (*she*), "wisdom" (*she*), "death" (*he*), are frequently personified and given the gender of the corresponding Latin word:

```
(14)   The moon had raised her pale shiny face in wonder
(15)   Old man river, he just keeps rolling along
(16)   I love Wisdom more than she loves me
```

15.3.7 If the sex of the persons referred to is unspecified, *he* is often used with reference to both male and female. This usage is sometimes felt to discriminate against women, however, in which case the most frequent alternatives are *he or she* and *they* (after indefinite pronouns):

```
(17a)  We need another language teacher, and he must be able to
       teach phonetics
(17b)  We need another language teacher, and he or she must be able
       to teach phonetics
(18)   If anyone calls, tell him/them I'm not in
```

**The Functions of *It* (15.4.1-15.4.8)**

15.4.1 *It*, as the neuter form, has the **regular** functions and types of reference of a personal pronoun in the 3rd person singular, in accordance with the above and § 13.6.1:

(1)  If *the phone* rings, don't answer *it*  (anaphoric reference)
(2)  Although *it* was zealously guarded, *the secret* was eventually leaked to the press  (cataphoric reference)

However, *it* also has a number of special functions:

15.4.2 *It* can have **anaphoric reference to a whole clause** (see further § 5.9):

(3)  They didn't believe her when she told them *she had been to prison*, but *it* was quite true

15.4.3 *It* can have **anaphoric reference to (part of) the predicate** of a clause (see also § 5.8):

(4)  I will *help you with your homework* this time, but I won't do *it* again

15.4.4 *It* can function as **preliminary subject**, and (in certain idioms) as **preliminary object**:

(5)  It is true that I didn't try to hurt her on purpose
     S=  V  SC                                    =S

(6)  Is *it* possible *to buy a drink there on Sundays*?

(7)  They saw to *it* that no one got hurt
     S    V    DO=      =DO

(8)  I take *it* you already know?

The functions as preliminary subject/object, as well as the functions described below in §§ 15.4.5-15.4.8, may be characterized as **"slot-filler"** functions. In the case of the (preliminary) subject, *it* simply fills the subject "slot" without referring to anything, simply because the structure requires a subject in initial position. See also § 6.2.

15.4.5 *It* can function as the **subject of a cleft clause**, which may be regarded as a type of preliminary-subject construction (see further § 5.4.2):

(9)  It was Brendon who stole Carlo's watch
     S=  V   SC        =S

(10) *It* was the watch *that Brendon stole*

15.4.6 *It* can function as the **subject of "identifying" utterances**:

```
(11)   Who is the gorgeous redhead in the corner? — It is our dean
(12)   Cliff answered the door — it was his father
(13)   Why do you look so unhappy? — It is all these utility bills
       I've just had
```

Note that *it* is neutral with respect to gender and number reference in this function.

If the utterance "defines" something rather than "identifying" it, *it* cannot be used:

```
(14)   What are "rivets"? — They are bolts for fastening metal
       plates
(15)   Who is Dorothy? — She is the manager
```

15.4.7  *It* is also just a slot-filler when used as subject in expressions about **weather/climate/environment**, as well as **distance** and **point in time**:

```
(16)   It is raining/snowing
(17)   It is foggy/windy
(18)   It's cold/awfully quiet in here
(19)   How far is it to the nearest garage?
(20)   What time is it? — It's two o'clock
(21)   It must be ages since I've seen him
```

If distance and time are conceived of as space to be covered (23), or space available (25), *there* is used instead of *it*. Compare:

```
(22)   It's a long way to Tipperary; it's a long way to go
(23)   There is still a long way to go before we can rest
(24)   It's time to say goodbye
(25)   There is still time to say goodbye
```

15.4.8  *It* as a mere slot-filler realizes various constituents in certain **idiomatic expressions**, of which the following are but a few:

```
(26)   It said in the papers that the government was ready to
       resign
(27)   That's it  ("the task is completed")
(28)   This is it, then  ("the time has come")
(29)   This is overdoing it
(30)   You've had it  (slang: "you will get no more chances")
(31)   Damn it!
(32)   Run for it!
```

**The Functions of the Pronominal Genitive (15.5.1-15.5.3)**

*Determiner: Genitive 1 (15.5.1-15.5.2)*

15.5.1  The genitive-1 forms (*my, his/her/its, your, our, their*) realize the determiner of a noun phrase:

```
(1)    My car had been stolen
       D   H
       ‾‾‾‾‾
        S
```

There are few restrictions on the use of pronominal genitives as determiner. The objective genitive frequently **replaces an *of*-postmodifier**, e.g.

```
(2)    He wanted to take my picture (cp. He wanted to take a
       picture of me)
```

However, the objective genitive cannot replace the *of*-postmodifier in a number of idiomatic expressions:

```
(3)    She doesn't like the look of him
(4)    On the face of it, his story seems unconvincing
(5)    I couldn't for the life of me see what was wrong
(6)    You'll soon get the hang of it
```

15.5.2 A noun phrase introduced by a genitive is most often definite specific, i.e. genitive 1 **alternates with the definite article**:

```
(7)    He got into his car and drove off
(8)    He got into the car and drove off
```

*His* makes the noun phrase definite specific through its reference to *he*. *The* presupposes that the identity of the car is already known to the addressee. The noun phrase may well refer to the same car, in (7) and (8).

Genitive 1 may also have a **reflexive function** (cp. § 16.3.1 ff.), i.e. the noun phrase in which it occurs refers to something which is "part of" what the subject refers to: parts of the subject's body, the subject's personal effects, clothing, or mental or physical processes. Here the definite article is not possible:

```
(9)    He put his hands in his pockets
(10)   They took off their shoes
(11)   We changed our minds
(12)   She lost her balance
```

On the other hand, the definite article, not the genitive, is used when the part of the body etc. belongs to the **object**, or to a subject representing the afficative case role in relation to an action (see § 6.4), as in passive clauses (15a) but cp. also (15b):

```
(13)   He took me by the hand
(14)   I shot him in the foot by accident
(15a)  He had been hit on the head with a blunt instrument
(15b)  He had received a blow on the head with a blunt instrument
```

The definite article in such cases is part of a noun phrase with a junctive (a prepositional phrase) functioning as adverbial.

Certain idiomatic, more or less metaphorical expressions, require the definite article rather than the genitive, e.g.

```
(16)   The child was choking and had turned blue in the face
(17)   She has rock music on the brain
(18)   We were armed to the teeth
```

### Head: Genitive 2 (15.5.3)

15.5.3 When the genitive of the personal pronoun does not realize the determiner, it has the form of genitive 2 (*mine, his/hers, yours, ours, theirs*)[34] and realizes the head:

(18)   His office is <u>next to *mine*</u>
     <u>J    H</u>
        A

(19)   <u>*Ours*</u> was never a romantic relationship
 <u>H</u>
  S

Sometimes it realizes the head of a rankshifted noun phrase:

(20)   <u>A friend of *hers*</u> bought it in China
               J   H
    <u>D    H      POM</u>
          S

See further §§ 14.3.6 and 14.3.8.

## -*SELF* FORMS (16.1-16.3.7)

### Definition (16.1)

16.1   The -*self* forms are morphologically related to the personal pronouns, cp. their distinctions in terms of person:

|  |  |  | Singular | Plural |
|---|---|---|---|---|
| **1st person** | Genitive case of pers. pron. |  | *myself* | *ourselves* |
| **2nd person** | + -*self/selves* |  | *yourself* | *yourselves* |
| **3rd person** | Objective case of pers. pron. + -*self/selves* | (masc.) (fem.) (neut.) | *himself* *herself* *itself* | *themselves* |

In addition, the generic pronoun *one* (see § 13.6.2) has a -*self* form, *oneself*.

---

34. As regards *its*, see § 14.2.2.

**Modification and Grammatical Systems (16.2)**

16.2    -self forms are rarely modified, though a postmodifier is sometimes found, realized by the form *alone*:

    (1)    The diary was intended for *himself alone*

The -self forms exhibit the same grammatical systems as the personal pronouns apart from the case system, which is irrelevant here, i.e. **number** (§ 15.3.1-15.3.2), **person** (§ 15.3.4) and **gender** (15.3.5-15.3.7). Regarding specification, see §§ 15.3.0 and 13.6.

**Functions (16.3.0-16.3.7)**

16.3.0  The functions of the -self forms are much more limited than those of the personal pronouns. Their two primary functions are the **reflexive** function (§ 16.3.1-16.3.5) and the **emphatic** function (§ 16.3.6).

*The reflexive function (16.3.1-16.3.5)*

16.3.1  The -self form is reflexive when, in a function **corresponding to an ordinary complement or adverbial**, it refers to the same person (etc.) as the subject of the clause:

    (1)    He shot *himself*   (cp. He shot *the fox*)
    (2)    I gave *myself* a book for Christmas   (cp. I gave *him* a
           book..)
    (3)    You are not *yourself*   (cp. You are not *George*)
    (4)    She was sitting *by herself*   (cp. She was sitting *by the
           window*)

In (3) and (4) the -self form gives the statement a special meaning, though it is structurally equivalent to other subject complements/adverbials.

16.3.2  A number of verbs can be constructed as either intransitive or reflexive (with a reflexive -self form as object), i.e. the -self form is **optional** in the sense that its presence or absence makes little difference in meaning:

    (5)    We'll call the party off if you don't *behave (yourself)*
    (6)    She won't *adjust (herself)* to new conditions
    (7)    They washed *(themselves)* carefully

These verbs do not need the -self form to indicate that the action is directed toward the subject. Rather, the -self form focuses on the action as a process, indicating that it represents a conscious effort. Cp. (8) with (7):

    (8)    They had to wash before dinner

Some of these verbs, e.g. *dress, shave, adjust, wash,* may also take a normal object, being in this respect like those of § 16.3.1 (e.g. *She washed the child*).

16.3.3  The *-self* form is reflexive when it is **part of a complex verb** (the object of an object verb, see § 7.9.3), in which case it is obligatory and cannot be replaced by another form:

```
(9)    I would like to avail myself of this opportunity to thank
       you
(10)   You're always trying to ingratiate yourself with the boss
(11)   If you make that statement while under oath you will
       be perjuring yourself
```

This small group of verbs also includes e.g. *absent oneself (from), demean oneself, pride oneself (on)*.

16.3.4  After junctives and prepositional verbs, the *-self* form occurs regularly in its reflexive function to indicate that the action (etc.) relates to the subject as opposed to somebody else:

```
(12)   He was talking to himself
(13)   They were laughing at themselves
(14)   She thinks only of herself
(15)   You take too much upon yourself (you should let somebody
       help you)
```

If the contrast between the subject and somebody else is irrelevant, a personal pronoun is usually used instead, even when the form is clearly used reflexively:

```
(16)   Ahead of him he could see the tail lights of a big car
(17)   They placed the chest between them
(18)   They shared the money between them   (i.e. they shared the
       money between themselves)
(19)   Would you take it upon you to write the invitations?
       (cp. (15))
```

16.3.5  When the complement is realized by a nonfinite clause, the latter has the reflexive *-self* form as subject:

```
(20)   He found himself unable to solve the problem
                  ‾‾‾‾‾‾  ‾‾‾‾‾‾‾‾‾‾‾‾‾‾‾‾‾‾‾‾‾‾‾
                    S              SC
       ‾‾ ‾‾‾‾‾‾
       S   V                     DO
```

The fact that the reflexive *-self* form always points back to the last subject means that a *-self form* placed later in the nonfinite clause will refer to the subject (perhaps understood) of the nonfinite clause, not the subject of the main clause:

```
(21)   Al persuaded Bill to get himself a new suit
                           ‾‾‾‾‾‾ ‾‾‾‾‾‾‾ ‾‾‾‾‾‾‾‾‾
                             V      IO      DO
       ‾‾ ‾‾‾‾‾‾‾‾‾ ‾‾‾‾
       S      V      DO              OC

       (Bill got a new suit)

(22)   Al persuaded Bill to get him a new suit  (Al got a new suit)
```

### The emphatic function (16.3.6)

16.3.6 *-self* forms used reflexively may of course receive emphatic stress:

```
(23)  They weren't laughing at 'you, but at them'selves
```

but *-self* forms also have a special emphatic function which is syntactically distinct from their reflexive use: to emphasize the head of a noun phrase, a *-self* form may be used **as modifier**. Unless the noun phrase realizes the subject, the *-self* form has to occur immediately after its head, as a postmodifier (apposition):

```
(24)  Visitors to the castle were received by the owner himself
(25)  The grounds were pleasant, though she did not like the
      building itself
```

If the noun phrase realizes the subject, its *-self* modifier has some additional possibilities with regard to position in the clause, corresponding to those of the adverbial (27)-(29):

```
(26)  I myself had never seen Kathy swim
(27)  Myself, I had never seen Kathy swim   (I-pos)
(28)  I had never myself seen Kathy swim    (V-pos)
      H ___  ____  ____    POM   _____
      S- V-   A     -S     -V         DO

(29)  I had never seen Kathy swim myself    (F-pos)
```

### Stylistically determined functions (16.3.7)

16.3.7 In some cases the use of *-self* forms is a matter of style, often adding a degree of formality to the sentence. As in its reflexive function, the *-self* form realizes the head of the noun phrase, but this (simple) noun phrase does not refer to the same person as the subject, in fact it may itself realize (part of) the subject (33). It is often found after the junctives, *and, as, like* and *than*.

```
(30)  There is always someone worse off than yourself (cp. There
      is always someone worse off than you)
(31)  She is a businesswoman like myself
(32)  This was explained to my wife and myself
```

Sometimes a *-self* form is used to avoid the choice between the subjective and the objective case, if the speaker is uncertain as to which form would be the "correct" one to use (see § 14.3.2 n.). However, this may in fact result in utterances which some speakers feel are incorrect:

```
(33)  My colleague and myself would be happy to show you around
```

## DEMONSTRATIVE PRONOUNS (17.1.1-17.5.10)

### Definition (17.1.1-17.1.2)

17.1.1  The **central demonstratives** are: *this* (pl. *these*)/*that* (pl. *those*).
The **marginal demonstratives** are: *here/there, now/then, hence, thus, therefore*, etc.
(i.e. the marginal demonstratives that function as adverbials); *the former, the latter*; *such, so*.

   Unless otherwise stated, the following description concerns only the central demonstratives. The marginal demonstratives will be dealt with in § 17.5.

17.1.2  The traditional name, "demonstrative pronouns," captures their characteristic function of pointing out, or pointing at, something which is present in the situation:

```
(1)    This is my husband George
(2)    That's the door to the stockroom
```

This is often referred to as their **deictic** function and explains why it is normal (unmarked) for the demonstratives to carry emphatic stress; whereas emphatic stress is the exception (the marked choice) as regards the personal pronouns, which may also have situational reference. Compare:

```
(3)    When I said I wanted to go out with George, I didn't mean
       that George — I wouldn't go out with 'him!
```

*That*, in (3), is automatically interpreted as having contrastive meaning and so is necessarily stressed, whereas *him* needs the stress for the meaning to be contrastive ("...though I would have gone out with the other one").

   Although their defining characteristic is their deictic function, the demonstrative pronouns can also have textual reference:

```
(4)    What she did was unfair, but that's beside the point
       (anaphoric)
(5)    I'm not at liberty to reveal his name, but I will tell you
       this: he is a man of considerable influence  (cataphoric)
(6)    Although he obviously can't spell, this is hardly reason
       enough to reject his application  (anaphoric)
```

Note that *that* cannot have cataphoric reference.

**Modification (17.2)**

17.2 The form *all* (with uncountable or plural meaning) is practically the only possible **premodifier** when the head of the noun phrase is a demonstrative pronoun:

```
(1)    You can't eat all that/those
```

*Both* and *half* occur in the same function in British English, but in American English they normally become head of a noun phrase with an *of*-postmodifier:[35]

```
(2)    He can have both these   (BE)
(2a)   He can have both of these   (AE & BE)
(3)    Half these are mine   (BE)
(3a)   Half of these are mine   (AE & BE)
```

The **postmodifier** of a demonstrative pronoun, on the other hand, can have almost the same realizations as that of a noun, especially if the demonstrative pronoun is *those*: relative clauses (4)-(5); nonfinite clauses (6)-(7), except infinitive clauses; noun phrases introduced by a junctive (prepositional phrases, as in (8)); adjectives (9) and adverbial particles (10):

```
(4)    When I came to pick up the boots, they gave me these, which
       are too small
(5)    We often seem to prefer what is familiar to that which is
       new and untried
(6)    Those wishing to dine at the hotel must make their
       reservation before three o'clock
(7)    He felt sorry for those left behind
(8)    The postmodifier of a demonstrative pronoun can have almost
       the same realizations as that of a noun
(9)    The damage must be paid for by those responsible
(10)   The examples below are less ambiguous than those above
```

**Grammatical Systems (17.3.1-17.3.6)**

17.3.1 The grammatical systems of the demonstrative pronouns are **number** and **proximity**:

|  | Near | Distant |
|---|---|---|
| **Singular and uncountable** | *this* | *that* |
| **Plural** | *these* | *those* |

---

35. In British English speech, *both these* and *half these* are probably more common than the *of*-construction.

17.3.2 **Specification** is not indicated formally. The demonstratives are like the personal pronouns (see § 13.6) in having either definite specific or generic reference, i.e. they cannot have indefinite specific reference:

(1)     You've met most of my friends, but you haven't met *these*
(2)     I don't have anything to write on — can I use *this*?
(3)     Heaven helps *those* who help themselves

Generic reference is much less common than with the personal pronouns, except when *that* and *those* function as "prop" words (3). See also § 17.2 (5) above, and § 17.4.2.

17.3.3 **Gender** is not indicated formally, either, though gender reference to persons/nonpersons does determine the syntactic function of the pronoun: the **singular** forms *this* and *that* can function as **head** of the noun phrase only if they refer to **nonpersons**:

(4)     He had found another stone, but *this* was too heavy to lift
(5)     *Those* at the back of the plane escaped  (not *\*That* at the back...)
(6)     Don't buy a used car from Nick Dixon. *That* man is not to be trusted  (not...*\*That* is not to be trusted)

As we can see, there are no such restrictions on the use of the demonstrative as determiner ((6), see § 17.4.1), or in the plural (5). *This* and *that*, furthermore, have personal reference when used as deictic substitutes for *it* as subject of "identifying" utterances (see § 15.4.6):

(7)     *This* is my daughter Liz
(8)     *That* must be the famous athlete

*Number (17.3.4)*

17.3.4 *This* and *that* have the plural forms *these* and *those*, see the table in § 17.3.1. The number of the demonstrative corresponds to the number, in terms of form or content, of what it refers to (see § 12):

(9)     *That* story is sick!
(10)    Look, I've found your keys! — But *those* aren't mine
(11)    *This* is a lot better than the food we had yesterday
(12)    *These* are the musicians I was telling you about
(13)    *That* was a delightful three weeks

*Proximity (17.3.5-17.3.6)*

17.3.5 The distinction between that which is close to (*this/these*), and that which is distant from (*that/those*), the speaker — in space, time, or in terms of real/unreal — can be found in several different categories of the language:

| Near: | Distant: | (in terms of:) |
|-------|----------|----------------|
| *this* | *that* | (person, place, time, reality) |
| *I* | *you/he* etc. | (person) |
| *here* | *there* | (place) |
| *come* | *go* | (direction) |
| *now* | *then* | (time) |
| *today* | *yesterday* | |
| *(he) does* | *(he) did* | |
| *(he) does* | *(I wish he) did* | (reality) |

Everything else being equal, in other words, *this* (*these*) tends to be used in contexts such as those expressed by the items in the "Near" column, whereas *that* (*those*) is likely to occur in the contexts represented by the items in the "Distant" column:

(14)   *This* is Dorothy Jenkins speaking — is *that* you, Mr. Thompson?
(15)   Come and get *this* one over here, if you can't use *those* over there
(16)   What was *that*? I thought I heard something
(17)   Yesterday it didn't sound so loud, but the noise *this* morning is killing me!
(18)   Don't argue with me! I want you to do *this* for me now
(19)   I wish you wouldn't do *that*

17.3.6   **"Attitudinal proximity":** The basic distinction between *this* and *that* is one of spatial meaning, as in examples (14) and (15) above. Other meanings associated with *this/that* may be regarded as more or less metaphorical extensions of this distinction between "near" and "distant." Attitude, in particular, is frequently associated with proximity (cp. statements such as "they are *close* friends," "he is somewhat *remote* by nature," "she gave me a *distant* smile"). It is not surprising, therefore, that *this* ("near") should often indicate a positive attitude, whereas *that* ("distant") frequently has negative overtones:

(20)   My great-grandmother used to wear a crinoline, but *that* was in the time of Queen Victoria. Nowadays a woman can dress more comfortably because she is allowed to show her figure
(21)   *This* is my husband, and *this* is my youngest son   (formal introduction)
(21a)  *This* is my husband, and '*that* is my youngest son! (*that* is used in mock indication that the speaker is ashamed of "the little brat")

The distinction between *this* and *that* in terms of textual reference is another, and related, manifestation of attitudinal proximity: when they refer to something in the text, like *that* in (20), *that* can only have **anaphoric** reference, whereas **cataphoric** reference (reference to what comes next, i.e. to what the speaker's interest is focusing on) is expressed by *this*. *This* may also have anaphoric reference, when something said previously is being made relevant or brought into focus:

(20a)   My great-grandmother used to wear a crinoline, but *this* was in the time of Queen Victoria, when the style of women's clothing was dictated less by considerations of comfort than by...

People and things that the speaker wants to bring "close," so that they come alive, to the addressee, are often referred to by *this* in **lively narrative** (colloquial) style — often when they are being introduced into the story, as in (23). Conversely, through its meaning of "distance," *that* often conveys a distinctly **negative attitude** (cp. also (21a)):

(22)    I didn't even have time to get out of the way — all I felt was *this* terrific punch in my stomach
(23)    Well, there is *this* friend of mine, who has *this* great big St. Bernard, and he was taking it for a walk when he met *this*...
(24)    *That* idiot! Look! He has scratched my new car
(25)    I want to have a word with *that* husband of yours

### Functions (17.4.1-17.4.4)

17.4.1   The main functions of the demonstratives are those as **head** and as **determiner** of the noun phrase. The two functions have been distinguished only sporadically above, as they differ little in terms of the grammatical systems of the pronoun, and as the noun phrase is used in much the same way whether the demonstrative realizes the head or the determiner.

A notable exception is the fact that *this* and *that* (i.e. the singular forms) can refer to persons only when they realize the determiner, not when they realize the head, see § 17.3.3.

Other differences include the fact that the use of noun phrases as adverbials, if they have a demonstrative as head, is limited to a few types, primarily manner adverbials introduced by the junctive *like*:

(1)    You have to do it *like this*
(2)    Don't act *like that*

whereas their adverbial uses are not quite so limited, nor is the junctive always necessary, if the demonstrative is the determiner:

(3)    You have to do it *this way*
(4)    *(In) this way* we'll get it done *this week* (etc.)

The following describes some special uses of the demonstrative, as head and determiner respectively, in a noun phrase which has a defining postmodifier; as well as its function as a modifier of degree in the adjective/adverb phrase.

17.4.2 When *that* and *those* are used as head of a defining postmodifier, they are called **prop words**, i.e. they are used simply because the postmodifier needs a head (see also § 2.7.9). *This* and *these* cannot be used as prop words. In its **generic** use as prop word, *that* refers to something uncountable, usually a concept, whereas *those* refers to people in the plural:

(5)     We tend to believe *that which we hope*
(6)     The postmodifier of a demonstrative pronoun can have almost the same realizations as *that of a noun*
(7)     For *those who can't read* there is television

*That which* alternates with *what*, when used generically, *what* being the more common/informal form (see also § 3.7.1):

(8)     I couldn't very well give them *what/that which* I don't have

The prop-word function is also possible with **specific** reference, in which case *that* is uncountable or singular, used in reference to nonpersons, whereas *those* is plural, referring to persons or nonpersons:

(9)     It is the same example as *that on top of page 3*
10)     You haven't read any detective stories if you haven't read *those by Agatha Christie*

Instead of *that* (with singular reference), it is more common to use *the one*:

(9a)    It is the same example as *the one on page 3*

17.4.3 The demonstrative sometimes **replaces the definite article** as determiner, in noun phrases with a defining postmodifier. This happens when the speaker is jogging the addressee's memory (10), or for contrast (11), or because another, preceding, postmodifier causes doubt as to what is the head of the relative clause (12):

(10)    *That blue dress you were wearing at Martha's wedding* — do you still have it?
(11)    Only *those patients who can afford it* can expect to receive treatment
(12)    Never open *that window in the dining room which overlooks the river*

17.4.4 *This* and *that*, finally, function as **modifiers** of degree **in the adjective/adverb phrase**. Notice how the system of proximity works even here.
As **premodifiers** (colloquial style):

(13)    It can't have been *(all) that difficult*
(14)    The boy must have been about *this tall*

As **postmodifiers**, introduced by *as* and *than*:

(15)    Are you trying to bribe me? You should know better *than that*!
(16)    Does it get as hot *as this* in New York?

**Marginal Demonstratives (17.5.1-17.5.10)**

*The proadverbials (17.5.1)*

17.5.1  Proadverbials are pro-forms which function almost exclusively as adverbials (see also § 15.0.4). Some of them reflect the system of proximity, corresponding to the distinction between *this* and *that*:

**Near:**        *here, now*
**Distant:**     *there, then*

*Hence, thus* and some compound forms indicating cause, time, place etc. can refer to previously mentioned events or states, and are often used much like adverbs linking sentences together (i.e. adverbs functioning as conjuncts, cp. *consequently, accordingly*, see § 4.4.3). Some of them, however, can also have deictic reference (e.g. *thus* in (2) below). *Hence*, which belongs to formal language, usually means "this/that is the reason for":

(1)    He is an actor who has just experienced a major comeback.
       *Hence* his elation

*Thus* means "in this/that way" or "for this/that reason":

(2)    You simply fasten the papers with a clip: *thus*
(3)    She did not leave the party until 10:30. *Thus* she could not
       have committed the murder even if she left by car

Most of the compound forms, except *therefore*, are used only in formal, written language: *henceforth, hereafter/thereafter, herein/therein, heretofore*, etc.

**There** *as preliminary subject (17.5.2)*

17.5.2  *There* loses its meaning of place and becomes a mere slot-filler when functioning as **preliminary subject** (cp. *it*, § 15.4.4, and see § 6.2), in clauses pointing out the existence of something. The verb is nearly always a copula verb, usually *be*:

(4)    There are two men at the door
        S=   V    =S       A
(5)    *There is going to be* a party
(6)    *There is* something I want to tell you
(7)    There appears to be trouble in the kitchen
        S=         V      =S         A
        S-    V              -S

In literary style, however, a few intransitive verbs can also be constructed with *there* if the real subject is a long and heavy one, e.g.

(8)    In that village *there lived* an old man who was famous
       throughout the kingdom as a sage and soothsayer
(9)    *There comes* a time when even the gentlest person has to
       wield the sword

The form of the finite verb is determined by the real subject; compare, for instance, (4) and (5) above. In colloquial language, however, the singular form of the verb is often used automatically, before the speaker's mind is made up as to whether the subject is going to be singular or plural:

(10) *There was* a police woman and two men in white jackets in the hall

### The former *and* the latter *(17.5.3)*

17.5.3 *The former* and *the latter*, used to point out which of two previously mentioned noun phrases we are referring to, have the structure of a complex noun phrase, which is either elliptical (determiner + ordinator) or precedes a head:

(11) He arranged the piece for both string quartet and solo piano; personally, I prefer *the former version* to *the latter*

### Such *(17.5.4-17.5.7)*

17.5.4 *Such* means "of that kind," and most often has textual reference. It can function as a noun-phrase **premodifier**, in which case it has the same meaning whether its position makes it a predeterminer or an ordinator 3 (§§ 10.3.1 and 10.4.3):

(12) *Such* a student/*such* students will go far     (PrD)
(13) *Such* courage is rare these days     -
(14) You will do no *such* thing!     (O3)
(15) We don't have many *such* students     -

or as **head**:

(16) Her anger was *such* as to render them speechless
(17) Our representative will need an office and a car, if *such* are available

If the noun phrase in which *such* is head realizes the subject, as in (17), the number concord is determined by the content.

17.5.5 *Such* has anaphoric reference in most of the above examples, but as head it may also refer to a postmodifier introduced by *as* or *that* (see also (16) above):[36]

(18) His expertise was <u>such</u> <u>that nobody dared challenge it</u>
                                  H                   POM
                                       SC

---

36. Note that the expression, *such as it is/was*, has negative implications (see also § 18.4.7):

    a. His expertise, *such as it was*, was yet sufficient to give him a high standing among his even less knowledgeable fellows.

In formal (archaic) language *such* is sometimes used as prop-word head of a relative clause introduced by *as*, with reference to persons:

    b. *Such as heard him* were full of praise.

(19)    This is happening in countries such as Poland and Czecho-
                                              H              POM→
                                    J      H              POM→
                                                            A→

slovakia
←POM
←POM
←A

The noun phrase in which *such* is head may be divided:

(20)    This is happening in such countries as Poland and Czecho-
                                   H                           POM→
                            J     M-       H              -M→
                                                     A→

slovakia
←POM
←M
←A

As subject complement, the noun phrase in which *such* is head is often divided so that *such* occurs in initial position, causing inversion (in accordance with § 4.2.3), whereas its postmodifier has final position. Compare (18) and (21):

(21)    Such was his expertise that nobody dared challenge it
        H                         POM
        SC-  V      S             -SC

**17.5.6** *Such*, furthermore, may have **deictic** reference, usually as predeterminer:

(22)    Why do you have *such* a funny look on your face?
(23)    Is there always *such* a big crowd waiting outside her office?

**17.5.7** Finally, *such* is used to express **emphasis**, as predeterminer:

(24)    We had *such* a good time at the party yesterday
(25)    They are *such* hypocrites

## So (17.5.8-17.5.10)

**17.5.8** *So* has anaphoric reference when as **complement** or **adverbial** it refers to a clause or (part of) a predicate; see also §§ 5.8 and 5.9:

(26)    Chris is a bigot — *So* is Tom
(27)    Do you think she will accept? — I hope *so*
(28)    This is a secret, *so* don't tell him anything!

*So* may have either anaphoric or cataphoric reference when realizing the **premodifier of an adjective/adverb phrase** (AP, see §§ 21.2.2 and 21.2.4). The AP functions as subject complement or adverbial in the clause, or as predeterminer or postmodifier in a noun phrase.
Anaphoric reference:

(29) We'll build ourselves a house as big as a palace — Why does it have to be *so big*?
(30) We must leave at five o'clock — Do we have to go *so soon*?
(31) This principle has guided the lives of our family for generations.
    (a) *So fundamental* a principle is not to be thrown away casually
    (b) A principle *so fundamental* is not to be thrown away casually

Cataphoric reference, to a postmodifier realized by an infinitive or a finite clause, introduced by *as* or *that*, respectively:

(32) Their loss was *so* vast *as to be almost incomprehensible*
(33) She was *so* angry *that she could not speak*

**17.5.9** *So*, furthermore, may have **deictic** reference, sometimes alternating with *this/that* (§ 17.4.4) or *thus* (§ 17.5.1):

(34) How tall was he? — About *so/this* tall
(35) Fasten the papers with a clip, *so/thus*
(36) What's *so* funny?

**17.5.10** Finally, *so* may be used to express **emphasis**:[37]

(37) I'm *so* glad you could come
(38) She is *so* unhappy

## RELATIVE PRONOUNS (18.1-18.5.4)

### Definition (18.1)

**18.1** The **central relatives** are: *who/whom/whose, which, that*/zero.
The **marginal relatives** are: *what, when, where, why, how; as; whoever, whichever, whatever*.

The relative pronouns are named after their typical function, viz. that of relating the postmodifier clause in which they occur to its head (see also § 3.7.1):

(1)   The customer *who* had stolen the camera
     D    H           POM

See further about functions, § 18.4.

---

37. Note the special use of *so* in expressions with *many/much*:
    a.   They just sat there like *so many* dummies ("as if they were all [something negative]")
    b.   We have only *so much* money to spend ("only a limited amount of")

**Modification (18.2)**

18.2    Relative pronouns are rarely modified, though *all, both* and *each* (see § 15.2) may occasionally occur as postmodifiers, e.g.

(2)    Joan and Peter, *who both* wanted to wish her goodbye

**Grammatical Systems (18.3.0-18.3.3)**

18.3.0  The grammatical systems of the relative pronouns are **case** (only *who/-m/-se*), **gender** (*who/which*) and **defining/nondefining** (see the table):

|              | Defining or nondefining | Defining only |
|--------------|-------------------------|---------------|
| **Person**   | *who*                   |               |
|              |                         | *that* / zero |
| **Nonperson**| *which*                 |               |

Neither **number** nor **specification** is indicated formally in the relative pronoun. When the pronoun is the subject of the relative clause, the form of the finite verb, in terms of number, is determined by the head (antecedent) of the relative clause:

(3)    The *girl* who *is* missing...
(4)    The *girls* who *are* missing...

*Case (18.3.1)*

18.3.1  The case system is reflected in the difference between *who* (the subjective case), *whom* (the objective case) and *whose* (the genitive case). The general use of the case system has been dealt with in § 14, see in particular § 14.2.3.

*Gender (18.3.2)*

18.3.2  The gender system is minimally represented in the relative pronouns, in the distinction between *who/-m* (person) and *which* (nonperson):

(5)    My *sister, who* is a librarian, has got a job in Washington D.C.
(6)    The *house, which* was old and decrepit, was torn down last week

There is no gender distinction when the relative realizes the determiner (see § 18.4.7):

(7)    My *sister,* whose husband has left her, is now staying with us
(8)    She bought an old *car,* whose wheels looked as if they were coming off

though the use of *whose* in reference to nonpersons is often avoided by some speakers:

(9)     She bought an old *car*, the wheels *of which* (*of which* the
        wheels) looked as if they were coming off
(10)    She bought an old *car*, *which* looked as if the wheels were
        coming off

*Who* cannot be used when the relative pronoun functions as subject complement:

(11)    He is not the mathematical genius *(that)* I thought he was
(12)    He is regarded as  a mathematical genius, *which* he is[38]

| | | PRM | PRM | H | | | |
|---|---|---|---|---|---|---|---|
| S | V | | SC | | SC | S | V |

*That* can be used about persons as well as nonpersons, but usage in this respect varies both according to the function of the relative and according to style (see § 18.4).

### Defining/nondefining (18.3.3)

18.3.3 **Defining relative clauses** (see also § 3.7.1) are clauses whose content is necessary for the definition and/or specification of the whole noun phrase. All relative pronouns can occur in defining relative clauses. As far as the central relatives are concerned, this means *who, which, that*/zero (zero cannot occur as subject):

(13)    Gamblers *who cheat* will be prosecuted
(14)    The building *which suffered the least damage* was the
        hospital
(15)    The letter *(that) you sent me* made me very unhappy

Only *who* and *which*, however, can occur in **nondefining relative clauses**, i.e. relative clauses which give additional information, but which are not needed for the sake of definition or specification:[39]

(16)    The gambler, *who had at first refused to play*, was finally
        persuaded to join them
(17)    She was particularly fond of the grandfather clock, *which
        she had inherited from her grandfather*

For the marginal relatives and their use in defining as opposed to nondefining relative clauses, see § 18.5.

---

38. ...*which he is* corresponds to a new main clause = "and he 'is (a mathematical genius)."
39. Nondefining relative clauses, sometimes also defining ones, frequently correspond to adverbial clauses; cp. (13), (16), (17) with:
        13a.    Gamblers will be prosecuted *if they cheat*.
        16a.    *Although he had at first refused to play*, the gambler was
                finally persuaded to join them.
        17a.    She was particularly fond of the grandfather clock, *because
                she had inherited it from her grandfather*.

### Functions as Head of NP (18.4.0-18.4.6)

18.4.0 Only functions in which the central relative pronouns are involved will be dealt with in §§ 18.4.0-18.4.7. Functions peculiar to the marginal relatives will be treated in §§ 18.5.1-18.5.4.

*The pronominal NP is subject (18.4.1)*

18.4.1 *Who* (person) and *which* (nonperson) can always be used as subject of a relative clause, defining or nondefining:

```
(1)    The boy who is always playing football has broken his leg
(2)    Harry, who was to have played for the team next Sunday, has
       broken his leg
(3)    The book which disappeared from the library yesterday has
       been found
(4)    This beautiful little book, which has been missing for
       months, has finally been found
```

*That*, which can occur only in defining relative clauses, is less frequent than *who*, in reference to persons, especially in written language. In fact, *that* as subject with reference to persons is only common when the antecedent is premodified by particular (pre-)determiners and ordinators: *all, any, every, no, only*, ordinal numbers and superlatives:

```
(5)    Any boy that wants to succeed must work hard
(6)    She is the only person that can help you
(7)    The first rescuer that spotted her was my father
(8)    Einstein was the greatest genius that ever lived
```

and in cleft clauses:

```
(9)    It is Mrs. Jenkins that makes the decisions, not her husband
```

*That* can also be used instead of *which*, in reference to nonpersons, but this depends on stylistic factors: *that* is preferred in colloquial, *which* in written, language:

```
(10)   He gave me the book that/which inspired me to make my first
       film
```

*The pronominal NP is object and/or follows junctive (18.4.2-18.4.4)*

18.4.2 *Who/-m* (persons) and *which* (nonpersons) can be used both in defining and nondefining relative clauses. *Whom* is not common outside formal language, except in nondefining clauses, and after a junctive (where *who* cannot be used); see also § 14.2.3:

```
(11)   The robber who you "recognized" has turned out to be
       somebody else
(12)   The girl, who(m) I had never met before, was younger than
       I had expected
(13)   He is one of those people of whom posterity will say that
       he did his best
```

*That* or zero, in defining relative clauses, is frequently preferred in informal language to *who/-m*, though neither *that* nor zero is possible after a junctive (cp. (13)):

```
(11a)  The  robber  (that)  you  "recognized"  has  turned  out  to  be
       somebody else
(14)   The  house  (that)  she put up for sale yesterday has already
       been sold
```

If the relative clause and its antecedent are separated by other postmodifiers, it is sometimes necessary to use *who/which* to avoid ambiguity:

```
(15)   The  man  with the squeaky voice  who you dislike
           ‾‾‾  ‾‾‾‾‾‾‾‾‾‾‾‾‾‾‾‾‾‾‾‾‾‾‾  ‾‾‾‾‾‾‾‾‾‾‾‾‾‾‾
            H          POM
       ‾‾‾‾‾‾‾‾‾‾‾‾‾‾‾‾‾‾‾‾‾‾‾‾‾‾‾  ‾‾‾‾‾‾‾‾‾‾‾‾‾‾‾‾‾‾‾‾‾
       PRM            H                      POM
```

```
(15a)  The  man  with  the  squeaky  voice  which you dislike
                  ‾‾‾‾  ‾‾‾  ‾‾‾‾‾‾‾  ‾‾‾‾‾  ‾‾‾‾  ‾‾‾‾‾‾‾‾‾‾‾
                   J    PRM    PRM     H      POM
       ‾‾‾  ‾‾‾  ‾‾‾‾‾‾‾‾‾‾‾‾‾‾‾‾‾‾‾‾‾‾‾‾‾‾
       PRM   H              POM
```

```
(16)   What  was  in  the  briefcase  belonging  to  the  member  of
       Parliament which/who you picked up at the bar?
```

**18.4.3** A junctive connecting the relative pronoun to the verb is more often placed after the verb than before the pronoun, especially when the junctive is part of a prepositional verb (as in (17) and (18), see also § 7.9.2):

```
(17)   The  person  (that)  they  turned to  for guidance...
       ‾‾‾  ‾‾‾‾‾‾  ‾‾‾‾‾‾  ‾‾‾‾  ‾‾‾‾‾‾‾‾‾  ‾‾‾‾‾‾‾‾‾‾‾‾
                     DO      S      V            A
       ‾‾‾  ‾‾‾‾‾‾‾‾‾‾‾‾‾‾‾‾‾‾‾‾‾‾‾‾‾‾‾‾‾‾‾‾
        D    H              POM
```

```
(18)   Their  teacher,  whose knowledge  the project  depended on
(19)   The  idea  (that)  he  died  for
                   ‾‾‾‾‾  ‾‾  ‾‾‾‾  ‾‾‾
                    H           J
                    A-    S    V    -A
       ‾‾‾  ‾‾‾‾  ‾‾‾‾‾‾‾‾‾‾‾‾‾‾‾‾‾‾‾‾
        D    H           POM
```

whereas in formal language the junctive is often placed before the relative pronoun (always *whom/whose* or *which*):

```
(20)   The  person  to whom  they  turned  for guidance
       ‾‾‾  ‾‾‾‾‾‾  ‾‾‾‾‾‾‾  ‾‾‾‾  ‾‾‾‾‾‾  ‾‾‾‾‾‾‾‾‾‾‾‾
                   V-  DO     S     -V         A
       ‾‾‾  ‾‾‾‾‾‾‾‾‾‾‾‾‾‾‾‾‾‾‾‾‾‾‾‾‾‾‾‾‾‾‾‾
        D    H              POM
```

```
(21)   Their  teacher,  on whose knowledge  the project  depended
(22)   The  idea  for which  he  died
                  ‾‾‾‾‾‾‾‾‾  ‾‾  ‾‾‾‾
                     A        S   V
       ‾‾‾  ‾‾‾‾  ‾‾‾‾‾‾‾‾‾‾‾‾‾‾‾‾
        D    H         POM
```

**18.4.4** As a postmodifier in the noun phrase, introduced by a junctive, the relative may remain in its position after the head while the whole noun phrase is moved to the front of the relative clause:

```
(23)   (They stole a large number of bicycles,)
       the  majority  of which  they  have  sold
       ‾‾‾  ‾‾‾‾‾‾‾‾  ‾‾‾‾‾‾‾
                       J    H
       ‾‾‾  ‾‾‾‾‾‾‾‾  ‾‾‾‾‾‾‾  ‾‾‾‾  ‾‾‾‾‾‾‾‾‾‾‾
        D    H         POM
       ‾‾‾‾‾‾‾‾‾‾‾‾‾‾‾‾‾‾‾‾‾‾  ‾‾‾‾  ‾‾‾‾‾‾‾‾‾‾‾
              DO               S        V
```

or junctive + relative are moved to the front whereas the rest of the noun phrase remains in its "normal" position:

```
(24)   ...of which they have sold the majority
         J   H
         POM                           D    H
         DO-        S        V              -DO
```

or, in colloquial language, the relative alone is moved to the front whereas the rest of the noun phrase as well as the junctive remain in their "normal" position:

```
(25)   ...which they have sold the majority   of
          H                                    J
          POM-                        D    H   -POM
          DO-    S        V               -DO
```

### *The pronominal NP is subject complement (18.4.5)*

18.4.5  Only *that*/zero can be used in defining relative clauses; only *which* can be used in nondefining ones:

```
(26)   He is not the mathematical genius (that) I thought he was
(27)   She is regarded as a mathematical genius, which she is
(28)   He said it was Tom, which it wasn't
```

### *The pronominal NP refers to a clause (18.4.6)*

18.4.6  The relative clause has no postmodifying function when *which* or *what*, functioning in a nondefining relative clause, refers to a clause (or to the predicate of one). *Which* has anaphoric reference, and the relative clause functions as a coordinated main clause (see § 3.7.1):

```
(29)   He was late, which was unusual
(30)   He looked like a foreigner, which is unfortunate when you
       are looking for a job
```

*What* has cataphoric reference, the relative clause functioning as conjunct in the way it relates the following main clause to the preceding one, while its evaluativeness in relation to the second main clause makes it akin to a modal disjunct:

```
(31)   His money and credit cards had been stolen, but what was
       even more serious, his passport was gone
```

### **Functions as Determiner (18.4.7)**

18.4.7  Relatives realizing the determiner are neutral in terms of gender, i.e. they can refer to persons as well as nonpersons. *Whose* always realizes the determiner, see § 18.3.2. *Which* is occasionally used as determiner, most often in noun phrases introduced by a junctive (prepositional phrases), and only when the relative clause is nondefining:

(32)   They were now waiting for Joan, *on which individual* the success of the entire operation depended
(32)   Sometimes they expect him to make a speech, *in which case* he is in a state of terrible anxiety throughout the meal

*What* (meaning "the little/few...") and *what-/whichever* (see § 18.5.3) are sometimes used as determiners. In this function they may be regarded as "misplaced" relatives to the extent that they preclude the use of a relative pronoun in the following relative clause with which they correlate:

(33)   *What* information *he had* was soon sold in exchange for tobacco
(34)   She invited *what* friends *she still had left*
(35)   *What-/whichever* solution *I choose* is bound to fail

The construction with *what* alternates with *such...as* (see also § 7.5.5 n.):

(36)   *Such* information *as he had* was soon sold in exchange for tobacco

## Marginal Relatives (18.5.1-18.5.4)

### What *(18.5.1)*

18.5.1  Some marginal relatives do not need an explicit antecedent, the antecedent being included in the meaning of the relative pronoun itself. *What* in this function can be paraphrased by *that which*, see also § 3.7.1 (as for the less frequent functions of *what*, see §§ 18.4.6 and 18.4.7):

(1)   What I don't understand is your enthusiasm *(that which)*
      DO  S        V
      _____
      H          POM
            S

### The proadverbials *(18.5.2)*

18.5.2  *When, where, why* and *how*, as relatives, are characterized by always realizing the adverbial of the relative clause, in reference to time, place, cause and manner (cp. § 15.0.4). **After an explicit antecedent,** *when* and *where* may either be defining or nondefining, whereas *why* can only be defining. (*how* cannot have an explicit antecedent); *when* and *why* as defining may be replaced by *that*, cp. (4a), (4b) and (5a):

(2)   I'll show you the village where I grew up
                              A  S   V
      _____           _____
      PRM    H              POM
            DO

(3)   She is not available in May, *when she will be away on her annual business trip*
(4a)  She told me the reason *why there are so few members*
(4b)  She told me the reason *(that) there are so few members*

(5a)   Do you have to arrive at that time in May? That's *the time
when/that I'll be away on my annual business trip*

**Without an explicit antecedent** they are all defining, *when, where* and *why* corresponding to *the time when, the place where*, and *the reason why*, cp. *what = that which* (§ 18.5.1). *How*, which is never preceded by an antecedent, cannot be paraphrased this way:[40]

(5b)   Do you have to arrive at that time in May? That's *[the time]
when I'll be away on my annual business trip*

   ...that's  <u>when</u>  <u>I'll</u>  <u>be</u>  <u>away</u>  <u>on my annual business trip</u>
            A    S   V    A           A

                <u>H</u>                    POM
         <u>   </u>  <u>  </u>
          S    V                   SC

(6)    That is *[the reason] why there are so few members*
(7)    Watch closely now, this is *how you operate it:* ...

Note that we regard proadverbials as simple (pronominal) noun phrases functioning as adverbials (see § 15.0.4), cp.

(2a)   (...the village) <u>where</u> <u>I</u> <u>grew up</u> = <u>in which</u> <u>I</u> <u>grew up</u>
                  A   S    V     J   H      S   V
                               A

(3a)   (...in May,) <u>when</u> <u>she</u> <u>will be</u>... = <u>at which time</u> <u>she</u>
                   A   S    V     J   PRM  H     S
                              A
   <u>will be</u> ...
      V

(7a)   ...<u>how</u> <u>you</u> <u>operate</u> <u>it</u> = (the way) <u>in which</u> <u>you</u> <u>operate</u> <u>it</u>
         A    S    V   DO         J   H        S   V   DO
                               A

In other words, the forms *when, where, why* and *how*, when used as relatives, are regarded as belonging to the same class of words (relative pronouns) as the other *wh*-forms, the only distinguishing feature being the fact that they can realize no other clause constituent than the adverbial. As we shall see (§ 19.2), a similar view of *wh*-proadverbials as pronouns is also implied in our account of their use in some interrogative clauses.

There is no need to regard these forms as relatives in examples like (8), where it seems more appropriate to describe them as adverbs functioning as a mixture of adverbial and junctive. The ambiguity (cp. (8) and (8a)) stems from the *wh*-clause functioning either as adverbial or as direct object (in case of the latter it is an interrogative clause):

---

40. Their function as relative, without an antecedent, is most clearly seen when these forms occur after a copula verb, as in (5b)-(7).

```
(8)     (Tell me)  when  the President  has  his breakfast
                   J(A)        S          V        DO
                                    A
```

i.e. "tell me at that point in time." Compare:

```
(8a)    (Tell me)  when  the President  has  his breakfast
                   J(A)        S          V        DO
                                   DO
```

i.e. " tell me when it is that..."

### The -ever forms (18.5.3)

18.5.3 *Whoever, whatever* and *whichever* (unlike the other *wh-* forms when they function as relatives) represent the same selectivity system as the interrogative pronouns (see § 19.3.3): *whichever* (referring to persons as well as nonpersons) selects from a limited group of possibilities, as opposed to *who-* and *whatever*.

Apart from the determiner function of *whatever* and *whichever* (see § 18.4.7), the *-ever* forms occur in relative clauses without an explicit antecedent, as in (9b) and (10b) below (cp. §§ 18.5.1-18.5.2). That an antecedent is contained in the meaning of the *-ever* form is perhaps seen most clearly if we compare with the construction where the relative is determiner ((9a) and (10a)): the similarity in meaning between (a) and (b) can only be accounted for if we accept that the relative clause functions as a noun-phrase postmodifier in both cases:

```
(9a)    Whichever book you choose will make her happy
                             S    V
        ───────── ──── ──────────
            D      H      POM
                    S
```

```
(9b)    Whichever you choose will make her happy
            DO      S    V
        ───────── ──────────
            H        POM
                 S
```

```
(10a)  Ask whatever child you meet
(10b)  Ask whoever you meet
```

### As (18.5.4)

18.5.4 *As* occurs only in defining relative clauses, and only if the antecedent contains *such* or *same* (cp. § 21.2.1, about *as* in the adjective/adverb phrase). *As* is occasionally replaced by *that* after *same*:

```
(11)   You must have had the same teacher as (that) I had
                                            J    (J)  S  V
                          ──── ──── ─────── ──────────
                          PRM  PRM    H        POM
                                    DO
```

```
(12)   Such information as he had was  soon  sold  in  exchange for
       tobacco
```

(13)   She would repeat her indignant account to *such as were still*
       *willing to listen to her*


## INTERROGATIVE PRONOUNS (19.1-19.5.2)


### Definition (19.1)

19.1   The **central interrogatives** are: *who/whom/whose, what, which.*
The **marginal interrogatives** are: *when, where, why, how*; note also the
interrogative junctives, *if* and *whether.*

These forms are to a large extent identical with the relative pronouns, so that
their main distinguishing feature is their function: Interrogative pronouns
introduce interrogative clauses, main clauses as well as subclauses (see §§ 5.2.2-
5.2.4):

(1)    *Who* is afraid of the big bad wolf?
(2)    Guess *who* is coming to dinner?

and whereas relative clauses usually realize the noun-phrase postmodifier,
interrogative subclauses realize the direct object more often than the noun-
phrase postmodifier (apposition, see also §§ 3.7.2-3.7.3). In other words,
interrogative subclause constructions such as:

(3)    We do not know where they hid their treasures
       S  V-  A   -V              DO

are more common than constructions like:

(3a)   We have no knowledge of where they hid their treasures
                  PRM    H                POM
       S     V                     DO

Note that relative clauses without an antecedent are analyzed as postmodifiers
in the noun phrase like other relative clauses, so that the difference between
interrogative and relative clauses in terms of meaning is brought out clearly by
the analysis in such examples as:

(4)    (Tell me) where the President has his breakfast
                   A        S        V    DO
                          DO

       (i.e. "where it is that..." — interrogative)

(5)    (Show me) <u>where</u> <u>the President</u> <u>has</u> <u>his breakfast</u>
                   A           S             V         DO
              _____
                   H                      POM
                              DO

(i.e. "the room where..." — relative)

Thus the analysis disambiguates sentences like the following, cp. (6a) and (6b):

(6a)   Do you remember *when (it was that) the French beat the English*?
       — I think it was in 1985

(6b)   Do you remember *(the time) when the French beat the English?*
       — Yes, there were fights in the streets all over the country

Another important distinguishing feature of the interrogatives is the selectivity system, see § 19.3.3.

**Modification (19.2)**

19.2    Interrogative pronouns as head of the noun phrase (including pronominal noun phrases that can only realize the adverbial of the clause, the so-called "proadverbials," as in (5) (7), cp. also §§ 18.5.2 and 19.5.1) can only be modified by a few types of postmodifier, e.g.

(1)    *Who ever* told you that?  (also one word: *whoever*)
(2)    *Which of you* will help me wash the car?
(3)    *What else/more* can we do?
(4)    *What the hell* do you mean?
(5)    *Where in London* is he staying?
(6)    *Where on earth* are you going to find such a thing?
(7)    *Why in the world* won't you listen?

*Which* is frequently modified by an *of*-postmodifier, as in (2).

**Grammatical Systems (19.3.0-19.3.3)**

19.3.0  The grammatical systems of the central interrogative pronouns are **case** (only *who/-m /-se*), **gender** (*who* vs. *what*) and **selectivity** ([*who, what*] vs. *which*).

   Neither **number** nor **specification** is indicated formally in the interrogative pronoun. When *who* is the subject of the interrogative clause, the finite verb usually has singular form, except when there is an explicit indication of number (3), or when there is an implied choice between a number of groups (4):

(1)    Who *knows*?
(2)    Now children, who *likes* chocolate?  (a likely answer, from each child, is *"I do"*)
(3)    Who *are* the culprits?
(4)    Who *tell* the best jokes? (the Irish)

When *who* is the subject complement followed by a subject in the plural, it is of course the subject which determines the form of the verb:

(5)    <u>Who</u> <u>are</u> <u>they</u>?   —  <u>They</u> <u>are</u> <u>the new lodgers</u>
        SC   V   S            S    V       SC

Note, however, that with *be* as copula verb, the analysis of *who* as either subject or subject complement may depend on the expected answer:

(6)    I didn't read the last chapter —
       <u>who</u> <u>was</u> <u>the murderer</u>?   (<u>The butler</u> <u>was</u>)
        S    V      SC                S         V

(7)    <u>Who</u> <u>are</u> <u>those boys over there</u>?   (<u>They</u> <u>are</u> <u>my cousins</u>)
        SC   V         S                        S    V     SC

### Case (19.3.1)

19.3.1   The case system is reflected in the difference between *who* (the subjective case), *whom* (the objective case) and *whose* (the genitive case). The general use of the case system has been dealt with in § 14, see in particular § 14.2.3.

### Gender (19.3.2)

19.3.2   The gender system is represented in the distinction between *who/-m/-se* (person) and *what* (nonperson). Note the following differences from the relative pronouns: *which* as an interrogative pronoun is neutral with regard to gender, cp. § 18.3.2; the gender reference of *whose* as an interrogative pronoun is exclusively personal (cp. § 18.4.7) —

(1)    *Who* did you see?
(2)    I know *who* you are and *whom* you represent
(4)    *Whose* bicycle is that?
(5)    *What* did he give you?
(6)    I don't know *what* to do about it

*What* refers to the "occupation" (classification), not the person (identification), in examples like:

(7)    *What* is she?   — She is a writer
(8)    Let me tell you *what* you are: a crook and a swindler, that's *what* you are

*What* is gender-neutral when used as a determiner (see § 19.4.1):

(9)    Can't you get the children to help you? — *What children?* I don't have any
(10)   They didn't know *what bus* to take

*Selectivity (19.3.3)*

19.3.3 *Which*, as opposed to *who* and *what*, is used when the speaker wants the addressee to select from a definite number of possible alternatives:

(11) I have some brandy, Scotch and bourbon. *Which* would you prefer?
(12) *Which* sister married the American?
(13) I want to know *which* of you is responsible

Cp. *which* and *what*, e.g.

(14a) *Which* did you do first? (wash the car or mow the lawn?)
(14b) *What* did you do in the meantime? (you must have been doing something)
(15a) They didn't know *which* bus to take (no. 1 or no. 9)
(15b) They didn't know *what* bus to take (there are so many)

(16a) *Which* policeman do you think accepted the bribe? (Johnson, Smith or Jones?)
(16b) *What* policeman would stoop to accepting bribes? (= what kind of policeman...)

Cp. *which* and *who* in questions of identity (a) and identification (b):

(17a) *Who* is Charles? — Charles is the new dean
(17b) *Which* is Charles? — the one in the green sweater

**Functions (19.4.1-19.4.4)**

19.4.1 The interrogative pronouns (all of them) can function as **head** of the noun phrase, e.g.

(1) *Who* are you?
(2) *Whose* is it?
(3) *What (ever)* is the matter with you?
(4) *Which (of them)* do you want?
(5) *Where (the hell)* did he go?
(6) *How (on earth)* did she manage that?

or as **determiner** (only *whose*, *which* and *what*):

(7) *Whose* book is that?
(8) *What* children are you talking about?
(9) *Which* way did they go?

19.4.2 Regardless of the function of the noun phrase in which they occur, interrogative pronouns have to appear in initial position in the interrogative clause.[41] This sometimes results in a divided subclause, to which the interrogative belongs,

---

41. Except in expressions of shocked surprise, of the type: *You did 'what?*

whereas it is the main clause which is treated as an interrogative clause (with inversion, see §§ 4.1.1 and 5.2.3):

```
(10)   Who  do you think  would be  interested?
        S                    V          SC
      ───  ──  ──  ──      ──────────  ────────
      DO-  V-  S   -V           -DO
```

19.4.3  A junctive connecting the interrogative pronoun to the verb is more often placed after the verb than before the pronoun, especially when the junctive is part of a prepositional verb (as in (11), see § 7.9.2):

```
(11)   Who(m) did they turn to for guidance?
(12)   Which bed did you sleep in?
```

whereas in formal language the junctive is often placed before the interrogative pronoun (any central interrogative except the form *who*):

```
(13)   To whom did they turn for guidance?
(14)   In which bed did you sleep?
```

See also § 5.2.3. Cp. the relative pronouns, § 18.4.3, for parallel examples and analyses.

19.4.4  *What, why* and *how* are often used in interjections (i.e. nonquestions): *what* is a predeterminer, *why* is outside the syntactic structure, and *how* premodifies an adjective (see § 19.5.1),

```
(15)   What an excellent idea!
(16)   What utter nonsense!
(17)   Why, it never occurred to me!
(18)   Why, that's wonderful!
(19)   How awful!
```

**Marginal Interrogatives (19.5.1-19.5.2)**

*The proadverbials (19.5.1)*

19.5.1  *When, where,*[42] *why* and *how*, as interrogatives, are characterized by always realizing the adverbial of the interrogative clause, in reference to time, place, cause and manner (cp. § 15.0.4):

```
(1)    When is she leaving?
(2)    Where are you going?
(3)    Why not have another drink?
(4)    How did you manage to open the safe?
```

---

42. Note also the compounds *whereabouts* and *wherein*, of which the latter is found only in very formal language:

```
     a.   Whereabouts do you live, in Boston?
     b.   Wherein lay her greatness? Time and history will provide the
          answer.
```

except that *how* may also function as a premodifier in the adjective/adverb - phrase:

(6)    *How old* are you?
(7)    *How soon* would you be able to come?

### The interrogative junctives (19.5.2)

19.5.2  *If* and *whether* are not pronouns, but junctives. They are mentioned here because, like the interrogative pronouns, they occur at the beginning of an interrogative clause. But whereas interrogative pronouns are constituents of a *wh*-interrogative clause (main- or subclause), *if* and *whether* are junctives introducing *yes/no* interrogative subclauses (see § 5.2.4):

(8)    He inquired *whether* his wife had checked in
(9)    She asked *if* she could be of any help

### INDEFINITE PRONOUNS (20.1-20.5.5)

### Definition (20.1)

20.1.1  **Central indefinite pronouns:**

1.      Those functioning in relation to the **specification** system:
        Indefinite specific:    *some, somebody/-one/-thing, one*
        Generic:                *any, anybody/-one/-thing*
        Generic negative:       *no(ne), nobody/-one[43]/-thing*

2.      The **universal** pronouns:
        Distributive (singular): *each, every (-body, -one, -thing)*
        Global:                  *all*

3.      Those relating to **duality**:
        Global (plural):        *both*
        Generic (singular):     *(n)either*
        Alternative:            *other*

---

43. The compound form *no one* is written as two words.

## 20.1.2 **Marginal indefinite pronouns:**

4.   Forms functioning        *any-, no-, some-, every-, elsewhere*
     as **adverbials**         *sometimes; some-, anyhow (-way); otherwise*

5.   Certain **quantifiers**:  *many/much, more, most*
                               *few/little, fewer/less, fewest/least*
                               *enough, half, several*
                               *plenty (of), lots/a lot (of), a good/great deal (of)*

20.1.3 The traditional name of these pronouns may be seen as a reflection of the fact that the *some(-)/any(-)* forms complement the personal pronouns, with which they share most of their syntactic functions, within the system of specification: Each of the personal pronouns usually has definite, and never indefinite, specific reference. By contrast, *some(-)* has indefinite specific, *any(-)* generic, reference. Compare e.g.

(1)   *She (someone/anyone)* might have left a note on your desk
(2)   I need the nails to close the box.
      Did you find *them (some/any)*?

### Modification (20.2.1-20.2.2)

20.2.1 Only postmodification is possible with the indefinite pronouns. With the **simple forms** of the pronouns, the most frequent type by far is the *of*-postmodifier with partitive meaning (see § 10.8.6), e.g.

(1)   She gave Fred *some of the money*
(2)   I don't recognize *any of these people*
(3)   *None of you* had bothered to check it out
(4)   He gave *each of us* an apple
(5)   And so say *all of us*
(6)   They would probably accept *both/either of us*

Relative clauses, too, may occur at POM:

(7)   *Some, who had not heard of his death*, sent him long admiring letters
(8)   *All I need* is love

20.2.2 The **compound forms** of the indefinite pronouns can take a wider range of postmodifiers,[44] corresponding almost to that of the nouns (see § 10.8):

---

44. The compound forms occasionally become full-fledged nouns with the possibility of premodification:

a.   "Here is *a little something for you*," said the kind-hearted Mrs. Hopkins.
b.   They may be important people in their own village, but they are *mere nobodies* here in town

```
(9)    He gave her everything that money can buy
(10)   There was nothing to be done about it
(11)   Why would someone like Jim go and steal a car?
       (like + NP only after any-, no-, some-)
(12)   I can't remember anything of what happened at the party
(13)   The prisoner who escaped must have had help from somebody
       outside
```

They allow postmodification by adjective phrases to a greater extent than nouns (see also § 10.8.9); the adjective phrase is either in the positive or in the comparative (see § 21.1.5 ff.):

```
(14)   There is something (very) peculiar going on here
(15)   It is nothing special, just ham and eggs
(16)   Can't you think of anything better to do?
```

They may also be postmodified by *else*, and by a phrase introduced by *but* (if the pronoun begins in *any-*, *no-* or *every-*):

```
(17)   Ask somebody else
(18)   Nothing else matters to her
(19)   I have told everyone but you
(20)   He wouldn't tell this to anyone (else) but you
(21)   She is anything but stupid
```

as well as by *more* (only forms ending in *-thing*) and *much* (only *nothing* and *anything*):

```
(22)   Did he tell you anything more? – Nothing much
```

### Grammatical Systems (20.3.0-20.3.12)

20.3.0  The grammatical systems of the indefinite pronouns are **specification** and **number** (see the tables in §§ 13.2 and 13.6.3), **gender** and **case** (only the compound forms), the **global/distributive** system and **selectivity**.

### *Specification (20.3.1-20.3.2)*

20.3.1  The general noun-phrase system of specification (§ 13) is represented in the indefinite pronouns by the following contrasts:

| | |
|---|---|
| Indefinite specific: | *some, somebody/-one/-thing, one* |
| Generic: | *any, anybody/-one/-thing* |
| Generic negative: | *no(ne), nobody/-one/-thing* |

*One* is often used as the singular of indefinite specific *some* (as distinct from generic *any*), which is why it is mentioned under specification. However, *one* does sometimes have (singular) generic reference, which is why it is more appropriately dealt with in terms of the number system, see § 20.3.3 (13)-(15).

*No(-)/none* is not a separate term in the specification system, being the negative version of *any(-)*.

20.3.2 *Any(-)*, i.e. generic reference, is particularly common in **negative, interrogative** and **conditional** clauses:

```
(1)    There wasn't anyone there
(2)    Will it do any good?
(3)    If you see anything suspicious, call the police
```

though *any(-)* may also occur in other clause types, just as *some(-)* may occur in negative, interrogative and conditional clauses, depending on the context: the use of *some(-)*, i.e. indefinite specific reference, presupposes the existence of a particular entity to which it refers, as opposed to *any(-)*,

```
(4)    Any ten-year-old will tell you that
(5)    Didn't some ten-year-old boy named Harry Sumner disappear
       about a month ago?
(6)    Anything you can do I can do better
(7)    Didn't I ask you to do something for me?
(8)    She did not recognize some of them (cp. ...any of them)
(9)    Will somebody close the door, please?  (cp. Will anybody
       ever know the truth?)
(10)   But if you saw someone in the building, why didn't you
       report it to the police?
(11)   If someone stops you, tell them you are here with my
       permission (the speaker regards it as likely that this will
       happen)
(11a)  If anyone stops you, tell them you are here with my
       permission (the speaker does not regard it as likely that
       this will happen)
```

*Some* is also used to specify a subclass, as opposed to *any*, which refers to the whole class:

```
(12)   Some people will always be afraid of the truth
```

### Number (20.3.3-20.3.4)

20.3.3 The general noun-phrase system of number (§ 12) is represented in the indefinite pronouns by the contrast between *one* (singular) and *some/any/none* (plural or uncountable) used as head:[45]

```
(13)   He gave me this box of chocolates.  (a) Have one!  (sg.)
                                           (b) Have some! (pl.)
(14)   I'll need money; can you give me some?  (uncount.)
(15)   Can I borrow your pencil? — I don't have one  (sg.)
(16)   I wanted some steaks but there weren't any/there were none
       (pl.)
(17)   I'll need money — I don't have any/I have none  (uncount.)
```

---

45. As determiners, *any, no* and (occasionally) *some* may also have singular reference, see §§ 20.4.6-20.4.7.

(See also §§ 20.4.20-20.4.22 on forms with duality meaning.) Noun phrases with *any* as head, with reference to a member or members of a group, usually take a verb in the plural when used as subject, as opposed to the compound forms (cp. § 20.3.4); *none* (and *not..any* before a relative clause), on the other hand, may govern either a singular or a plural verb:

(18)    *Have any/none of you* seen her yet?
(19a)   I tried on a number of coats, but *none was/were* exactly what
        I wanted
(19b)   ...but I did*n't* see *any* that *was/were* exactly right

20.3.4  In formal style, the following indefinite pronouns which have only one form show **singular concord** (verbal as well as pronominal) when used as subject: the compound indefinite pronouns, ending in *-body*, *-one* or *-thing*, *each* and *(n)either*:

(20)    *Everybody* who *is* anybody *was* there
(21)    *Anybody* in *his* right mind would deny that
(22)    *Each* of them had to answer questions about *his* or *her*
        political convictions
(23)    If *either* of them *has* anything to complain about, *she* will
        have to see me personally

In informal style, they often show plural pronominal concord (to avoid the question of gender and/or because they are felt to have plural reference). *Neither*, in addition, sometimes takes plural verbal concord (cp. *none*, § 20.3.3):

(24)    *Somebody* has left *their* briefcase here
(25)    *Each* of them was asked to show *their* ticket
(26)    The twins both promised to come, but *neither* of them
        *has/have* arrived

### Gender and case (20.3.5)

20.3.5  These two grammatical systems apply only to the compound indefinite pronouns. **Gender** is represented by the distinction between *-body/-one* (person) and *-thing* (nonperson):

(27)    *Everybody* is supposed to bring *something* to the party

**Case** involves the same distinction between the common and the genitive case as for the nouns (see § 14), cp. the above common-case forms with the genitive:

(28)    I think he stole *somebody's* briefcase
(29)    It isn't *anybody's* fault, really

### The global/distributive system (20.3.6-20.3.8)

20.3.6  *All* and *both* have global reference to the group, without singling out the individual member, as opposed to *every* and *each*, which refer to the individual member (this is called "distributive" meaning):

| | Group of three or more | Group of two |
|---|---|---|
| **Global** | *all* | *both* |
| **Distributive** | *every/each* | *each* |

(30)  *All/both* (of) the children were there
(31)  *Every/each* state in the Union has a flag of its own
(32)  *Each* of the twins was rewarded

*All* (= "the whole of") may also occur in singular and uncountable noun phrases, see the following and § 20.4.19:

(33)  Why not take *all* of it?
(34)  She wants *all* or nothing

20.3.7  *All* and the compound *every-* forms can sometimes be used more or less interchangeably:

(35)  They dream of a new world where there will be food enough for *all/everybody*
(36)  Tell me *all/everything* about it

though with reference to persons *all* rarely appears as head of a simple noun phrase, as opposed to *everybody/-one*:

(37)  *All of them* came – *They all* came
(38)  *Everybody* came

*All* and *everything* are often interchangeable with very little difference of meaning:

(39)  After *all/everything* I have done for you and you still won't help!

However, their distribution is not identical. *All*, by comparison with *everything*, tends to be used in contexts where it has a limiting effect:

(40)  *All* he bought was a tie
(41)  *Everything* he bought was always of the best quality
(42)  That's *all* I can do for you
(43)  Why do I have to do *everything* for you?

20.3.8  Note the difference in meaning between the following sentences with *all* (a) and *each* (b):

(44a)  She put *all* the applications in a separate file      (many applications, one file)
(44b)  She put *each* of the applications in a separate file      (many applications and as many files)

### Selectivity (20.3.9-20.3.12)

20.3.9 The choice between *each* and *every* can be accounted for in terms of selectivity (cp. the interrogative pronouns, § 19.3.3) vs. accumulation: *Each* selects, one by one, the individual members of a limited group (often defined by an *of*-postmodifier). *Every(-)*, too, refers to the individual members of a group, but it is accumulative, not selective, and the group does not have to be well-defined or even limited:

```
(45a)  Each of them wanted to say hello to her
(45b)  Everybody wanted to say hello to her
(46a)  Each school has a library
(46b)  Every school has a library
```

20.3.10 Because *every(-)* is nonselective and universal, its meaning, in positive declarative clauses, comes close to that of generic *any(-)*:

```
(47a)  Every member of the party could have committed the murder
       ("both Peter and Paul and Mary and...")
(47b)  Any member of the party could have committed the murder
       ("whether we take Peter or Paul or Mary or...")
```

whereas *every(-)* and *any(-)* differ considerably in negative, interrogative and conditional clauses:

```
(48)  You haven't met every-/anyone yet
(49)  Did the burglar take every-/anything?
(50)  If you tell them every-/anything, I won't ever speak to you
      again
```

20.3.11 Greater emphasis on the all inclusiveness of the reference is achieved when the simple forms are followed by *one* (head) + an *of*-postmodifier:

```
(51)  Any 'one of us could do that
(52)  Each 'one of you has helped win this prize
(53)  Every (single) 'one of them had misunderstood the question
```

### Functions (20.4.0-20.4.14)

20.4.0 The following deals with the syntactic functions of the central indefinite pronouns. Simple as well as compound forms can realize the **head of the noun phrase** (see §§ 20.4.1-20.4.4), whereas only simple forms realize the **determiner of the noun phrase** (§§ 20.4.5-20.4.11), the **noun-phrase postmodifier** (20.4.12) and **constituents of the adjective/adverb phrase** (§§ 20.4.13-20.4.14).

In addition, each of the forms *one, all, both, (n)either* and *other* has some special characteristics, which will be dealt with separately (§§ 20.4.15-20.4.22).

For the functions of the marginal indefinite pronouns, see §§ 20.5.1-20.5.5.

*As head of the NP (20.4.1-20.4.4)*

20.4.1  The **simple forms** except *no* and *every* may function as head of the noun phrase, see the examples in §§ 20.2.1 and 20.3.3-20.3.4 above. They usually have **textual reference** to a noun phrase, changing its specification and/or adding partitive meaning (as in (2)):

(1)     We went looking for *some juicy steaks*, but there weren't *any* (anaphoric reference)
(2)     *Some* of *the students* would like to study abroad (cataphoric reference to noun phrase at POM)

They may also select the individual members of a group:

(3)     The princess greeted *the patients*, shaking hands with *each* in turn
(4)     *Each* of *the boxes* was decorated with a single pearl

20.4.2  *Some* (and, usually in formal language, *any* and *none*) may have **situational reference** to persons in the plural:

(5)     *Some* would say he had it coming to him, others regard him as a victim of intolerance
(6)     Such deeds are perpetrated by *none* but the most hardened criminals/...not perpetrated by *any* but the most hardened criminals

For the form *others* (5), see § 20.4.22.

20.4.3  The **compound forms**, ending in *-body, -one* or *-thing*, always realize the head of a noun phrase (see also §§ 20.2.2 and 20.3.4), usually having situational, i.e. nontextual, reference:

(7)     *Someone (else)* must have done it
(8)     George built *everything* himself
(9)     *Anybody* can ride a bicycle
(10)    You must tell this to *no one (but your father)*

Note the difference in reference between simple and compound forms, as between (a) *some* and (b) *something* in:

(11)    I don't want any money —
        (a)    I still want to give you *some* (money) to make it worth your while
        (b)    I still want to give you *something* (not necessarily money) to make it worth your while

20.4.4  Together with an *of*-postmodifier, constructions with *-thing* as head mean "of that quality," as opposed to the same construction with a simple form as head, which has partitive meaning (metaphorically speaking). Compare e.g.

(12a)   There is *something of the gipsy* about her   (i.e. the same kind of appearance or character)

(12b)  She has *some of her sister's innocent charm* (i.e. she has some innocent charm, but not as much as her sister)
(13)   Apart from my hair, there is *nothing of the dumb blonde about me*

### As determiner (20.4.5-20.4.11)

20.4.5  All simple forms of the central indefinite pronouns (except *none*)[46] may realize the determiner, as opposed to the compound forms. *Some* and *any*, as determiner, complement the articles in making up the general specification system of the noun phrase (see the table in § 13.2). Examples with *some, any, no*:

(14)   Please send us *some brochures/literature* on your micro-wave ovens
(15)   *Any excuse* will do
(16)   I couldn't find *any cigars/tobacco*
(17)   *No man* is an island
(18)   They have *no water, no electricity, no facilities* whatsoever

20.4.6  *Some* is unstressed in common examples like (14), and is not normally used in the singular. Bearing main stress, however, *some* may occur in the singular to indicate that the speaker cannot or does not wish to be specific:

(19)   For *some reason (or other)* your name was omitted
(20)   *Some hooligan* threw a stone at me
(21)   You must come and visit me *some day*

20.4.7  In colloquial language, stressed *some* is used in the singular in expressions of emotion (22)-(23); and unstressed *some* is used in the singular when immediately followed by *other* (24):

(22)   '*Some 'friend* "you are — you won't do anything to help me
(23)   That was '*some 'speech* you gave the other day (= "quite a...")
(24)   If you don't trust 'me ask *some 'other teacher*

20.4.8  *Some* means "fairly large" or "better than nothing" in (more or less idiomatic) expressions like:

(25)   The discussion went on for *some time*
(26)   They went to *some lengths* to help her
(27)   There is at least *some chance* that it will work

20.4.9  *Some* means "approximately" when occurring before a numeral:

(28)   This university has received *some 250 new students*

The numeral does not change the basic meaning of *any* or *no* (cp. § 20.3.8):

---

46. Though *none* does realize the determiner in the expression, *none other than: It was none other than the famous Mr. Watson himself.*

```
(29)   This box could not have been carried by any one man
(30)   No two persons have identical fingerprints
```

As for *every* before a numeral, see § 20.4.11.

20.4.10 *Each* (cp. *each* as head, § 20.3.4) and *every* are used only with nouns in the singular and with singular verbal concord:

```
(31)   The building has four floors, and each floor has six rooms
(32)   England expects every man to do his duty
(33)   Every man, woman and child was expected to help defend their
       home
```

See also §§ 20.3.6-20.3.7.

20.4.11 Even before a numeral, the basic meaning of *every* is easily discernible, in expressions of frequency:

```
(34)   You must take his temperature every two hours   (i.e. "once
       for every period of...")
(35)   She visits us (a) every two/three years
                     (b) every second/other/third year
(36)   The government changes every five years
(37)   I go there about once every six months
(38)   Since 1980, eight women have lost jobs for every five men
       (i.e. "for every count of...")
```

### As noun-phrase postmodifier (20.4.12)

20.4.12 *Each, all, both* and *neither* may enter into a construction where they function as postmodifier of a noun phrase realizing the subject, the indirect object, or the direct object; as part of the subject NP, the postmodifier follows the positional rules for adverbials in verb-neighbor position, cp. (39) and (40), and see § 4.4.0:

```
(39)   They each/all/both wrote to her and explained their views

(40)   The unsuccessful escapees have each/all been taken to a
       PRM      PRM          H              POM
                       S-             V-    -S           -V        A→

       separate prison
              ←A

(41)   They sent us all/both letters
(42)   They asked us all/both to wait
```

The head of the noun phrase may be a noun if the noun phrase functions as subject, as in (40). Otherwise the head of the noun phrase can only be a pronoun, as in (41) and (42).

*Each* can also have final position, cp. the following examples with (39) and (41) above:

```
(39a) They wrote a letter each
       H                   POM
       S-    V      DO    -S
```

```
(41a) They sent us a letter each   (i.e. They sent each of us a
                  H        POM
       ─── ─── ──── ──── ─────
        S   V  IO-  DO    -IO

      letter)
```

*(N)either* (+ *of* + pronoun) as postmodifier only occurs in noun phrases realizing the subject. Its position follows the rules for adverbials in verb-neighbor (cp. (39) and (40) above) or final position. Note that verb-neighbor position is **after** the (simple) verb phrase when the main verb is *be* (44a):

```
(43)   We neither of us care very much for him
(44a)  We were neither of us very happy about it
(44b)  We weren't happy about it, either of us
```

### Any *and* no(ne) *in the AP (20.4.13-20.4.14)*

20.4.13 Besides having functions in the noun phrase, *any* and *no* may function as premodifiers in the adjective/adverb phrase:[47]

```
(45)   She won't see me any more
(46)   He took the matter no further
(47)   You're no better than the other pilot   ("you're just as
       bad")
(48)   Last year he ran that distance in no more than 30 minutes
       and 17 seconds  ("in as little as...")
```

### Cp. (47) and (48) with

```
(47a)  You're not better than the other pilot   ("but you may be
       just as good")
(48a)  He ran the distance in not more than 30 minutes  ("in 30
       minutes at the outside")
```

20.4.14 Note the construction *any/none* + *the* + the comparative, in a few idioms:

```
(49)   Although I have taken my medicine regularly, I don't feel
       any the better for it
(50)   If we take just one piece of cake each, Mother will be none
       the wiser
```

Cp. the form of the adverb *nonetheless*.

### One *(20.4.15-20.4.18)*

20.4.15 *One* is used in a variety of ways, some of which have already been treated under different headings. This and the following paragraphs contain a summary of its most important functions other than that of a mere numeral:

---

47. In colloquial American English, the functions of *any* and *some* include those of an adverb of degree:

```
      Then she cried some, but it didn't bother me any.
```

*One*, with indefinite specific or generic reference, **complements** *some* **and** *any* in the number/specification system when referring to a countable noun phrase (see also § 20.3.3):

(51)   The city has *one* of *the largest airports in the world*
(52)   Can I borrow your pen? — I don't have *one*

20.4.16   *One* is a **"prop word"** when substituting, not for a whole noun phrase, but for a countable noun as head (see also § 10.1.4). In this function *one* is obligatory after premodifiers realized by adjectives in the positive, and nouns:

(53)   These bags are too small, give me *the large ones*
(54)   He tried to keep up with the horses and grabbed hold of *the black one's tail*
(55)   She wants a teak table with square legs — I want *an oak one with round legs*

As the examples show, the prop word *one* is declined exactly like a noun, and can be pre- and postmodified like one. Note its use in formal subject-complement constructions, as in — instead of *His decision was courageous* —

(56)   His decision was *a courageous one/one of courage*[48]

Prop-word *one* never occurs (immediately) after genitives, *own*, and cardinal numbers:

(57)   Your bike is no good. I need *Joan's*
(58)   I thought I had six cups, but I only have *five*. Be sure to bring your *own*!

and is usually left out after demonstrative pronouns in the plural, after superlatives, and occasionally after two adjectives in juxtaposition:

(59)   There aren't enough glasses on the table, so you'd better take *these*
(60)   Of all the great fighters in this century, Muhamed Ali was *the greatest*
(61)   They were sitting close together, his right hand in her *left*

20.4.17   *One* is used with **reference to persons** in a number of more or less idiomatic constructions:[49]

(62)   Bill is *the fat one at the bar*
(63)   *One* can't be too careful these days   (see § 13.6.2)
(64)   Tom is *a great one for football*
(65)   Sheila is not *one to underestimate the difficulties*

---

48. Note the alternative (formal) construction with genitive 2: *His was a courageous decision* (§ 15.5.3).
49. *Young one(s)* may also refer to animals:

The bird was busy looking after its *young (ones)*.

20.4.18 *One* may be used as a **determiner**:

(66)  *One day* she came to ask me for a loan
(67)  There is *one Mr. Smith* to see you
(68)  *One person I'd like to meet* is Dustin Hoffman[50]


**All (20.4.19)**

20.4.19 *All* as **head** is usually followed by a postmodifier (for examples where it is not, see § 20.3.7), and may be of singular, plural or uncountable content:

(69)  What do you think of this book? — Well, not *all of it* is bad
(70)  *All of you* are to be back here at five
(71)  *All I want* is a little butter

*All* with singular reference is relatively infrequent, except when it governs a pronominal *of-* postmodifier (69), and in formal language:

(72)  Caesar's actions were applauded by *all (of) the Roman world*

The alternative construction is one with *the whole of*: *The whole (of the) Roman world applauded him*.

For *all* as **postmodifier**, see § 20.4.12.

In the version without *of*, in (72) above, *all* functions as **predeterminer**. Both functions (head and predeterminer) can occur before a determiner with definite specific reference, cp. also:

(73a)  (She has lived) all of her life (in New York)
                            J   D    H
                 H          POM

(73b)  (She has lived) all her life (in New York)
                        PrD  D    H

(74)  *All (the) prisoners/of the prisoners* were released
(75)  Not *all good literature* is expensive

See also §§ 20.3.6-20.3.8.

---

50. Although there is an element of quantification in the meaning of *one* in (68), it is the element of specification which seems central. We can use (68) to give an **example** of a person we "would like to meet" (*one* can be stressed, unlike the indefinite article). We are not saying that we want to meet (only) one person. Consequently we regard *one* as a determiner here, rather than as an ordinator.

### Both, (n)either, other (20.4.20-20.4.22)

20.4.20 These forms have duality meaning, i.e. they presuppose a group or class consisting of two members.[51]

Both corresponds to global all. It functions as head, predeterminer or postmodifier (see § 20.4.12) in a noun phrase with plural, definite specific, reference. As head, it may be with or without a postmodifier:

(76)   *Both of us* love Beethoven   (*We both...*)
(77)   I didn't know which of my boyfriends to invite, so I invited *both*
(78)   *Both (of) the students* were there
(79)   *Both students* were there

20.4.21 Technically, *either* and *neither* have generic reference, corresponding to *any* and *no(ne)*, respectively. They function as head, determiner or postmodifier (see § 20.4.12). As head, they may be with or without a postmodifier themselves. In the case of *either*, the noun phrase is always singular:

(80)   *Neither of them* was much good   (*They* were *neither of them...*)
(81)   *Either answer* is acceptable
(82)   Paul and Harry both want to marry me, but I know I wouldn't be happy with *either (of them)*

(See § 20.3.4 with regard to concord.) *Either* may be synonymous with *both* or *each*:

(83)   There were office buildings on *either side* of the street
(84)   There was an armchair at *either end* of the long table

20.4.22 *Other* indicates an alternative, having specific (definite or indefinite) reference. It functions as head or as ordinator (see §§ 10.4.1-10.4.2) in a noun phrase which is either singular or plural. As head it has the form *others* in the plural. The indefinite article and the pronoun are written as one word, *another*, as in (86). The reference may be textual (e.g. (85) and (89)) or situational (e.g. (86) and (88)):

(85)   I have found one shoe, but I can't find *the other*
(86)   Pour yourself *another drink*
(87)   I haven't found *any other references* to this
(88)   We aren't all here yet. Where are *the others*?
(89)   Some were getting ready to go home, *others* had already left

---

51. *Both* and *(n)either* are **junctives**, not pronouns, in examples like:
    a.   *Both* Peter *and* Kathy would have to leave
    b.   *(N)either* Peter *(n)or* Kathy would have to leave
*(N)either* is a **conjunct** in:
    c.   Peter would not have to leave, *nor/neither* would Kathy
    d.   Peter wouldn't leave, and Kathy wouldn't *either*

The compound forms *each other* and *one another*, each of them written as two words, have **reciprocal** meaning, cp.

```
(90)   The kittens were washing themselves   (reflexive)
(91)   The kittens were washing each other    (reciprocal)
```

When *other* is followed by a *than*-postmodifier, it may appear as a divided modifier (see §§ 10.8.7 and 17.5.5), cp.

```
(92)   (He did it) for no other reason than sheer malice
                           H                POM
            J   D   M-      H               -M
```

```
(93)   (I have) no possessions other than the house and a little
                                  H          POM→
              D        H                       POM→
```

```
       furniture
        ←POM
        ←POM
```

## Marginal Indefinite Pronouns (20.5.1-20.5.5)

### The proadverbials (20.5.1)

20.5.1  The proadverbials (see § 15.0.4) function as —
**Adverbials of place:** *any-, no-, some-, every-, elsewhere*

```
(1)    She can't find him anywhere
(2)    He was nowhere to be found
(3)    If it isn't there you must look somewhere else
(4)    He will have to look elsewhere for a suitable partner
(5)    Are you sure you've looked everywhere?
```

**Adverbials of time:** *sometimes, sometime*

```
(6)    I sometimes wonder if she told me the truth   ("once in a
       while")
(7)    You'll see her somewhere, sometime   ("some day")
```

As indicated by the parenthesis in (7), the temporal meaning corresponding to that of *sometime* is often expressed by a noun phrase.

**Adverbials of manner:** *somehow/-way, (anyhow, otherwise)*

```
(8)    We'll find a way somehow
(9)    Someway we'll manage to do it   (informal AE)
(10)   The clothes were all jumbled in anyhow
(11)   You mustn't blame him; he was incapable of acting otherwise
```

*Anyhow* (alternating with *anyway*) and *otherwise* more often function as **conjuncts**:

```
(12)   He doesn't care what you say, he'll do it anyhow/anyway
```

```
(13)   I know he can be a bore, but anyhow/anyway, Bill and I have
       decided to invite him to the party
(14)   I must catch the bus. Otherwise I won't get home for dinner
```

### Quantifiers (20.5.2-20.5.5)

**20.5.2** Most of these contribute to a system of comparison (cp. the adjective/adverb phrase, Ch. VI):

| **Positive**<br>Count./uncount. | **Comparative**<br>Count./uncount. | **Superlative**<br>Count./uncount. |
|---|---|---|
| *many/much* | *more* | *most* |
| *(a) few/(a) little* | *fewer/less* | *fewest/least*[52] |

and are to some extent gradable by modifiers, e.g. (positive) *very many/ much* etc., (comparative) *many more (..than..), considerably less (..than..)*.

Quantifiers include items like *enough, half, several, plenty (of), a lot (of), a good/ great deal (of)*.

**20.5.3** The quantifiers, as might be expected, most often function as **ordinators** (see § 10.4) in the noun-phrase premodification:

```
(15)   The many/few people who had turned up were not disappointed
(16)   They now had little/more/less money to spend
(17)   More/fewer/most people are aware now of the origin of that
       tradition
(18)   They are the ones with (the) fewest mistakes
(19)   This  is  the  item  that  will  attract  (the)  most/least
       attention
```

*Much* (see § 2.5.5), *enough,* and the compound forms, e.g. *a few/a little* (= "some"), *a lot of,* realize the **determiner** when functioning in the premodification, see § 10.3.2.

**20.5.4** The quantifiers, furthermore, may realize the **head** of the noun phrase, usually with textual reference:

```
(20a)  Many people are for it, many more are against it
(20b)  Many people are for it, a few are against it
(20c)  Many people are for it, few are against it
(21)   Some of the furniture was sold, but most of it was stored
       away
```

---

52. In informal language, *less* and *least* are often used with countable noun phrases, synonymously with *fewer* and *fewest*:

```
a.      There used to be more people working in agriculture than in
        industry, but now there are less/fewer
b.      They are the ones with the least/fewest mistakes
```

This practice is regarded by purists as "incorrect."

(22)   I asked her for some money, but she did not have *much to give*

though some forms may occasionally have situational (nontextual) reference:

(23)   *Much/little* has been said about the cost of this project
(24)   You'd better let Chris drive — he has had *less than you*
(25)   That's *(quite) enough*, thank you!

including *many* and *few* with reference to people (formal style):

(26)   We have lived for too long in a system where the *few* rule the *many*

20.5.5 Note that *many* and *much* are primarily used in negative and interrogative contexts (i.e. contexts where *much* complements *any*):

(27)   She did not receive *much/any* money
(28)   He doesn't have *many* friends
(29)   Did you have *much/any* difficulty finding a place to stay?
(30)   What did he say? — Not *much/hardly anything*
(31)   Were there *many* spectators?

In positive declarative clauses, in informal style, *many* and *much* are only common after certain modifiers of degree (*as, so, too*):

(32)   There is *so/too much* violence on television
(33)   He bought *as many* books as he could carry

Otherwise the compound forms are preferred, in informal style:

(27a)  She received *a lot of* money
(33a)  He bought *lots of* books
(36)   We have *plenty of* time
(37)   He said *a great deal*

In formal style, *many* and *much* without premodification are not uncommon in positive declarative clauses (cp. also (23)):

(37)   *Much energy* has been expended trying to solve this problem
(38)   *Many people* cannot afford to travel abroad

# VI. THE ADJECTIVE/ADVERB PHRASE

## Introduction (21.0.1-21.0.2)

21.0.1 Adjective and adverb phrases share some formal and semantic characteristics, which makes it natural to treat them as members of the same type of phrase, the adjective/adverb phrase (AP).

**Formal** similarities: The root of the word realizing the head is usually the same for both adjective and adverb phrases, as in *handsome/ handsomely*. Secondly, simple adjective/adverb phrases are expanded by the same types of modifier; cp.

(1a)  Our statement must be *as clear as possible/very clear*
(1b)  We must state this *as clearly as possible/very clearly*

(2a)  She is *more handsome than I would have thought*
(2b)  She paid him *more handsomely than I would have thought*

**Semantic** similarities: The modifiers of adjective as well as adverb phrases indicate to what degree the quality expressed by their head is manifest (see the examples above).

21.0.2 Phrases with an adjective as head are adjective phrases, but after a definite article the adjective phrase realizes the head of a noun phrase (see also §§ 10.1.2 and 10.3.2). Compare:

(3)  My uncle is *very rich*  (AP)
(4)  Only *the very rich* can afford such luxury  (NP)
(5)  You are *the nicest of all the people I know*  (NP)

## THE STRUCTURE OF THE ADJECTIVE/ADVERB PHRASE (21.1.0-21.5.2)

### Head: Adjectives and Adverbs (21.1.0-21.1.9)

21.1.0 The head of the adjective/adverb phrase is almost invariably an adjective or an adverb. The form realizing the head, furthermore, is important in determining not only the function, but also the structure, of the phrase. Our point of departure, therefore, will be a description of the adjective and the adverb, as word classes, on the basis of functional as well as morphological criteria.

*Functional characteristics (21.1.1-21.1.2)*

21.1.1  In principle, the adjective and the adverb always realize the head of the adjective/adverb phrase. Adjective/adverb phrases are frequently simple, i.e. consisting of head only:

(1)     This is an *awkward* situation
(2)     They were treated *brutally* by the enemy

Thus *awkward* in (1) is a simple adjective phrase functioning as a premodifier in the noun phrase; *brutally* in (2) is a simple adverb phrase functioning as the adverbial constituent of the clause.

However, adjective/adverb phrases can be complex, too: adjectives and adverbs are typically premodified by adverb phrases, e.g. simple ones like *very* and *quite*,

(1a)    This is a very awkward situation
                   (H)
                   PRM       H

(2a)    They were treated *quite brutally* by the enemy

or by complex ones like *much more*,

(1b)    This is a much more awkward situation
                   PRM    H
                         PRM        H

(2b)    This time they were treated *much more brutally*

21.1.2  The head of the adjective/adverb phrase is rarely realized by anything but an adjective or an adverb, though there are exceptions, as when occasionally the head of the adjective/adverb phrase is realized by a noun phrase. Compare:

(3a)    An elderly *upper-class* gentleman
(3b)    An elderly, *very upper-class* gentleman

In (3a) *gentleman* is premodified by a noun phrase, *upper class*. In (3b), however, *gentleman* is premodified by an adjective phrase, *very upper-class*, which has a noun phrase as head (see also § 10.7.1).

*The derivation of adverbs from adjectives (21.1.3-21.1.4)*

21.1.3  Adverbs are typically derived from adjectives by means of the suffix *-ly (-y, -ally)*, which is added to an adjectival root. Compare:

(4)     Clear/clear*ly*,    happy/happi*ly*,    probable/probab*ly*,
        romantic/romantic*ally*

It must be emphasized, however, that the *-ly* suffix is not the **criterion** of an adverb. For example, of the forms

(a) *soon*     (b) *friendly*     (c) *hard*     (d) *kindly*

(a) is an adverb, (b) is an adjective, and (c) and (d) can each function both as an adjective and as an adverb.

21.1.4    Some forms occur both with and without *-ly* when functioning as adverbials. Sometimes there is a difference of meaning involved. In other cases the choice is determined by style or idiomatic usage:

```
(5a)   The sniper aimed too high
(5b)   I think highly of him

(6a)   The prisoner got clear away
(6b)   I can't see clearly in this light

(7a)   I was with her right till the end
(7b)   She rightly refused to answer  (i.e. she was right in
       refusing)

(8a)   Until it blows over, all we can do is to sit tight¹
(8b)   She screwed the lid on tight(ly)
(8c)   Your seat belt must be tightly fastened

(9a)   All our plans went wrong
(9b)   He was wrongly accused of embezzlement

(10a)  Go/come quick!  (informal style)
(10b)  He moved quickly and noiselessly

(11a)  That's easier said than done  (informal style)
(11b)  That's more easily said than done
(11c)  I can easily get it for you
```

*The system of comparison (21.1.5-21.1.9)*

21.1.5    Adjectives and adverbs share the system of comparison, which has three **degrees**: positive, comparative, superlative. They also share the formal indicators of degree, both word classes distinguishing between comparison by premodifier and comparison by suffix:

     **Comparison by premodifier** is done by means of the forms *more (less), most (least)*, in the comparative and the superlative, respectively —

```
(12)   More (less) graceful, most (least) graceful
(13)   More (less) gracefully, most (least) gracefully
```

Comparison by premodifier, because it includes expressions of a smaller/the smallest degree, is the more versatile type of comparison.

     **Comparison by suffix** is done by adding the suffixes *-er* (the comparative) and *-est* (the superlative), which express a higher/the highest degree:

---

1. Some of these expressions are perhaps better regarded as idiomatic copula constructions, with an adjective as subject complement, as in *to stand/hold firm* (cp. I am *firmly* against it).

```
(14)   Big, bigger, biggest
(15)   Soon, sooner, soonest
```

21.1.6  The choice between comparison by premodifier and comparison by suffix is primarily determined by the phonological make-up of the adjective/adverb, e.g. the number of syllables, the structure of the syllables, and accentuation:

**Words of one syllable** usually take comparison by suffix, see also (14) and (15) —

```
(16)   Tough, tougher, toughest
(17)   Hard, harder, hardest
```

**Words of two syllables** ending in *-er, -ow, -y,* or in a consonant followed by *-le,* usually take comparison by suffix —

```
(18)   Clever, cleverer, cleverest
(19)   Narrow, narrower, narrowest
(20)   Early, earlier, earliest
(21)   Simple, simpler, simplest
```

Also a few common two-syllable words which do not meet these requirements may occasionally take comparison by suffix, e.g. *common, handsome, pleasant, quiet, polite.*

Other words of two syllables generally take comparison by premodifier, see also (12) above, including adverbs derived from adjectives by means of *-ly,*

```
(22)   Afraid, more afraid, most afraid
(23)   Abstract, more abstract, most abstract
(24)   Strictly, more strictly, most strictly
```

**Words of three syllables** or more, as well as **participles**, generally take comparison by premodifier:

```
(25)   Important, more important, most important
(26)   Tired, more tired, most tired
(27)   Cunning, more cunning, most cunning
```

21.1.7  When two (or more) adjectives compared by premodifier are coordinated, one occurrence of *more* (etc.) will usually do for both:

```
(28)   Her dress was more elegant and tasteful than her sister's
```

The last adjective tends to carry more weight, in accordance with the end-weight principle (see § 4.2.0).

If an adjective of the type that normally takes comparison by suffix is coordinated with one which takes comparison by premodifier, the adjective with the suffix tends to come first:

```
(29)   His explanation is simpler and more profound than those of
       his predecessors
```

However, most adjectives taking comparison by suffix, especially those of two syllables like *simple* in (29), can also be compared by premodification. This often happens in particular syntactic or stylistic contexts. Thus, in the case of coordination (29), we may want to give more weight to the adjective *simple*, which means reverting to the pattern exemplified by (28):

(29a) His explanation is *more profound and simple* than...

Note that *more* (*less*) is not a premodifier in the construction where two qualities describing the same object are being compared, of the type:

(30)    He is *more silly than stupid*

In fact, the reason why *more* cannot be replaced by a suffix here is that it is the head of an adverb phrase realizing a degree adjunct. Thus the analysis, in (30a), corresponds to the meaning, "He is silly *more than (he is) stupid*":

(30a) (He is) more silly than stupid
          ———————     ——————————
                         J      SC
             H           ——————————
          ——————  ——————       POM
            A-      SC          -A

21.1.8  With a few highly frequent words, the forms of the comparison are **irregular**, e.g. *good* (*well*)/*better*/*best*, and *bad* (*badly,ill*)/*worse*/*worst*. In a few other cases, irregular forms of comparison involve idiomatic differences of meaning:

    *Far* has two sets of forms in the comparative and superlative: *farther*/ *farthest* (with concrete meaning only), and *further*/*furthest* (with concrete as well as figurative meaning):

(31)    He couldn't walk any *farther/further*
(32)    She stood at the *farthest/furthest* possible point from the entrance
(33)    Closed until *further* notice

    *Late* has *later*/*latest* about time, and *latter*/*last* about the relative order of two or more items:

(34)    A meeting will be held at a *later* date
(35)    What's the *latest* news
(36)    This development was not apparent until the *latter* half of the century
(37)    This is the *last* letter we received from him before his death

Note that *last* in (37) would have been ambiguous without the adverbial (*before his death*), meaning either "the last ever" or "the most recent."

    *Near* has two superlatives, corresponding to *latest/last*: *nearest* about place, and *next* about the relative order of things conceived of as points along a line. Compare:

(38)    The *nearest* bar is two miles away
(39)    The *next* bar is two miles away

*Little*, with reference to countable entities, uses as forms of comparison *smaller/smallest*. With reference to quantity it has *less/least*, whereas the form *lesser* is used in a qualitative sense:

(40)    Maybe he is not so *little*, but he is certainly *smaller* than you
(41)    This method will attract *little/less/(the) least* attention
(42)    For lack of evidence linking him to the murder, the police are holding him on some *lesser* charges

*Old* used about age normally has the regular forms, *older/oldest*, in the comparative/superlative. With reference to order of birth, usually among members of a family, the forms *elder/eldest* may be used, though only in formal language:

(43)    The *oldest* building dates back to the early 16th century
(44)    He has an *elder/older* sister in France
(45)    My *eldest/oldest* (son) wants to join the army

21.1.9    A series of adjectives have only a positive[2] and a superlative form, the superlative being formed by means of the suffix *-most*: *inner/in(ner)most, outer/out(er)most, nether/nethermost, upper/up(per)most, hind/hindmost*. A few of them have only the superlative form and can only be used in an absolute sense: *foremost, topmost, utmost*.

(46)    There is still a lot of social unrest in the *inner* cities
(47)    He was able to read her *innermost* thoughts
(48)    You must promise to treat this with the *utmost* discretion

**Modifiers (21.2.0-21.5.2)**

*Correlation (21.2.0)*

21.2.0    One of the characteristic features of the adjective/adverb phrase is the fact that it frequently contains modifiers which express **degree** (see further § 23). Such modifiers often **correlate** (are said to be **correlates**), i.e. the presence of one modifier is made necessary by the presence of another:

(1)    (I am)    <u>as</u> <u>happy</u> <u>as you are</u>
                  PRM    H        POM

(2)    (He was)    <u>more</u> <u>considerate</u> <u>than I had expected</u>
                    PRM        H                POM

In most cases, depending on the context, the postmodifier can in fact be left out by way of ellipsis:

---

2. Those ending in *-er* are original comparatives having acquired absolute meaning.

(3)     I can't use him, he's *too* stupid (for me to be able to
        use him)

Adjective/adverb phrases in the positive can be divided into two main
categories: (A) those whose modifiers are correlates, (B) those whose modifiers
are not. Looking first at those whose modifiers are correlates, we will
distinguish, in the following, between three types of correlative modifier.

### Modifiers of the Positive (21.2.1-21.2.6)

### *Correlative modifiers (21.2.1-21.2.3)*

21.2.1  **As + H + *as*-clause/NP**; the first *as* is often submodified by e.g. *just* and *quite*,
as indicated in (4) and (5):

(4)     She has worked (just) as hard as you
                        PRM    H
                        ‾‾‾‾‾‾‾‾‾‾  ‾‾‾‾‾  ‾‾‾‾‾
                         PRM        H      POM

*So* sometimes replaces *as* in negative clauses, in British (but rarely in American)
English:

(5)     His lecture was not *(quite) as/so* interesting *as I had hoped*

*So* is used when the *as*-correlate is a *to*-infinitive clause:

(6)     Would you be *so* kind *as to tell me what this is all about?*

21.2.2  **So + H + *that*-clause**; *that* can be left out:

(7)     The suitcase was *so* heavy *(that) she couldn't lift it*

21.2.3  ***Too* + H + *to*-infinitive clause/*for*-NP:**

(8)     It's *too* good *to be true*
(9)     Mexican food is *too* hot *for me*

### *Non-correlative modifiers (21.2.4-21.2.6)*

21.2.4  The most important modifiers which do not have a correlate are a series of
forms (mostly adverbs) functioning as **premodifiers of degree**, e.g. *very, highly,
damn, rather, quite, real* (informal AE), *really* (BE and formal AE), *so, (not all) that*:

(10)    She recovered *very* quickly
(11)    It was a *highly* satisfactory solution
(12)    You knew *damn* well this would happen
(13)    The noise was *quite* loud
(14)    That will make him *real(ly)* happy
(15)    The house is *so* beautiful!
(16)    He isn't *all that* strong, you know

The superlative form, *most*, has absolute meaning when used in a positive adjective phrase, without a correlate (cp. §§ 21.4-21.5):

(17)    The prince was *most* charming

*Very* and *much* complement each other as modifiers of degree: *Very* tends to modify adjectives and adverbs in the positive, as well as adjectives forming the superlative by means of the suffix:

(18)    You explained that *very well*
(19)    I want a *very good*/the *very best* wine

*Much*, on the other hand, is used in the comparative:

(20)    You are *much more dependable* than him
(21)    She came *much sooner* than they expected

and, in conservative language, before certain adjectives beginning in unstressed *a-*, such as *afraid, alike, ashamed*:

(22a)   They are *much afraid* of what will happen

but the language is changing, making *very* more frequent:

(22b)   They are *very afraid* of what will happen

Note, however, the common construction with *very much*:

(22c)   They are *very much afraid* of what will happen

Participles modified by *very* have lost their verbal content, becoming full-fledged (E1) adjectives, as opposed to those modified by *much*, see §§ 10.5.1-10.5.2:

(23)    (He is) a    politician much admired for his rhetoric
                                      A     V        A
                  D     H        POM

(24)             ... a very distinguished politician
                     PRM        H
                  D         E1              H

### 21.2.5 **Premodifiers of measure** realized by a noun phrase:

(25)    The street is *a mile* long
(26)    The girl is only *three years* old

### 21.2.6 **Postmodifiers, after particular adjectives**:

(27)    He is responsible *for the death of thousands*
(28)    This is tantamount *to an ultimatum*
(29)    She was aware *of his presence/of being observed*
(30)    It's worth *several million/trying*
(31)    Are you afraid *of snakes/to admit you are wrong*?
(32)    Are you afraid *(that) she will talk*

As these examples show, the postmodifier of such adjectives can be realized by a noun phrase introduced by a junctive (a prepositional phrase), as well as by a finite or nonfinite clause (*worth* is the only form which is never followed by a junctive, see (30)).

Note that with some of these adjectives the postmodifier is obligatory, as in (28)-(30).[3]

Observe further that *enough* can be followed by a postmodifier (a *for*-NP or a *to*-infinitive clause)[4] even when functioning in the noun-phrase modification; cp.

(33)    (That's) trouble <u>enough</u> <u>for one day</u>
                         H         POM
        <u>————————————————</u>  <u>————————</u>
                H              POM

(34)    (They have) <u>enough</u> dynamite <u>to blow up the entire town</u>
                     H                          POM
                   <u>————</u>   ————————   <u>——————————————————————————</u>
                    M-          H                  -M

### Modifiers of the Comparative (21.3.0-21.3.3)

21.3.0 The comparative, as opposed to the superlative, normally cannot have absolute meaning in English ("a relatively high degree"). Instead, it expresses a higher degree *than* something else, i.e. the *than*-postmodifier is a correlate of the comparative morpheme (*more/less* or *-er*). This does not mean that the postmodifier is always obligatory, only that a contrast is at least understood or implied (see also § 21.2.0):

(1)     Peter is strong, but John is even *stronger* (than Peter)
(2)     This is one of his *longer/better* novels

Likewise, expressions such as *higher education, Lower East Side, the upper classes, the younger generation, the more advanced students* presuppose obvious contrasts. Only a small series of Latin comparatives can be used with absolute meaning, as in *an inferior product, a girl of superior talent, a major disaster, a minor accident.*

### *Premodifiers of the comparative (21.3.1)*

21.3.1 The following are examples of premodifiers (in italics) which are peculiar to the comparative; (5) and (6) represent colloquial language:

---

3. *Aware* does not have a postmodifier when used in the sense of "generally attentive or alert":
    Young people are not *as politically aware* as they were during the seventies.

4. In addition, *enough* is frequently postmodified by a *that*-clause in American English; cp. (34) with:
    The people who lived here were privileged. Engineers and academicians, people with *enough* skill *that the State wanted to look after them and their needs.*

```
(2)     (Her attitude is now) much more mature
                              PRM   H
                                PRM      H
```

```
(3)     (This is) far better than I had expected
                  PRM   H          POM
```

```
(4)     He is no smarter/not any smarter than the rest of us⁵
(5)     These pictures are (a hell of) a lot more interesting
(6)     That horse ran a damn sight faster than we thought
(7)     That horse ran a good/great deal faster than we thought
```

The comparative may also be preceded by the definite article, e.g. in connection with an *of*-postmodifier (see § 21.4.1), or in idiomatic expressions with two comparatives which correlate:

```
(8)     The older she gets, the more beautiful she becomes
(9)     I want it done soon — the sooner the better
```

### Postmodifiers of the comparative (21.3.2)

21.3.2 The typical postmodifier of the comparative is a clause or noun phrase introduced by *than*:

```
(10)    They accomplished this more easily than I had expected
                                  PRM   H          POM
```

```
(11)    She is more dependable than her husband
```

The comparative may also be followed by an *of*-postmodifier, see § 21.4.1.

### Sequential modification (21.3.3)

21.3.3 Some of the adjectives with a postmodifier which were mentioned in § 21.2.6 may realize the head of an adjective phrase in the comparative, in which case we have sequential modification (see § 10.9.2):

```
(12)    (I'm) more afraid of snakes than you
                     H      POM
              PRM       H           POM
```

## Modifiers Shared by Comparative and Superlative (21.4.1-21.4.3)

21.4.1 The meaning of the comparative may come very close to the typical meaning of the superlative ("the highest degree"), when in formal language it is used to compare the members of a group consisting of two. This is why such an

---

5. Expressions like, *he's no good, it wasn't much/any good*, should not be seen as exceptions to the rule that *no* and *not much/any* only modify the comparative: they are peculiar to the word *good*, and should be regarded as idiomatic variants of corresponding expressions with the noun *use* (*it's no use; it wasn't much/any use*).

adjective phrase functions within the same structural framework (the noun phrase) as the superlative, cp. the definite article and the *of*-postmodifier:

```
(1)    Chris is the most intolerant (person) of them all
(2)    Pam is the more outgoing of the two sisters
```

In less formal language, the superlative is used in either case:

```
(3)    Pam is the most outgoing of the two sisters
```

The *of*-postmodifier may take clause-initial position, like an adverbial:

```
(4)    Of these three sisters, Emily was probably the most gifted
(5)    Of the two, Sullivan was the more musical
```

21.4.2 The idiomatic use of the definite article in corresponding adverb phrases is not consistent:

```
(6)    John handled the situation the most/least deftly of them all
(7)    Of my two benefactors, I liked Peter (the) better
```

The article is obligatory when *more/most, less/least* function as premodifiers (6). With comparison by suffix ((7)-(8)) and when *more/most, less/least* function as head ((9)-(11)), the article occurs in formal style:

```
(8)    She works the hardest of us all
(9)    He admires her (the) most
```

whereas the article is not possible in certain fixed expressions with a postmodifier:

```
(10)   I like Peter best of all
(11)   He would like that most of all
```

21.4.3 Apart from the *of*-postmodifier, the comparative occasionally shares with the superlative the expressions *easily, by far* and *(by) far and away*, which precede or follow (only *by far*) the comparative/superlative. These expressions are perhaps to be regarded as special adverbials (of degree) rather than as modifiers:

```
(12)   (He is) by far the better/best player⁶
                    PRM        H
          ____    PRM        H        ____
          _____    H
                         PRM
                         SC
```

**or**

```
(12a)  ... by far the better/best player
              PRM        PRM        H
          A                SC
```

6. The analysis is not quite satisfactory: in showing that *by far* modifies *the better/best*, we have at the same time obscured the function of the article (*the*) as determiner in relation to *player*.

```
(13)    He is the better/best player by far
(14)    He is far and away the better/best player
(15)    She is easily the more/most competent teacher
```

### Modifiers of the Superlative (21.5.1-21.5.2)

21.5.1  Apart from its typical, relative, meaning ("the highest degree"), the superlative can also have absolute meaning ("a very high degree"). Absolute meaning is usually conveyed by *most*, whereas absolute use of *-(e)st* is rarely found outside certain polite clichés (3). Absolute meaning is characterized by the fact that no correlate is needed or understood (as opposed to superlatives with relative meaning, see §§ 21.4 and 21.5.2):

```
(1)     It was a most delightful evening
(2)     He sang most wonderfully
(3)     My (very) best wishes
```

*Least* can have absolute meaning only in *not (in) the least*:

```
(4)     I was not the least ashamed/not ashamed in the least
```

21.5.2  Adjective phrases in the superlative almost invariably function in the noun phrase, see §§ 10.1.2 and 21.4. For modifiers of the superlative which can occur also with the comparative, in particular the *of*-postmodifier, see § 21.4. Two modifiers, finally, are peculiar to adjective phrases in the superlative, viz. the *that*-clause and the adverb *ever*, both postmodifiers (apart from this function, *ever* frequently occurs as an adverbial of the *that*-clause, as in (5)):

```
(5)     That's the worst (excuse) (that) I've ever heard
(6)     It's the best (thing) (that) I can do for you
(7)     It's the biggest (earthquake) ever
```

For analysis, cp. § 10.8.7.

## THE FUNCTIONS OF THE ADJECTIVE/ADVERB PHRASE (22.0-22.2.6)

### Introduction (22.0)

22.0    The adjective phrase and the adverb phrase have so far been treated together because they share the same basic structure. Functionally they are quite distinct, however, which is why in this section we shall deal with them separately.
        The **adjective phrase**, first, has the following functions:

| *In the clause:* | as subject complement[7] and object complement |
| *In the noun phrase:* | as premodifier, head and postmodifier |
| *In the adjective phrase:* | as head |

The **adverb phrase** has the following functions:

| *In the clause:* | as adverbial |
| *In the noun phrase:* | as postmodifier |
| *In the adjective/adverb phrase:* | as premodifier and postmodifier |
| *In the adverb phrase:* | as head |

## Functions of the Adjective Phrase (22.1.1-22.1.8)

### The function as Subject/Object Complement (22.1.1-22.1.2)

22.1.1 The adjective phrase functions as subject complement and object complement:

(1)    The wind was *stronger than I had expected*
(2)    Her words made me *very angry*

22.1.2 For some adjective phrases with particular adjectives as head, the function as complement is either the only one ((3)-(8)), or the adjective changes its meaning when used in the noun-phrase premodifier. This is true of a number of **adjectives beginning in unstressed *a-*** (see also § 21.2.4), e.g.

| (3)  He was *afraid* | (6) She is *asleep* |
| (4)  They are *alike* | (7) I want to be *alone* |
| (5)  I'm *ashamed* | (8) We must keep them *alive* |

as well as certain **adjectives with a non-correlative postmodifier** (see § 21.2.6):

(9)    She is *able* to come and go as she pleases  (cp. an *able* young doctor)
(10)  I'll be *content* with a smile and a friendly nod
(11)  Her smile was *devoid* of mirth
(12)  He is *fond* of you  (cp. his *fond* parents)
(13)  I'm *glad/sorry* you changed your mind  (cp. *glad* tidings/ a *sorry* sight)
(14)  She is *keen* on jazz  (cp. a *keen* wind)

and some **adjectives pertaining to health**: *faint, ill, poorly* (colloquial), *sick, (un)well*:

(15)  She felt faint/poorly/unwell and had to go to bed  (cp. a *faint* smile)
(16)  He is *ill*, which is why he hasn't been to work  (cp. *ill* health)

---

7. And, occasionally, as subject (e.g. *Black is beautiful*), but this function is not common.

(17)  I need some fresh air — I feel *sick*  (i.e. nauseous)
      (cp. She has a *sick* husband, i.e. her husband is *ill*)

In American English, *sick* can be used synonymously with *ill* also when functioning as subject complement: *Her husband is sick; they say it's cancer.*

### The function as Noun-Phrase Premodifier (22.1.3-22.1.4)

22.1.3 Another typical function of the adjective phrase is that of realizing the noun-phrase premodifier (see also § 10.5.1 ff.):

(18)  A *very interesting* lecture, a *little* boy, a *light-blue* dress, a *German* car

22.1.4 For some adjective phrases with particular adjectives as head, **the function as noun-phrase premodifier is the only one:**
**Adjectives denoting type, field or material** (N2 adjectives, § 10.6.2):

(19)  The *industrial* revolution, *medical* attention, a *wooden* bowl

**Adjectives whose superlative form ends in *-most***  (see § 21.1.9): *inner, outer, nether, upper, hind,* as in

(20)  The *Inner* City, the *upper* classes

The participles *drunken, shrunken* and *sunken,* which have lost most of their verbal content, as well as the adjectives *joint* and *live*:

(21)  A *drunken* sailor (cp. the sailor was *drunk*); the old man's *shrunken* hands; *sunken* ships (i.e ships lying on the bottom of the sea)

(22)  A *joint* enterprise, *live* animals

A number of **restricting adjectives** (O3, see § 10.4.3), e.g. *chief, entire, main, sheer, single, whole*:

(23)  The *entire* army, the *main* problem, a *single* mistake

### The function as Noun-Phrase Head (22.1.5)

22.1.5 Adjective phrases used in this way have **generic reference**, either to persons in the plural or to uncountable abstracts, see also § 10.1.2-3:

(24)  The *weak* need the protection of the *powerful*
(25)  The *Dutch* are famous for their clogs, canals and windmills
(26)  Their plan unfortunately did not allow for the *unforeseen*

**Specific reference** occurs only when an adjective phrase has the superlative structure (occasionally shared by the comparative) described in § 21.4.1, and when it belongs to the group of nationality adjectives ending in *-ese* (§ 10.1.3):

(27)  She is the *nicest* of all the people I know
(28)  She is the *elder* of the two sisters
(29)  The two *Japanese* were being told how to find the lecture
      room

besides a few idiomatic expressions, e.g. *the accused, the Almighty, the condemned*[8]
(see also § 20.4.17 n.):

(30)  The *accused* must state his name and occupation

### The function as Noun-Phrase Postmodifier (22.1.6-22.1.7)

22.1.6  As a noun-phrase postmodifier, the adjective phrase frequently corresponds to
the subject complement of a relative clause:

(31)  A custom *common among several tribes*
(32)  A weapon *simple* but *devastating*
(33)  Something *completely different*

The adjective phrase can normally function as postmodifier if it contains a
postmodifier of its own (31), or if several adjectives are coordinated (32). If the
head of the noun phrase is an indefinite pronoun (33), an adjective phrase can
only function as postmodifier. Otherwise, the function as noun-phrase
postmodifier is linked to particular adjectives, see §§ 10.8.8-10.8.11 for further
details.

22.1.7  Adjective phrases with a postmodifier are often **divided** by the head of the noun
phrase in which they function (for analysis, see also § 10.8.7):

(34)  That is a *different* project *from/than the one I am talking
      about*[9]
(35)  It is a *much more complicated* problem *than we thought*
(36)  She is the *most prolific* writer *of her generation*

In the positive, with correlative modifiers (see § 21.2.1-21.2.3), the premodifier
and head of the adjective phrase precede the noun-phrase determiner:

(37)  (She was) as   different a person  from Peter  as you can
                        H                   POM
            PRM       H-                    -H            POM→
                    M-        D    H                     -M→

      imagine

      ←POM
       ←M

---

8. In American English, *crazy* frequently occurs as head of a noun phrase of indefinite, singular
or plural, form and reference. In other words, it occurs as an ordinary countable noun:
      a.      It was the work of a criminal psychopath, *a crazy*, a nut.
      b.      *Crazies* have a logic all their own.

9. In British English, using *than* after *different* is often regarded as "incorrect" by purists.

(38)   It is *so easy* a thing *to say that you have to be careful not to say it*   (cp. It is a thing *so easy to say that...*)
(39)   This is *too difficult* a problem *for me to tackle alone*

Adjective phrases are also occasionally divided when they function outside the noun phrase, e.g. as subject complement of the clause:

(40)   It is <u>so</u> <u>difficult</u> to solve this problem <u>that we need more</u>
           PRM  H                        POM→
   S=  V     SC-              =S           -SC→

   <u>time</u>
   ←POM
   ←SC

### The function as Head of the Adjective Phrase (22.1.8)

22.1.8 The adjective phrase may realize the head of another adjective phrase:

(41)   (John is) <u>so</u>   <u>extremely gullible</u>
                   PRM      H
       PRM          H

## Functions of the Adverb phrase (22.2.1-22.2.6)

### The function as Adverbial (22.2.1)

22.2.1 Modified adverbs most often function as manner adjuncts, less frequently as other types of adverbial, e.g.

(1)   They work *extremely hard*   (manner adjunct)
(2)   He moved *so quickly that his pursuers did not have time to aim their guns at him*   (manner adjunct)
(3)   They have *most likely* left for home by now   (modal disjunct)
(4)   I don't think that's such a good idea, *quite honestly* (style disjunct)
(5)   *Never before* had she experienced such callousness   (time adjunct)
(6)   We didn't see each other *very often*   (frequency adjunct)
(7)   She drove *straight ahead*   (adjunct of place (direction))
(8)   He *very generously* paid for my dinner   (subject-related adjunct)

### The function as Postmodifier in the Noun Phrase (22.2.2)

22.2.2 Simple adverb phrases (with an adverbial particle as head, see § 10.8.12) can realize the postmodifier in a noun phrase:

(9)   I'm used to a more comfortable life style — you know, meals *out* and holidays *abroad*

### The function as Head of the Adverb phrase (22.2.3)

22.2.3  The adverb phrase may realize the head of another adverb phrase:

```
(10)   (They work) so   extremely hard
                          PRM      H
       ___  _____
       PRM            H
```

### The function as Premodifier in the AP (22.2.4)

22.2.4  Most adverb phrases realizing the premodifier of an adjective/adverb phrase express degree:

```
(11)   He is (so) very young and innocent
(12)   This question is (much) more complicated
(13)   She sang (ever) so beautifully
```

though if they correspond to adjuncts, they frequently retain that meaning as premodifiers in the adjective phrase:

```
(14)   Her attitude was quietly assertive   (manner)
(15)   We couldn't think of a financially sound solution to this
       problem   (viewpoint)
```

If they correspond to disjuncts, or if they are premodifiers in the adverb phrase, they invariably express degree:

```
(16)   He is surprisingly competent (i.e. competent to a surprising
       degree)
(17)   He sings surprisingly well
```

### The function as Postmodifier in the AP (22.2.5)

22.2.5  Adverb phrases with *enough* and *by far* as head can realize the postmodifier of another adjective/adverb phrase:

```
(18)   The shutters are not strong enough (to withstand the press-
       ure)
(19)   None of them could run fast enough (to catch up with me)
(20)   This is better by far
```

### Marginal functions (22.2.6)

22.2.6  The second component of a phrasal verb (§ 7.9.1) is occasionally modified by an adverb, which makes it structurally similar to an adverb phrase. Here the phrasal verb can no longer be said to constitute one (complex) lexical item; instead, it can be analyzed as a simple main verb with an obligatory postmodifier (this is the only case where a verb phrase has a postmodifier):

```
(21)   She got right up and left
                     PRM  H
            ___  _____
            H       POM
       ___  _____  ___  ___
        S        V            J    V
```

(22)   He went straight through with his plan
                    PRM        H
       _____
       __  H          POM          _____
       S          V                    A

The junctive, too, (regardless of whether it introduces a clause or a phrase) is sometimes intensified by an adverb, so that its realization becomes structurally similar to an adjective/adverb phrase:

(23)   (I have loved you) ever since that first day
                          PRM   H    ____  _____  ___
                                  J      PRM   PRM   H

(24)   She is *dead against* the plan/building a hotel on that site
(25)   His adversary swept him *clean off* the floor


## GRADATION (23.0-23.3)


### Introduction (23.0)

23.0   In this final section we shall look at an important aspect of the semantics of the adjective/adverb phrase, looking first at the difference between adjectives which allow gradation and those which do not. Then we will deal with types of semantic relationship between head and modifiers in a gradable AP (intensification/downtoning, and comparison), and discuss the basis of the comparison.


### Gradable and Nongradable Adjectives/Adverbs (23.1.1-23.1.4)

23.1.1   We have already seen (§ 10.5.1) that there is a fundamental distinction between gradable and nongradable adjectives, to the extent that adjective phrases with a gradable adjective as head have their own slot (E1) in the noun-phrase premodification:

(1)    A (very) tired German soldier
         E1         N1
(2)    A (very) ugly yellow house
         E1        E4
(3)    A (very) chic young woman
         E1        E3

In semantic terms, this is because they denote relatively **transient and/or subjective** qualities, as opposed to other types of adjectives, which express more **permanent and/or objective** qualities: *tired* in (1) is more transient than *German*;

*ugly* in (2) is more subjective than *yellow*; and *chic* in (3) is more transient/subjective than *young*.

23.1.2 Even among gradable adjectives some are more transient/subjective than others: *careful* describes a certain behavior which can change from one moment to the next, as opposed to e.g. *tall*. Therefore *careful*, but not *tall*, allows construction with the progressive, i.e. the dynamic/stative distinction of the verbs is found also with the adjectives:

```
(4)    She is only being careful
(5)    *She is only being tall
```

As with the verbs, the same adjective (as well as a corresponding noun) can often be used both statively and dynamically. Thus *fool(ish)* is stative in (6) but dynamic in (7):

```
(6)    The boy is foolish/a fool   (general characteristic)
(7)    Brian is being foolish/a fool  ("behaving foolishly")
```

23.1.3 We saw in § 23.1.1 that a gradable adjective denotes a quality which may be present to a greater or lesser extent. If it is present to an extent which does not deviate from the **norm** for what we are describing, we do not mention it: we do not say about a house that it is ugly unless it is uglier than houses in general; conversely, when we do say about a house that it is ugly, we mean that it has that quality **to a greater extent than** the norm.

Thus we see that a gradable adjective does not depend on modifiers to express gradation: the mere mention of it represents gradation. This is not true of adjectives occurring outside E1. For instance, *yellow* in example (2) does not mean "more yellow than the norm," denoting instead a color which is different from red, blue, brown, etc.; *German* in (1) refers to a soldier who is non-English, non-French, etc.; and *young* as an E3 adjective, in (3), means "in that age bracket."

23.1.4 The same distinction applies to adverbs: adverbs are gradable if they denote a frequency or manner (etc.) which is greater or more marked than the norm for the action (etc.) concerned:

```
(8)    His boss replied (very) coldly
(9)    Revolutions happen (very) frequently in that part of the
       world
```

If, on the other hand, their meaning is inherently absolute, gradation is not possible. Thus we have (a) but not (b), in each of the following pairs:

```
(10a)  He cleaned the car very thoroughly
(10b)  *He cleaned the car very completely

(11a)  She leaves very soon
(11b)  *She leaves very immediately
```

**Intensification/downtoning (23.2)**

23.2    We saw in §§ 23.1.3-23.1.4 that the very presence of a gradable adjective (and,
for instance, most manner adverbs) indicates a higher degree of the quality
concerned than the norm. This relatively high degree can be further intensified,
or can be toned down, by means of the most important of the non-correlative
modifiers, the degree adverbs (see § 21.2.4).

**Intensification:**

```
(1)    His book is extremely boring
(2)    The food was most delicious
(3)    Her mother answered very coldly
```

**Downtoning:**

```
(4)    The situation seems pretty hopeless
(5)    The man was rather tall
(6)    Her mother answered somewhat coldly
```

**The Basis of Comparison (23.3)**

23.3    We have so far been discussing the concept of degree in relation to an **implicit**
norm. We shall finish by looking at it in relation to an **explicit** norm, or basis
of comparison. This relationship is represented by correlative modifiers
(§ 21.2.1 ff.), of which the first correlate expresses the degree, the second correlate (POM) containing the norm to which the expression of degree has to be
related:

```
(1)    She was as good as her word
(2)    He played so beautifully that it brought tears to my eyes
(3)    It's too good to be true
(4)    He is more mature than his classmates
(5)    She visits him less frequently than before
(6)    Tom is the most diligent of my students
```

The difference between the comparative and the superlative, usually described
in terms of degree, also involves the basis of comparison:

```
(7)    Sheila is the most intelligent of the three children
(8)    Sheila is more intelligent than her two brothers
```

With the superlative (7), that which is being compared ("Sheila's intelligence")
is itself represented on the scale which constitutes the norm ("the intelligence
of the three children"); in other words, that which is being compared is itself a
member of the category which is the basis of comparison. We know there are
only two other children besides Sheila, in (7), precisely because we have made
inclusive reference to a category.

    With the comparative (8), on the other hand, that which is being compared is not itself a member of the category which is the basis of comparison. This makes the comparison arbitrary: we might as well have compared Sheila with her sisters, if she has any, the point being that we do not know how many siblings there are, or whether her two brothers are mentioned in their capacity as family or as fellow members of some other category ("Sheila is more intelligent than her two brothers, but not as intelligent as some of the other students in her class").

Note, finally, that, when the comparative is used to compare two entities (see § 21.4.1), the basis of comparison is of the same type as that of the superlative:

(9)    Sheila is *the more* intelligent *of the two children*

# SELECT BIBLIOGRAPHY

Arndt, H., Preisler, B., Østergaard, F.
1977    *Kompendium i engelsk grammatik.* Copenhagen: Akademisk Forlag.

Arndt, H. & Ryan A.
1986    "An Ordered Inventory of Communicative Functions of General FLT." In Gabriele Kasper (ed.) *Learning, Teaching and Communication in the Foreign Language Classroom.* Aarhus University Press.

Brown, G. & Yule, G.
1983    *Discourse Analysis.* Cambridge University Press.

*Collins Cobuild English Grammar*
1990    London & Glasgow.

Crystal, D.
1990    *Rediscover Grammar with David Crystal.* London: Longman.

Dijk, T.A. van
1977    *Text and Context.* London: Longman.

Dik, S.C.
1978    *Functional Grammar.* Amsterdam: North-Holland.

Egersten, E.
1964    *Amerikansk engelska.* Stockholm: Svenska Bokförlaget.

Fillmore, C.J.
1968    "The Case for Case." In Bach, E. & Harms, R.T. (eds.) *Universals in Linguistic Theory.* New York: Holt, Rinehart & Winston.

Freeborn, D.
1987    *A Course Book in English Grammar.* Basingstoke: Macmillan.

Halliday, M.A.K.
1961    "Categories of the Theory of Grammar." In *Word* 17, 241-92.

Halliday, M.A.K.
1967    "Notes on Transitivity and Theme in English." In *Journal of Linguistics* 3, 37-81, 199-244; 4, 179-215.

Halliday, M.A.K.
1985    *An Introduction to Functional Grammar.* London: Arnold.

Huddleston, R.
1984    *Introduction to the Grammar of English.* Cambridge University Press.

Jespersen, O.
1933      *Essentials of English Grammar*. London: Allen & Unwin.

Kirchner, G.
1970-72 *Die Syntaktischen Eigentümlichkeiten des amerikanischen Englisch*. 2 volumes. München:
           Max Hueber.

Leech, G. & Svartvik, J.
1975      *A Communicative Grammar of English*. London: Longman.

Marckwardt, A.H.
1958      *American English*. Oxford University Press.

Mencken H.L.
1979      (ed. by R.I. McDavid, Jr.) *The American Language: An Inquiry into the Development of
           English in the United States*. New York: Knopf.

Quirk, R. & Greenbaum, S.
1973      *A University Grammar of English*. London: Longman.

Quirk, R., Greenbaum, S., Leech, G., Svartvik, J.
1985      *A Comprehensive Grammar of the English Language*. London: Longman.

Scott, F.S. et al.
1968      *English Grammar: A Linguistic Study of its Classes and Structures*. London: Heinemann.

Searle, J.R.
1969      *Speech Acts: An Essay in the Philosophy of Language*. Cambridge University Press.

Strevens, P.
1972      *British and American English*. London: Collier-Macmillan.

Swan, M.
1980      *Practical English Usage*. Oxford University Press.

Sørensen, K. & Steller, P.
1988      *Engelsk Grammatik*. Copenhagen: Munksgaard.

Trudgill, P. & Hannah, J.
1982      *International English*. London: Arnold.

Vestergaard, T.
1985      *Engelsk Grammatik*. Copenhagen: Schønberg.

# INDEX

*Linguistic forms* are in italics. *Grammatical concepts* (as entry heads) are capitalized. In the case of several references, boldfaced ones indicate where the central information is to be found.